SINATRA

and the

JACK PACK

SINATRA

and the

JACK PACK

The Extraordinary Friendship between Frank Sinatra and
John F. Kennedy—Why They Bonded and What Went Wrong

MICHAEL SHERIDAN
WITH DAVID HARVEY

Skyhorse Publishing

Skyhorse Publishing books may be purchased in bulk at special discounts for sales promotion, corporate gifts, fund-raising, or educational purposes. Special editions can also be created to specifications. For details, contact the Special Sales Department, Skyhorse Publishing, 307 West 36th Street, 11th Floor, New York, NY 10018 or info@skyhorsepublishing.com.

Skyhorse® and Skyhorse Publishing® are registered trademarks of Skyhorse Publishing, Inc.®, a Delaware corporation.

Visit our website at www.skyhorsepublishing.com.

10 9 8 7 6 5 4 3 2 1

Library of Congress Cataloging-in-Publication Data is available on file.

Cover design by Rain Saukas
Front cover photograph: AFP

Print ISBN: 978-1-51070-362-9
Ebook ISBN: 978-1-51070-371-1

Printed in the United States of America

For a comprehensive bibliography, please visit www.circlefilms.tv/jackpack.

CONTENTS

———◆———

Chapter 1: The Beginnings

———————◆———————

4̲15 MONROE STREET was an unremarkable building on an unremarkable street in the unremarkable town that is Hoboken, New Jersey. A four-story tenement surrounded by many of similar size and some much smaller, one and two story, the sort of buildings that defined the immigrant communities that grew up on both sides of New York's Hudson River in the late nineteenth and early twentieth centuries. From the top of the building, located just twelve blocks from the shoreline, you could see the three churches of St. Ann, St. Francis, and Our Lady of Grace and St. Joseph, established in the area to cater to the optimistic Catholic emigrants who had streamed into the town hoping for a new life in America. Beyond these places of worship was the growing skyline of Manhattan, where some of the neighborhood's residents traveled daily to try to make a living.

For many people, the American dream had come to a crashing halt in Hoboken, just five miles from where they had entered the United States at Ellis Island, the nation's busiest immigration inspection station from around the turn of the nineteenth century. For Italian peasants from as far apart as the picturesque shores of Lake Como in northern Lombardy to the arid and tiny towns of Ragusa in southern Sicily, the hope of wealth and prosperity had given way to the harsh reality of life at the bottom of the immigrant ladder in the New World. At the time, German merchant classes occupied the top rung, a trend that would decline rapidly as a result of anti-German sentiment at the outbreak of World War I. Their dominance was followed by the Irish, who controlled the police and fire services, leaving the scraps for the Italians, many of whom arrived in the country without papers, prompting the denigrating nickname "WOP."

Saverio Antonino Martino Sinatra was just twelve when he passed through the Ellis Island inspection in 1904 with his mother, Rosa, and his sisters, Angela and Dorotea. Francesco, his father, had traveled ahead and was already working in a pencil factory when his family arrived. Rosa appears not to have considered education essential to her son's advancement, and Saverio, who had adopted the more Americanized moniker of "Marty," remained illiterate. First apprenticed as a shoemaker, he turned in his late teens to prizefighting, adopting the pseudonym "Marty O'Brien," possibly to ingratiate himself with the Irish locals but more likely because Italians were not allowed in the fight game. Marty had tattoos drawn all over his arms, but with a slight build and an asthmatic condition, he did not come across as fearsome or threatening, neither to his opponents nor to the local street gangs. He was also too laid back in personality to make any impact either in, or outside, the ring.

He had, however, made an impact on Natalie "Dolly" Garavente, another Italian immigrant who lived nearby. Dolly had left the town of Rossi in Liguria, northern Italy in the late 1800s and had settled with her family in Hoboken. Dolly and Marty had been seeing each other since late 1910, when she had just turned fifteen and he was eighteen, and Dolly would dress up in her brothers clothes, hair bunched up under his cap, to go to Marty's bouts in a time when women were not allowed at boxing matches. Dolly's brother, Dominick, was also a disguised Italian fighter and regular opponent of Marty's.

The Ligurian Garaventes had little time for the Sicilian Sinatras and regarded the illiterate Marty as highly unsuitable for the daughter of a family keen on bettering itself. As a result, Dolly's parents refused to countenance the relationship. When the Garaventes refused point blank to host a wedding, Dolly and Marty eloped. The most romantic destination within their means was Jersey City, four miles down the road, and it was there, in the city hall, on Valentine's Day 1914, that they were married. The bridegroom's occupation was registered as athlete, and the couple's friends Anna Caruso and Harry Marrotta witnessed the ceremony. It was a tribute to Dolly's courage to go down this path without her parents' blessing and against the background of the importance of the act of marriage in the staunchly Catholic ethos of Italian culture, and all the more so among the immigrant community. It was also a vote of confidence in Marty who, although kind and decent in every respect, did not engender much confidence as a potential breadwinner. The couple would not starve though, because of the money Dolly's mother made at her grocery store. But they had two great assets, the bond that had kept them together and Dolly's ambition and maturity beyond her tender years.

When the dust from the secret wedding eventually settled, Dolly's parents grudgingly accepted the union and the couple settled on Monroe Street. It was in a small, dark room of the tenement house, on December 12 of the following year, that the most life-changing event of the young couple's lives was to occur. Dolly had become pregnant in the late spring, and as she began her labor the local midwife attended her, as was the custom in the community. Professional medical care was beyond the means of most, and with her sister and mother by her side, Dolly knew she would be delivering her baby with the most experience and attention at hand that she could hope for. After hours of labor, things seemed to stop abruptly, and Dolly was suddenly in great distress. This was most likely because at less than five feet in height, she had a small pelvic area, and the baby was so large that she couldn't push any longer because of exhaustion. At once, everyone in the room became increasingly worried by the progress of the birth. Sensing danger and realizing that the solution was beyond her skills, the midwife called the local doctor. Ten minutes later he arrived, quickly recognized that this had to be a forceps procedure, and literally ripped the baby from the exhausted mother's womb. The action, however crude, had been a matter of life and death. The doctor had not had time for niceties, knowing full well the potential consequence of two deaths as opposed to one. Safely delivering the child while making sure the mother survived was his priority in a time when infant mortality was extremely high.

A baby boy, weighing an enormous thirteen and a half pounds, was delivered with wounds to the left side of the head, including a scarred ear and a perforated eardrum. These would have a lifelong consequence for the baby, and the awful difficulty of the birth and its conclusion would ensure that Dolly would never give birth again. But nobody was inclined to blame the doctor, who after the delivery turned his medical attention to the mother and, in effect, played the role of lifesaver. The baby's grandmother, concerned that the baby appeared lifeless, put him under a cold tap until he started to cry. In a time when most, if not all, births in deprived areas were at home and the chances of survival up to a year were less than fifty-fifty, the event was unremarkable for the denizens of this Italian ghetto, who were preparing to gather whatever meager means they could for Christmas. Generations later there would be more reason to remember it as the day that Francis Albert Sinatra entered this world.

From the start of their tenancy of the Monroe Street address, Dolly had cast her eyes on a better life, and the birth of Francis Albert provided a fresh impetus to her aspiration to leave the stench of poverty behind. As far as she was concerned, their tenancy of number 415 was to be as brief as possible, and no source of retrospective pride. She had her sights firmly set on the better side of the city, and that meant that she was not going to subscribe to the traditional role of stay-at-home mother. The money had to come in, and whatever that took she was prepared to do. This meant that for the foreseeable future her beloved son would be minded and brought up by the extended family. If the possible consequences of this for little Francis ever crossed Dolly's mind, she stuck it in some mental drawer and threw away the key.

Hoboken was not the worst place to be if you lived on the right side or you took, or were given, decent opportunities, although being

Italian was a definite minus in that regard. The Hoboken community had been formed as a township in 1849, and after a referendum six years later attained the status of a city. By the late part of the century, shipping lines were using it as a terminal port, and a railroad terminal was established on the waterfront. It was a bustling area with the busy Hudson River as its commercial focus. Hoboken was the major destination of the Hamburg line, the main carrier of immigrants from Germany to the United States, hence the large German population in the city and its environs. Shipbuilding and dry-dock activity had also become a major source of employment, as had some rapidly growing manufacturing enterprises and big companies such as Maxwell House and Lipton's Tea. There was always work if you knew the right people, and Dolly set about acquiring some skills and cultivating connections, which, somewhat unusually for an Italian, were based among the Irish community.

Her first move in that direction came while she was recovering from the birth and planning little Frank's baptism, which she would not attend. She bucked the long-established Italian tradition of choosing godparents from within the close family circle by asking Frank Garrick, an Irish friend of Marty's, to be godfather. Garrick's father, Thomas, happened to be a local police captain, and Dolly felt he could potentially do much more for her Frank than any Italian relative or friend. The godmother, Anna Gatto, was Italian though, and the ceremony took place in St. Francis Church on April 2, 1916, when Frank was four months old.

Dolly had been planning her next move. She knew how valued midwives were in the community, and how they always retained a strong residual loyalty from those whose babies they had brought into the world. So as soon as she was fit and able, Dolly elected to become one. Her informal training consisted of accompanying doctors who were called to home births until such time that she was able to do it on her own. A doctor was not within the budget of most of the Little Italy occupiers and other immigrant groupings all over the greater New York area, so the midwife became the principal assistance at birth. In time, Dolly would be seen running around the neighborhood carrying a little black bag and looking like a medical professional. The best of midwives were very good but, as Dolly's personal experience had illustrated, often not good enough when complications arose in the process of giving birth.

If her newfound role was in some way inspired by the horror she endured when bringing her son into the world, her later "diversification" of her services would confirm Dolly's ruthless drive to acquire the means to improve the family's social status. That drive would not be interrupted by any moral considerations or religious constraints. Within a couple of years she had amended her midwife role, one which was charged with assisting the safe passage of the unborn, to assisting the very opposite. Dolly Sinatra became a backstreet abortionist and did so because destroying the unborn was more lucrative than saving it. The instruments of the abortionist were simple and crude; the modus operandi was to break the amniotic sac inside the womb with a sharp instrument. For Dolly, it was a long hatpin regarded as a fashion item of the time, giving her the nickname "Hatpin Dolly."

For over half a century there had been a somewhat ambivalent attitude toward abortion. The church and most doctors opposed it and the press vilified it, but the law in general accommodated it, probably because rich and powerful society figures availed of the service to avoid shame or diminution of reputation. The most famous American abortionist was Mrs. Ann Lohman, aka Madame Restell, or Madame Killer, as she was better known. She operated a high-class abortion clinic in Manhattan but franchised her services to others including a woman in Hoboken by the name of Frederika Loss. This female abortionist and tavern owner who had a farm in the Hoboken and Weekhaven area had become a major player in one of the most famous and sensational unsolved murder cases in American criminal history. The case involved a beautiful young woman by the name of Mary Rogers, who worked in a famous Manhattan cigar shop owned by John Anderson. In July 1841 she sought, in some sense of desperation, a loan for an "emergency," and her employer duly obliged without explanation of the nature of the emergency. On the weekend of July 25 she told her widowed mother, who ran a boarding house, and her fiancé, a boarder, that she was going to visit an aunt and other family. Three days later her battered body, with severe blunt trauma to the face, was fished from the Hudson River in Hoboken. The coroner found strange wounds in the area of the vagina. The beauty of the victim and the strange circumstances of the case created a media frenzy, and all sorts of theories arose to explain the case, not helped by a totally incompetent police investigation.

In November 1842, Frederika Loss came forward and gave a sworn statement that the death was a result of a failed abortion attempt, but she was ignored by the police despite the fact that items of the victim's clothing had been found on the farm and that it was well known that the tavern served as an abortion location for Madame Restell's operations. The crime remained unsolved, but the Police Gazette of February 21, 1846 produced an unequivocal attack on Madame Killer:

> It is well known that females die in ordinary childbirth. How many then who enter her halls of death may be supposed to expire under her execrable butchery? An obscure hole in the earth; a consignment to the savage skill of the dissecting knife or a splash in the cold wave, with the scream of the night blast, for a requiem, is the only death service bestowed upon her victims. Witness this ye shores of Hudson. Witness this Hoboken beach!

Three decades later, there was still demand for abortion, and Hatpin Dolly was carrying on the long-established tradition in Hoboken. Despite the threat of prosecution if caught, she would have been very aware that her clients would, almost always, keep their silence and thereby make any legal action almost certain to fail. Dolly had by this time become something of a politician. She had a great ear for language and dialect and would get involved as a translator for her fellow Italian immigrants when they appeared before the courts. She also hooked up with the Democratic machine of New Jersey's Hudson Company and acted as a conduit between Italians and city hall. Helping to deliver votes, and ensuring that favors were organized and returned, put her in an increasingly strong position in both the Italian and Irish communities, and her tenacious, organized approach to political clientelism ensured that she was very quickly becoming someone to be respected. She was rewarded for her unstinting work when she was appointed leader of the third ward in the ninth district, a position never before held by a woman. This was by no means a sinecure, as it was not a paid job, but Dolly knew full well that when the time came she would be able to reap whatever reward she might seek.

As Dolly expanded her business and developed her local connections, there was an unexpected boost for her fortunes when in April 1917 the United States entered the First World War. The first local consequence was the taking over of the Hamburg American line piers and the establishment of federal control over the port. The German domination of the commerce of Hoboken came to an abrupt end with martial law imposed on the area. Many of the local German families were summarily removed to Ellis Island while others simply left the city. The Irish now firmly occupied the top rung of the local immigrant ladder, and Dolly, with her connections, was poised to profit from her work on behalf of her political masters. The exit of her family to a better side of the city was moving closer to reality.

* * *

On October 7, 1914, the same year that Marty and Dolly had married, another couple had tied the knot two hundred miles away and in very different circumstances. Their antecedents, however, were not so far removed from the origins of the Sinatras. Another aspect that provided an echo to their situation was the resistance of the parents of the bride to the bridegroom. In terms of wealth and influence the marriage of Joseph P. Kennedy and Rose Fitzgerald united two of the most powerful Irish families in the Boston area. But their origins, in particular on the Kennedy side, could have been easily forgotten by the passage of time, as often happens when money and position conspire to obliterate the facts of the past. The history of all Irish immigrant families, at the time, was grounded in extreme poverty.

In 1849 Patrick Kennedy had left his family, who farmed twenty-five acres in Dunganstown, County Wexford, Ireland, and had made his way to Liverpool and boarded the *Washington Irving* bound for America and a better life. Onboard he met Bridget Murphy, also from Wexford and also fleeing the famine-torn land in which millions had perished. From the depths of despair and the specter of the unknown emerged not only hope but also love. Thus on the Atlantic, in the steerage of an ocean liner, was the foundation stone laid for a great American dynasty.

Having reached Boston, the couple married on September 26, 1849 and settled in the slum area in the east of the city, where dreadful living conditions and overcrowding facilitated the spread of disease, cholera in particular. In the lower depths of East Boston in shanties and dark, water-filled tenement basements, adults and children perished in droves. The area was known as a place where children were born to die. The average life expectancy of the Irish immigrant was five to six years after arrival. The tenement building on Liverpool Street where they settled was a three-story wooden house with an open stairway at the back, situated in a row of houses distinguished by a common backyard full of rubbish and open, stinking sewers. A public health commission from the time described the conditions for the inhabitants of such tenement buildings:

> "Huddled together like brutes, without any regard to sex or age, or sense of decency; grown men and women sleeping together in the same apartment, and sometimes wife and husband, brothers and sisters in the same bed ... self-respect, forethought, all high and noble virtues soon die out (and

in their place) sullen indifference and despair or disorder, intemperance and utter degradation."

Patrick Kennedy found work as a cooper and the couple had five children, three daughters and two sons, one of whom died in infancy from the dreaded cholera. The disease also made a widow of Bridget when Patrick succumbed to it, at just thirty-five, in 1858, the same year their last-born child, their remaining son, Patrick Joseph, was born. Bridget would prove more than able to overcome the premature death of her husband. The family moved to Border Street near the docks, where she somehow found the money to open a stationery and notions store, selling ribbons and sewing goods on the ground floor of the house, in time expanding it into a grocery and liquor store. Young Patrick, known as PJ, left school at fourteen and worked as a stevedore on the Boston docks. He saved as much money as he could and, later borrowing some from his mother, took over the ruin of a saloon on Haymarket Square and transformed it into the most popular drinking venue in East Boston. The venture moved him into wholesale and then importation of liquor.

Only in his mid-twenties, a handsome, solidly built young man with a mop of auburn hair and sporting the then-fashionable handlebar moustache, there was little doubt that he would escape his tenement origins. Loyalty to his fellow Irish immigrants made him unwilling, however, to desert the customers who had supported the creation of his good fortune. So, while of course minding the profits, he dispensed help and advice to some of the less-fortunate Irish immigrants who visited his premises. PJ was a young man of vision, and it quickly struck him that commercial success alone would not guarantee him influence and power in his area. He began to turn his sharp eye and considerable talent to politics.

In 1885 he ran as a representative of East Boston for the Massachusetts state legislature, was elected, and would go on to serve no fewer than five terms. In the interim his sisters had all married and his mother was happily running her own small business. In the twenty-seven years since the death of the family patriarch when the only surviving son was just over ten months old, the Kennedy family had thrived by the old-fashioned virtues of hard work, faith, and self-belief. PJ also knew that wealth alone would not move him up the class ladder. The upper echelons of Boston society of the time were tightly controlled by the "Brahmins," descendants of old families, some of whom could trace their lineage back to the original English settlers of the northeastern United States.

In 1887 PJ married "upwardly." His bride, Mary Augusta Hickey, was the daughter of a businessman and the sister of a police lieutenant. The Hickeys lived in a big mansion in Brockton and had all the trappings of wealth, including servants. After the marriage ceremony at the Church of the Holy Redeemer, the couple moved into an apartment on Meridian Street in the center of East Boston. A year later, their firstborn was named Joseph Patrick, and they would go on to have another boy, who died in infancy, and two daughters. Poignantly, and with an echo of her husband's passing, Bridget died later the same year in December 1888, with the consolation, at least, of seeing the Kennedy name assured for the future. Young Joseph would continue where his grandmother and father had left off, but with a ruthless determination and single-mindedness which would, in time, make him one of the most significant Irish American political operators of the twentieth century.

In the North End of Boston, another Irish immigrant family had similar origins and ambitions as Joseph P. Kennedy. Thomas Fitzgerald had fled the Irish Famine in the company of an uncle and cousin on a ship bound for New York City. A huge storm had caused the vessel to be diverted to the alternative destination of Boston, and it was here that the Fitzgeralds had begun to put down roots. At the other end of the city from the Kennedys, the Fitzgeralds had experienced a parallel rise from poverty to prosperity in both business and politics.

In 1879, Thomas lost his wife, Rosanna, who was pregnant at the time, to a stroke. The couple had already lost two children in infancy

and a young daughter to cholera, but there were no less than nine
sons remaining. The most energetic and enterprising was John, and
his father decided to send him to Boston Latin School and Harvard
Medical School, but the boy had no interest in practicing medicine.
Just six years later, when Thomas followed his wife to the grave,
Johnny found himself in charge of the family. He began to amass
property, involved himself in local politics with the Democrats, married Mary Josephine Hannon, and went on to have five children.

The firstborn daughter, Rose, arrived on July 22, 1890. As her other
siblings, Eunice, Agnes, John F. Junior, and Thomas, duly arrived, her
father concentrated less on family and more on politics. In 1894 he
targeted a US congressional seat, running against Joseph O' Neill,
who was backed by some city bosses including PJ Kennedy. But the
Wall Street panic of the previous year helped Fitzgerald over the line
much to the irritation of PJ Kennedy. On the morning after his primary election victory, he shook hands with Kennedy, saying, "Now
that the fight is over, PJ, let's shake hands." The handshake worked
to Kennedy's advantage, for the victorious congressman would ultimately put his considerable political machine behind the man who
was once his rival. It was the forerunner of an alliance of far greater
political significance, which neither of the men, with all their astute-
ness and vision, could ever have predicted.

"Honey Fitz," as John Fitzgerald was now nicknamed, had a close
affinity to his daughter Rose, and she would accompany him on long
walks through his little empire, the North End. She first met Joe
Kennedy when she was five and he seven on Old Orchard Beach in
Maine, where the Fitzgeralds, Kennedys, and other up-and-coming
Irish families spent time in the summer months. The next time they
met was on the same beach when Rose was a sixteen-year-old, highly
intelligent beauty and Joseph Patrick a lean, handsome young man
of eighteen years with a fulsome head of dark hair, a charming personality, and a winning smile. There was obviously a strong attraction. Rose recalled later that Joe had "the most wonderful smile that
lit up his entire face from within and made an instant impression

on everyone he met." Regardless of his close and protective relationship with his eldest daughter, Honey Fitz viewed any development
of romance with a Kennedy with alarm. The Irish American community had made great progress in New England. From their mid-
nineteenth-century position at the bottom of the social ladder, the
immigrant Irish had risen dramatically, particularly in Boston. The
Irish ran the fire and police departments, and in the mayor's office,
the surnames of the incumbent had changed from Brahmin names
like Quincy and Lincoln to unmistakably Irish names like O'Brien
and Collins. But there was a very definite pecking order, and the
Kennedys, despite their newly found financial status, had insufficient
influence for a union between Joe and the precious Rose to be a matter for consideration.

There is a very telling photograph of both family groups taken on
the Old Orchard Beach in 1907. PJ Kennedy is second from the left
with his characteristic handlebar moustache. Rose is next beside him
in a long dress, flanked by her father, his fit frame in a bathing suit
with a top. Second from the right is young Joe with his hair drawn
back over what appears to be a defiant expression on his face. Rose is
the only one in the frozen image with a shadow of a smile on her face.
The photograph provides a portent of things to come.

The month after the photograph was taken, Joe went to Harvard
while Rose travelled to Europe and then to a convent school in the
Netherlands. In the normal order of Catholics in East Boston, boys
would go to the colleges of the religion, Boston College or Holy Cross,
but PJ and Mary, whose brother John had also attended, wanted the
best for their son, and Boston Latin, the largely Protestant preserve of
the Boston aristocrats, was chosen despite the constant exhortations
of the city Cardinal for Catholics not to darken its august doors. PJ
was a realist and knew full well that the Kennedy future would stag-
nate if confined to East Boston and the parochial politics of the Irish
in the area. There were also the Boston Brahmins to contend with.
Despite the progress of the Irish Americans, they still ruled the city
beyond the Kennedy and Fitzgerald bailiwicks and had created an

impregnable white Anglo-Saxon protestant empire. Knowing he and his family couldn't beat the Brahmins, PJ's logic was that they might have a better chance by joining them—so after school, Joe was sent to Harvard.

At Harvard, Joe performed indifferently in academic terms, and he never gained entry to the most prestigious clubs such as Porecellian, AD, or Fly. He just managed to be elected to a minor one, the Hasty Pudding. This would prove a bitter lesson in the club mentality of the ruling class of Boston, but one that would provide great motivation to better that class by any means available to him in his future business career.

One incident in his final year gave a firm indication of the modus operandi employed by the Kennedys when confronted with such obstacles. At Boston Latin he had excelled at baseball, making the school's first team four years in a row and acting as captain for two. But while making the team in his final year in Harvard, he was not getting to play on the diamond at all. During the ninth inning in the final game of the year against Yale, with Harvard leading four to one, Chick McLaughlin, the pitcher and captain of their side, requested that Kennedy be brought on to play, which seemed to all a most unusual decision in the circumstances.

The Yale batter hit a sluggish return and was put out at first base by Kennedy. Kennedy's move won the game for his team and gave Joe his varsity letter. When McLaughlin requested the winning ball Joe refused saying he had got the putout. So why had McLaughlin, someone clearly not enamored of Kennedy, brought Joe on in the first place? Sometime before the game a representative of PJ came to see the captain whom it was known would be looking for a movie theatre license after his graduation. He was made an offer he could not refuse. To get the license he would have to put Joe Kennedy in to play.

Graduating in 1912 with a BA in economics, Joe began to court Rose in a more serious fashion, later saying that he had no real interest in anyone else. His first job was as a state-employed bank examiner. A year later, the Columbia Trust Bank, in which his father had a significant stake, was the subject of a hostile takeover bid, and Joe borrowed $45,000 from family and friends and succeeded in beating off the predators. As a reward, the shareholders elected him as president of the bank, and at twenty-five years of age he boasted to the press that he was the youngest man in that position in the United States.

That may or may not have been true, but what reporter was going to trawl through a list of the banks in the most remote regions of the country to contradict the story? Joseph P. Kennedy had learned a lesson about the importance of manipulating the media to suit his own purposes. On this occasion he did it for two reasons: The first, no doubt, for career advancement. The second, to put Honey Fitz in his place and make a union with his daughter seem more attractive. The circulating rumors of a scandal involving Honey's alleged dalliance with a cigarette girl must have weakened his moral imperative, because on October 7, 1914, Joseph P. Kennedy and Rose Elizabeth Fitzgerald were married and after a two-week honeymoon settled in a nice and growing Boston suburb by the name of Brookline, at the address of 83 Beals Street.

Their first child, Joseph Patrick, was born at the Kennedy summer home in Hull, Massachusetts, on July 28, 1915. He, in turn, was followed by John Fitzgerald Kennedy, born at the Beals Street residence on May 29, 1917, with the aid of the best medical care money could buy. The proud father already had plans in his mind for the advancement of his children, and he, like Dolly Sinatra, would ruthlessly and without any moral compass pursue his own dreams and make sure that those he didn't achieve happened vicariously through his children.

Chapter 2: The Matriarch

———————◆———————

WHILE DOLLY SINATRA was furthering her ambitions for her family, young Frank was looked after each day by his grandmother, Dolly's mother, Rosa. When he began elementary school she collected him every day, obsessive about her grandson. Marty retired from his ignominious career in the ring after breaking both his wrists, but with no culture of men as child minders in those days, he would spend his days drinking coffee in various joints with men in a similar position of unemployment. To label Marty as a bum may be a little unfair, but it's clear he had no ambition, was held back significantly by his illiteracy, and, with a forceful, go-getting wife, was happy to take a backseat.

To complicate domestic matters further, a cousin of Marty's, Vincent Mazolla, had arrived from Italy and joined the household. A veteran of the First World War, he had sustained injuries, which left him with a limp and, possibly, a mild case of PTSD. All in all, he was a poor candidate for employment and therefore held in low regard by Dolly. For a while "Chit U," as he was known, was given the housework Dolly didn't have time to do. She had a superhuman appetite for work, but even she could not carry two adults as well as a child, and tapped her political masters to find the two some gainful employment and additional revenue for the household.

She found Chit U a job as a steward's assistant on the docks. Next stop was the mayor's office at city hall, where she informed an assistant that she wanted a job in the fire department for her husband. When she was told there was no vacancy, her reply was, "Make one." Dolly's attitude was simple: she never said no when asked to deliver votes, and she was not prepared to accept a negative when she needed delivery of a favor in return.

On August 1, 1926, Marty was appointed to the fire department, where he joined the predominantly Irish workforce on a salary of $2,000 per annum plus a pension. With three sets of wages coming in, and the addition of another role to her own portfolio—that of a weekend chocolate dipper in an ice cream parlor—after a tenancy of over a decade she was ready to think very seriously of abandoning the co-op in Monroe Street.

She found what she was looking for ten blocks away: a three-bedroom apartment at 703 Park Avenue for the not-inconsiderable-at-the-time sum of $65 a month. But it bought the respectability that Dolly craved, and the family moved there in September 1927. She was by now also compensating for being an absent mother by lavishing Frank with clothes and pocket money. He was shy and quiet by nature, but being the best-dressed kid in the neighborhood ensured that he got the attention that his character might not have attracted. Kids twelve years of age are naturally drawn to a contemporary whose pockets jingle, and Frank became popular among the boys from the Park Avenue Athletic Club as he shared his mother's spoils with them and as she slipped them the occasional treat at the ice cream parlor. If Dolly's parenting methods were coming up short, they simply reflected the theory and practice of her own life: everyone had their price, and most people could be bought. But the money was no substitute for love and attention, nor would it lessen the effects of the outbursts of her famous rage.

When that rage was focused on Frank she would beat him with a stick, on one occasion pushing him down the stairs, knocking him out. She alternated these displays of violent cruelty with hugs and kisses, which often followed directly after the beating. It left him in a constant state of confusion and alert, never knowing why or when she would turn on him. Dolly could have not chosen a better type of parental misbehavior to send a message of confusion to her only child. Her love was mixed with a liberal dose of hate, her generosity was tainted by cruelty, her attention was crossed with neglect, and it was all salted with desperately unpredictable emotive explosion, leaving psychological scars to match the physical ones he had received at birth. In later life, Frank would be prone to similar emotional explosions.

Love, in his experience, was already equated with an impermanent elation and hatred, the other side of the emotional coin forming an alliance with depression. And in his early adolescence, relentless spoiling further complicated this psychological maelstrom. The trouble was amplified by the fact that Frank was not like his father, the calm, almost laid-back Marty. He was, in temperament, anyway, the reflection of his mother. The adult Sinatra would later relate the emotional impact his mother had left on his younger self to Shirley McLaine: "She was a pisser. She scared the shit outta me. Never knew what she'd hate that I'd do." He told Pete Hamill, the author of *Why Sinatra Matters*, "When I would get outta hand she would give me a rap with that little club; then she'd hug me to her breast." It is well documented that the child who is a victim of such parental abuse can in later life turn full circle and become the abuser, and this is certainly true of Frank. And yet, to further confuse this tangled relationship, there is no doubt that without the help of Dolly, Frank Sinatra would have quickly faded into the shadows of anonymity and would never have gotten beyond the borders of Hoboken. Having assumed the singular role of carrying the family along her chosen path on her tiny but not frail shoulders, she was determined to see it through.

In June 1931 Frank graduated from junior high and lasted just two months as a student in A. J. Demarest High School. In the midst of the worst depression in the country's history, he had abandoned his education, the one thing that might help him ride with the economic tide, whenever that came. The Great Depression, which was putting millions out of work across the country, doesn't appear to have bitten too deeply in the Sinatra household, however. Dolly had just purchased a Lincoln convertible for $65 but didn't need a hungry, unemployed mouth to feed, so in her usual fashion, she decided to chase down a favor.

It was not for nothing she had chosen Frank Garrick, by then the circulation manager of the *Jersey Observer* newspaper, to be her son's godfather. Arriving at his office, she asked him for a job for Frank, and he was given one bundling newspapers on a delivery truck, a stark contrast to driving the convertible around Hoboken. Tiring quickly of this lowly occupation and believing that he was destined for greater things, Frank decided he wanted to be on the editorial staff as a sportswriter. But the manner in which he attempted to achieve this ambition was blatantly and ludicrously insensitive and showed the sense of entitlement that his mother had knocked into him.

A vacancy arose when a member of the sportswriting staff was killed in an automobile accident. Frank abandoned the delivery truck and sat in the office, in the seat previously occupied by the late-departed writer. Spotted by the editor who, understandably, inquired about his presence, he replied that Frank Garrick had appointed him to the position. When Frank was called and asked what had prompted the circulation manager to make an editorial appointment, the editor dispatched him to fire the disrespectful and insensitive employee. When Garrick imparted the bad news to Frank, he was met with a tirade of foul-mouthed abuse proving he was indeed his mother's son, whose curses would bring a blush to the cheek of the most experienced of stevedores.

Garrick would recall many years later to Kitty Kelley in her 1986 biography *His Way*, the verbal abuse he was subjected by the spotty, skinny little teenager: "Oh the temper and the words and the filthy names he called me, like he was going to kill me. He called me every name in the book and then he stormed out." Dolly never spoke to her son's godfather again, which was entirely typical. The most innocuous of slights was sufficient to see someone permanently dismissed, persona non grata. That was Dolly, and it would become Frank.

Insofar as a career was concerned, Dolly wanted Frank to follow convention. In the immigrant world of northern New Jersey, decent employment meant factory work or, if you were Irish (or Italian if you had a wife like Dolly), a fireman or a policeman or a government worker. These positions were respectable, they were permanent with the protection of a strong union, and they were pensionable. By these criteria, being a singer did not constitute a job. By her own standards, education was not a prerequisite to gaining a profession as she had proved with midwifery, and Frank's forty-seven days in the New Jersey High School system clearly took him out of the running for any employment that required any form of advanced education. The fact that this view fitted perfectly with a singing career escaped Dolly at the time, as did the huge rewards then available for those who achieved success.

The temptations and the incentives that a career in entertainment could bring had certainly not escaped her son. As he began to dabble in the singing world, he was keenly observing those beginning to carve out careers. At the top of the list was Bing Crosby, who had moved from performing with the Rhythm Boys to the Gus Arnheim Orchestra, and made his national radio debut with CBS, having signed with Brunswick Records in 1931. By 1932 he had appeared in his eighth movie, *The Big Broadcast*, a film in which he played himself, such was his notoriety. Crosby's delivery was a soft, conversational tone, leading to the labeling of crooner-sentimental as a singing genre. While Crosby was the king, inspiring the young Sinatra to reflect the great crooner's image by sticking a pipe in his mouth, Rudy Vallee and Russ Columbo also provided role models for the aspiring singer. So incensed was his mother with the idea of his following a professional singing career that Dolly completely lost the plot one evening upon seeing a picture of Crosby on Frank's bedroom wall, throwing a shoe at it and screaming that he was only a bum.

From the outside it might have been hard to disagree with her. After all, the United States was in the midst of the Great Depression with large-scale unemployment, misery, and poverty. This teenage layabout, as she saw it, was fantasizing about singing and refusing to take on a job that might involve the minimum of drudgery. Her son wanted to be a star but was refusing to dirty his hands on the way. The irony was that, in his own way, he had an even greater sense of entitlement than Dolly. The urge to get Frank to take onboard the concept of employment was normal but was now amplified by the fact that at the end of 1931 the family had taken another step up the social ladder, having purchased a house at 841 Garden Street for the then-enormous sum of $13,400. Dolly's view was that the least she might expect was a financial contribution from the youngest and, herself excepted, most-energetic member of the household.

Frank knew she would eventually capitulate, and she did, giving him money for sheet music, which he used to ingratiate himself with local musical combos, a favor that was returned by occasionally letting him onstage to sing a song. And she could see that he was hustling all the time to get a break, so she helped him by getting him into the Union Club on Hudson Street in Hoboken. Afterward, he did stints in Italian social clubs. It was small-fry stuff, but he had to start somewhere. The other, less-obvious work he did was to assiduously study the methods of the singers he admired, namely Crosby, Columbo, and Vallee, and the routes they had chosen to stardom. The map appeared to be fairly straightforward: get the singing spot with a band or orchestra, and do some touring and nightclub spots; exposure on radio was essential, and from there, to Hollywood. The key ingredient was talent, and, as the world would eventually discover, Frank had plenty of that. The skinny, young singer was doing the fieldwork and, in common with any such player, he needed a good bounce of the ball to get a break.

Given the financial disasters and general hardship caused by the depression, Sinatra's timing might have been considered questionable. But, although he had no idea at the time, in fact it could not have been better, as critic and author John Lahr observed, "While record sales had collapsed to $5.5 million in the early years of the depression as the 1930s progressed they would rise and rise to $48.4 million at the end of the decade and by 1945 to $109 million. By 1938 half of all broadcast programs were recordings of, mostly live, popular music."

In addition, between 1933 and 1939 the number of jukeboxes grew almost tenfold and, three years later, to close to half a million. There would be no quick fix; Frank would have to serve an apprenticeship, which was by his standards long, but, in reality, pretty short. As Lahr put it, "By the time he emerged from his apprenticeship as a dance band ballad singer with touring bands, the technology for success was all in place." Dolly eventually came to realize that there was no point in resisting her son's aspirations, so she subsidized his drive to break into a band by buying him portable speakers and a microphone.

Combined with the Lincoln convertible, Frank was suddenly a very attractive ally to any struggling band, and Dolly got him spots at roadhouses, nightclubs, and Democratic Party meetings. In 1934 there was an unexpected vacancy at the top table of crooners with the unexpected death of Russ Columbo, and while Frank was not then in a position to exploit the opportunity, he certainly would be later. In more than one way he had a closer affinity to Columbo than Bing Crosby. Like himself, Columbo was born to Italian immigrants in 1908, the twelfth child of a musician who then lived in Camden, New Jersey, about a hundred miles from Hoboken.

Like Sinatra he possessed both talent and drive and knew what he wanted from an early age. He left school at seventeen to travel the country with various bands in which he doubled on violin and vocals. He also played nightclubs and progressed to running one of his own. He had also starred in a few movies and would go on to have a relationship with the movie star Carole Lombard before being shot in a bizarre accident, at twenty-six, by the well-known celebrity photographer Lansing Brown. He was a classic example of the phrase "the beautiful and the damned." While the young Sinatra could not have avoided taking in an event that matched the passing of Valentino, Columbo's life and career probably spurred him on, as opposed to his wondering about the efficacy of pursuing a dream that might translate into a nightmare.

One way or another Frank was pursuing his journey. From pestering radio stations in New Jersey for appearance spots (without any immediate success) to pushing himself at every band that came his way, he was not behind when it came to putting himself forward. Local outfit The Three Flashes, made up of youngsters Jimmy Petrozelli, Patty Principe, and Freddy Tamburro, was just one of the groups Frank targeted.

Since 1922, regular entertainments were broadcast live, and in the later part of the decade the sponsored musical feature was the most popular program format, with the shows called after the name of the sponsor. As an indication of just how influential these shows were, in the same year that Sinatra was pushing himself, George Gershwin had been hosting his own program. It was vital for any aspiring entertainer to get on the airwaves, and the composer of the American classic "Rhapsody in Blue" was no exception. The programs at the time were almost always live because the inferior quality of phonographic discs discouraged the radio networks from making recorded programs. As a result, prime-time shows would be performed twice, once for each coast of the country. For fame, wide reach, and promotion of the orchestra, band, and individual artist, radio was the biggest game in town.

The biggest radio act of the time was the talent show. As if to demonstrate the obvious that there is nothing truly new in any era, including the entertainment business, *Major Bowes Original Amateur Hour* was the *America's Got Talent* of its time. Edward Bowes had been a hugely successful real estate investor who had lost his fortune in the California earthquake of 1906. Moving to New York, he reinvented himself as a show-business impresario, becoming managing director of the famous Capitol Theatre in the city. He had brought his amateur-hour talent show to New York City station WHN in April

1934, and the program had become a phenomenon. Every week Bowes talked to contestants and listened to performances, and his short attention span, interjections, and the use of a loud bell or gong to get rid of acts earned his title of "Major," like the clichéd bully in the playground. With a keen eye for talent and an ability to cash in on the success of the show, he was not averse to exploiting the successful acts, many of whom he sent off on franchised tours around New York, New Jersey, and beyond.

In 1935, the first year of the network broadcasts of the show, more than thirty thousand acts were auditioned. The Three Flashes had been performing at a venue called the Rustic Cabin, in Englewood Cliffs, half an hour north of Hoboken, in a spot with Harold Arlen and his orchestra. The Rustic Cabin had a wire link to WHN, which took live broadcast segments of the performances. The group had been using Frank as a chauffeur (using the Lincoln) while resisting his constant entreaties to sing, but they didn't reckon on Dolly, who visited the Tamburro family, and a deal was done for Sinatra to join.

The odds of getting anywhere from the talent pool on the *Original Amateur Hour* were quite staggering. Over ten thousand applied weekly and of that number five hundred to seven hundred were auditioned. This number was whittled down to twenty, who would appear on the night of the show. Even then, an act could be the victim of the infamous gong even before the performance had finished. Edward Bowes had auditioned the Flashes on April 9, 1935. On the foot of the application form, their act was described, in a fairly far-fetched way, as "singing, dancing, and comedy." Whatever Dolly promised the Tamburros had obviously worked, because the name submitted on the form was "Frank Sinatra and the Three Flashes," a rapid promotion for the most recently recruited member of the group. The leader's address was given as 841 Garden Street, Hoboken, telephone number supplied, followed by the others: Freddy Tamburro (Freddy Tamby), Adam Street, Hoboken; Jimmy Petrozelli (Jimmy Skelly), 214 Monroe Street, Hoboken (Frank's old neighborhood), and Patty Principe (Patty Prince), West New York.

The song submitted and chosen was "Shine," a recent hit for black quartet the Mills Brothers, who had also appeared with Crosby in *The Big Broadcast* in 1932. Bowes, unilaterally deciding that the name of the group didn't work, changed it to the Hoboken Four. The competition date was set for September 8, 1935. Whatever the outcome, Frank Sinatra must have felt that destiny was calling and that the opportunity to prove that his avoidance of respectable employment was justified, was about to present itself. On the evening of the show, the Hoboken Four trouped on stage to be met by the imperious Bowes: "Four boys in fine-looking suits, singing and dancing fools." He went on to say, "they seem so happy I guess and they make everyone else happy." He asked who would speak for the group, and Frank said he would, adding, "We're lookin' for jobs, how about it?" Tamburro introduced himself and the others and said where he, Petrozelli, and Principe worked. "What about that one?" inquired the Major, pointing at Sinatra. "Oh, he never worked a day in his life," came the reply to roars of laughter from the audience.

It was clear even before they got to sing that the Hoboken Four had made an impression on the audience and, most importantly, on Bowes. The group and their song not only elicited the best audience reaction of all the acts but also won in great style with forty thousand call-in votes, the largest to date in the show's history. Bowes remarked that they had "walked right into the hearts of their audience," and he promptly signed the group on a six-month contract to one of his lucrative touring shows. Within weeks the Hoboken Four had realized that the touring was lucrative solely for Bowes and that they would have to be content with the exposure. The tour involved long hours on the road, staying in dives, doing singing promotions in grocery stores, and generally adding to the already-stuffed coffers of their mentor. The grueling apprenticeship quickly knocked the sheen off their newly won celebrity, and that life-changing night in the Capitol Theatre increasingly seemed like a very pleasant dream.

The drudgery was worse for Frank than for the others. They were happy to ditch the menial jobs they had abandoned for the short-term glamour of singing. Sinatra, on the other hand, had never ever really worked and, used to being cossetted by his mother, was unhappy to be pushed around, particularly when the "contract" with Bowes turned out to be outrageously one sided. The only consolation was that the females in the audience zoned in on him, and he was having the time of his life bedding as many as possible while the other group members got to sign autographs. Internal tensions increased, and there were fights, including a physical one in which Tamburro knocked Frank out for getting a fit of giggles with the others onstage. The honeymoon was over for the Hoboken Four, and after three months Sinatra left the tour and returned home. He was keen to progress his career in a direction he could have some control over. He was also keen to spend time with Nancy Barbato, a local girl he had been intermittently dating, much to the disapproval of her parents, who wanted her to find a nice guy with a proper job.

While the touring had been a bit of a disaster, the victory on Bowes's hugely popular radio show and the subsequent publicity was something Frank could exploit to his own advantage. He now knew he wanted to be a professional singer, to be heard, to be admired, even adored. He had glimpsed it briefly on the tour, and it was clear to all who met and heard him that he had something, not just the voice but also an unforced charisma. Exploiting his talent was something he would have to do quickly, because as long as he was living at home he would have his mother to deal with, and the fifteen seconds of fame would soon disappear from Dolly's consciousness. It was hard to know if the fear of Dolly or the fear of failure was worse, but he was staring both in the face.

Chapter 3: The Patriarch

———————◆———————

IN STARK CONTRAST to Francis Albert Sinatra, the most important influence on the young John Fitzgerald Kennedy, and on his siblings, was, and would continue to be, his father. Joseph P. Kennedy would, for long periods of his children's formative years, be absent from the family home. Despite his efforts to give the contrary impression, Joseph P. Kennedy was anything but a family man. He was passionately interested in the welfare of his wife and children, but genuine fatherhood was a secondary consideration in his overall scheme of things.

His primary objectives were the attainment of power and status and the accumulation of wealth. He had set out to achieve these goals as fast as possible and at any cost to anybody but himself. From the outset, he played the game of money by a rule book of which he was the principal author, the first precept of which was that money was the root of all power. By his definition, the role of a financier was to use other people's money to increase his own wealth and to never, if at all possible, risk his own. In the pursuit of money, he considered hard cash to be the beating heart of business, and he believed in conducting his business on his own terms or not at all. He had a healthy disrespect for institutions, which, in his opinion, were there to be used, just like investors, to accommodate his quest to become rich. As Doris Kearns Goodwin, author of *The Fitzgeralds and the Kennedys*, put it:

Joe decided early on that he would build his life on his own foundation without depending on the loyalty of any place or institution.

That belief could, in part, be explained by the rejection by the top, Brahmin-controlled clubs he had experienced at Harvard. He had sensed that this institutionalized anti-Irish racism would follow in business life in Boston where the WASPs would never let an East Boston Irish Catholic share in the control of the wealth of the city. Kennedy instinctively knew he would have to look beyond the boundaries of his native place to find a bit more empathy for a descendant of poor Irish immigrants such as himself. The steel in his character, inherited from PJ, gave him a cold and ruthless modus operandi in the conduct of business. He took no account of moral or personal consequence or, indeed, any consequence other than the pursuit of profit.

His recognition of his place as an outsider and his hatred of the Boston Brahmins and their equivalents were summed up some years later when he told a young lawyer at the SEC (Securities and Exchange Commission): "You have to take everything from the business elite, even the gold in their teeth." In that respect, he certainly was not his father's son. PJ was an excellent businessman, tough but fair. His high standards had included honesty in all of his dealings and a deep-rooted kindness toward deprived sections of his community. He was a charitable man at heart, and his altruistic actions among the people he represented were not motivated by political hypocrisy. He was also a man of genuine empathy who understood that others from the Old Country were not as fortunate as he and deserved his compassion. None of these qualities rubbed off on the young Joe who, despite the negative experiences associated with his Irishness, remained entirely lacking in empathy, viewing the many people helped by his father as parasites as opposed to victims.

In every sense, Joe was a man driven by self-interest, with little or no grasp of the impact of his ruthless nature on others, either in his business or his personal life. His good looks, charm, and charisma ensured that this nasty persona remained hidden and his excesses tolerated. He believed that the perception of a man was more important than the reality, and he became an expert in the creation of that perception. His widespread promotion of himself as the country's youngest bank president after the failed Columbia Trust takeover bid is evidence of his talent as an arch manipulator. The bank was, in any event, a fairly modest financial institution, and Joe was also always careful not to mention the family investment, which would have greatly diluted the significance of the appointment.

He did not enlist when America entered the First World War in 1917 because, as Doris Kearns Goodwin observed, "The truth is that his abstract feelings of patriotism and justice were not as strong as his fundamental principle of self-interest." There is no doubt that abstract is the correct word in the context, but Joseph Kennedy made absolutely sure that there could be no perception that he had shirked his duty by not exposing himself to danger on the battlefields of Europe. The reality was, however, that he wanted, and sought, an exemption from the draft. He had no intention of risking his life and the future of his family, not to mention his fledgling career in the field of finance. Any reticence on his part had nothing to do with being of Irish descent or believing, as many immigrant Irish did, that joining up would make him an ally of the British Empire.

Instead Joe performed his patriotic duty at home, as assistant general manager of Boston Bethlehem Steel Shipyard, a giant company with a government contract to build destroyers at its Fore River facility. It was an enormous operation and Kennedy, with his managerial and organizational flair, along with his huge natural energy, made a significant contribution to its success. To all around him he appeared to work assiduously for the good of the war effort but, as in everything he did, there was always an eye on the main chance. In this case it was in a developing friendship with the up-and-coming Franklin Delano Roosevelt, the assistant secretary of the US Navy. He had also been hired by three of the top executives of the company, one of whom a lawyer by the name of Guy Currier. Currier would loom large in the development of Kennedy's financial empire.

His insatiable appetite for work would, for the first—but not the last—time, affect his health, leading to a physical collapse and a period of rest and recuperation. By the summer of 1919, he had had enough of the steel business, and, anxious also to restart his career, he resigned from Boston Bethlehem. He joined a small but influential securities firm, Hayden Stone, as manager of the brokerage department. That was the day job, but he also made money by stock investing and speculating on the real estate market. While he and fellow speculators operated in a very lax regulatory environment, it was still easy to lose one's own, and one's client's, money. But having insider information, the license to use it, and the know-how to employ a variety of dubious financial instruments, such as stock manipulation, provided the advantage, which Joe Kennedy could easily translate into significant financial windfalls.

David Kennedy, author of *Freedom from Fear*, puts the Wall Street of the time in perspective:

> It was a strikingly information-starved environment. Many firms whose securities were publicly traded published no regular reports or issued reports whose data was so arbitrarily selected and capriciously audited as to be worse than useless. It was this circumstance that had conferred such awesome power on a handful of investment bankers like JP Morgan because they commanded a virtual monopoly on the information necessary for making sound financial decisions. Especially in the secondary markets where reliable information was all but impossible for the average investor to come by, opportunities abounded for insider manipulation and wildcat speculation.

Such an uneven playing field provided rich pickings for a smart, young man like Joe. He had a natural instinct for a good bet and a quick return, and he and his investing partners would also pay off journalists to hype up reports on their chosen shares, guaranteeing significant interest in the stock.

In the meantime, Rose had been delivering one child after another. Rosemary was born on September 13, 1918, and Kathleen, nicknamed "Kick," arrived on February 20, 1920. All was well, and then something occurred that should have given the patriarch of the burgeoning Kennedy family long pause for thought, not to mention the realization of the fragility of his dreams and the frailty of human nature. In 1920, three-year-old Jack fell ill and was diagnosed with scarlet fever. His condition deteriorated rapidly, and he was admitted to Boston Hospital. He would spend eight weeks there with the fever fluctuating dangerously. Joe, beside himself with worry, spent every afternoon with his very ill son, casting aside most of his work. He also prayed daily and, in a form of epiphany, vowed to change his habits, spend more time with his family, and donate generously to charity. When Jack recovered after two months' recuperation in Maine, he kept one of his promises, a large monetary donation to the church. The personal reforms were, not surprisingly, set aside, and no softer or more generous aspect emerged. The crisis over, it was business as usual, and the family man stepped back onto the wings of commerce.

Joe's ruthless drive and insatiable desire for wealth was not all in the name of self-aggrandizement. He was motivated by the desire to see his family set up for life but, at the same time, could see no down-side to the fact that his general absence might have an effect on his wife and children.

Just one month and three days before Kick's birth, the Eighteenth Amendment of the Constitution was enacted, introducing a nation-wide ban on the sale, production, importation, and transportation of alcohol. The Prohibition era began, and a force of 1,500 prohibition agents were appointed to enforce the law. Myths naturally surround humans like Joe Kennedy who have exceptional talent, and, in Joe's case, it became a long-standing belief that the young businessman was, in the 1920s, partners with notorious Italian gangland figures in bootlegging, the illegal manufacturing and distribution of alcohol. Despite the many illegal activities that Kennedy had been associated with to date, or would be in the future, not one whit of real or documentary evidence has ever been put forward to support this myth. All that exists is the word of two or three notorious underworld figures. In an exhaustive search through FBI files, author Seymour Hersh could find no link between Joe and bootlegging, and no one else has succeeded in producing anything credible to back it up.

Biographer David Nasaw, who received unrivaled access to the Kennedy private papers, also concurs with the view in his book *The Patriarch*:

> Not only is there no evidence of Kennedy being a bootlegger, but it flies in the face of everything we know about him. As an East Boston Irish Catholic outsider struggling to be allowed inside, he was willing to take financial risks, but not those associated with bootlegging. Most of the stories about bootlegging originated in unsubstantiated, usually off-the-cuff remarks made in the 1970s and 1980s by Meyer Lansky, Frank Costello, Joe Bonnanno, and other Mob figures not particularly known for their truth telling.

In truth, Kennedy had neither the time nor inclination to risk his rising career by consorting with gangsters. In time this would change, but right then there was no advantage to his associating with the loose ragtag of local gangs involved in bootlegging. The Mafia, as the world would come to know it, would not emerge as the controlling force in gambling, prostitution, racketeering, and, later, drugs, for many years. Besides, Joe was making very good legal money in a variety of commercial pursuits and had begun to cast his eye toward the huge opportunities that the movie business was offering.

Joe saw his position at Hayden Stone as a stepping stone. There was no way he would become a multimillionaire by managing the brokerage department or even by eventually running the firm. But while he was eager to make his next move, he was profiting from stock speculation—in one deal he netted over $500,000. His eagerness, impatience even, was somewhat understandable. As someone intimately familiar with the markets, he knew well that regulation would eventually catch up with some of the finance industry's more unethical practices such as manipulation and stock pooling. The practice of stock pooling, in particular, was widespread. A syndicate bought up the stock until the public jumped in, driving the price up even further, before the syndicate sold at a huge profit, leaving the public out of pocket when the price collapsed. Kennedy and his associates were benefitting handsomely from this method of speculation, but the regulators, crude and all as they were, were beginning to close in on such activities.

By 1921 there was another addition to the growing Kennedy family when Eunice Mary brought the number to five, two boys and three girls. Jack was the only one who seemed to catch every bug going and was ill again in January of 1922. Fearing another crisis, his father was on alert again, but his business was not affected.

By the end of 1922, Joe was reaching the limit of his patience working for someone else and, after his chief supporter and mentor in the firm, Galen Stone, announced that he was going to retire, promptly handed in his resignation. He started the new year working out of Guy Currier's office and the Kennedy family home at Brookline. Currier, a lawyer and businessman, as well as a powerful political lobbyist, had been hugely impressed by the enterprise and drive of Kennedy at Boston Bethlehem, and was committed to helping him in every way possible, something that he would live to regret.

Around this time Joe hired Edward Moore, who had formerly worked for his father-in-law, Honey Fitz, as his right-hand man. In every sense—looks, dress, and demeanor—Moore was different from Kennedy, quiet and efficient with a dry sense of humor and the very soul of discretion. He also possessed the attributes of paramount importance to Joe: he was totally and unswervingly loyal and trustworthy. He and his wife, Mary, with no children of their own, became, literally, a part of the family. Joe and Rose naming their youngest child Edward Moore Kennedy evidenced just how important Eddie would become to the family.

With the knowledge that Eddie would look after the business at home, Joe began to spend even more time away pursuing different commercial opportunities. Two years previously he had invested $80,000, a very considerable sum at the time, in Hallmark Pictures, and lost every cent when the already teetering company went bust. It would have been enough to put most sensible investors off the movie business for good, but Kennedy was convinced that even someone like him, who knew nothing about the production of movies, could make a lot of money if he could get a foothold in a business that was rapidly capturing the imagination of the American public.

This was based on the fairly simple premise that if the big studios like MGM and Paramount were making millions, then there must be opportunities for other smart businesspeople like himself. "Look at those pants-pressers in Hollywood making themselves millionaires. I could take the whole business away from them," Kennedy is reputed to have boasted. The "pants-pressers" remark was a reference to the Jewish control of the rag trade, but the exaggerated, anti-Semitic boast was a clear insult to studio moguls like Louis B. Mayer, Adolph Zukor, and Sam Goldwyn. These three Hollywood pioneers, in particular, were first-generation immigrants who had escaped backgrounds of abject poverty and Jewish oppression to achieve positions of great power. As an immigrant descendant, with the same experiences and inclinations (although unlike the aforementioned movie moguls, Joe had been born into a certain degree of privilege), Kennedy should have empathized with them, not insulted them. Would he like to have been referred to as a potato farmer or road digger?

The irony would be that the Jewish moguls of Hollywood gave the Catholic access to their circle, which the Protestant elite of his hometown had denied him. For example, Carl Laemmle, the boss of Universal, sold Kennedy the distribution rights to New England before he made a concentrated foray into the business. For Joe, though, this was only a foot in the door, because his real ambition was to own and control his own movie company. Having been burnt on the Hallmark deal, he was also determined to avoid using his own money again and, instead, set out to persuade investors to back his acquisitions.

Not surprisingly, Joe was an ideal candidate for the job of movie mogul. He was handsome and had a natural bent for promoting himself and his projects, particularly through his expert manipulation of the media. But underpinning all this was his conviction that the glamour of movie production was a just a marketing tool, and the industry was subject to the same economic reality as any other commercial activity. As a commercial predator he could see the opportunities he had seen in the stock market and real estate. Hollywood was no different in his view. The main thrust of his efforts was to identify and exploit companies that were in trouble, buy them cheap, build them up, and sell for a big profit when the time was right. Joe Kennedy was a corporate raider long before the term was invented. Also appealing to him, as a sexual predator, was the added incentive of a ready supply of willing young and beautiful women in Hollywood Babylon.

But Joe didn't have to travel to California to meet women. Before acquiring a property there, the Kennedys rented a beach house at Hyannis Port on Cape Cod for four months every summer. The stunning scenery, combined with the long-unspoiled beaches from Provincetown at the tip of the cape right back to the Sagamore Bridge, made the area perfect for a family vacation. Joe would visit on weekends, spending his weekday evenings in Boston or New York in the company of a string of beautiful women. From the early years of his marriage, Joe had acquired a reputation as a ladies' man, and the ladies, for the most part, could not resist the combination of his good looks, charm, and money. His many mistresses occupied a place of minor importance in the scheme of his life and were treated as conquests, often cast aside without explanation. The young screen actress Betty Compson, who had starred in *The Miracle Man* alongside the famed horror actor Lon Chaney, was one of Joe's regular dates. When she discovered his simultaneous relationship with a chorus girl and confronted him with the evidence, it was she who was shown the door.

As Harvey Klemmer put it, "He liked women and women liked him. But he regarded them as a kind of food—to be consumed."

There would be one exception to the rule, but even then he did not lose his head. However, whether he chose to think about it or not, his dalliances did nothing for the dignity or self-esteem of his wife. How Joe could imagine that his Rose would not suffer humiliation as a consequence of his very public infidelities is hard to imagine, but suffer she did. By 1920 she was so unhappy that she moved back to her father's house. Rose declared herself thoroughly fed up with what was, in effect, a sham of a marriage, with only one partner observing the marriage vows and the other continuing to live the carefree life of a bachelor.

Three weeks later, Honey Fitz told his favored daughter to go back where she belonged, telling her, "The old days are gone. Your children need you and your husband needs you. You can make things work." Honey Fitz was in no position to confront the errant husband on the matter. His own dalliance with a cigarette girl and reputed prostitute, Elizabeth "Toodles" Ryan, who was the same age as Rose at the time of the fling, had recently been uncovered thanks to a poison pen letter from a political rival. It clearly did not occur to either Joe or Honey Fitz that their behavior was a ludicrous hypocrisy for so-called pillars of the community who presented themselves as devoted family men and devout Catholics. Rose was spoken to as if it was she who had done something wrong. Her father must have had more than a fair idea that his son-in-law would not be changing his way-wardness, so his advice was, in effect, to grin and bear it. Rose was both sustained and restrained by her religious faith. Separation was one thing, but divorce was not an option.

Acceptance of one's lot for the greater good is an essential part of religious belief and faith. Rose was not going to rock the boat but now took charge of it with the same rigor and control exercised

of her husband in the commercial sphere. Unlike Joe, she was a
devout Catholic and acted like one, attending Mass and receiving
Communion daily. She may, however, have taken the Old Testament
too literally when doling out punishment to her children. Her weap-
ons of choice were a coat hanger or a ruler employed on the burgeoning number of backsides in the house.

Like her husband, she wanted only the best for her children
but constantly reminded them of the responsibility that came with
privilege. The Catholic faith underpinned everything she taught, and,
leading by example, she encouraged her family to practice it without
question. Even taking into account the fault at the center of the marriage and the vast difference in attitude to sexuality, the patriarch of
the Kennedy family could not but have admired his wife's devotion
to, and expert handling of, the domestic operation.

Brad Darrach provided a close-up of that operation in an article
for *Life* magazine:

> The molding of the family was largely left to Rose and she did
> an astonishing job. She organized the household like a small
> town and ran it like a mayor, supervising a staff of cooks, nan-
> nies, maids, and secretaries. She was the health department:
> she made sure teeth were brushed after every meal, drove the
> gang to the dentist every few weeks, and kept a medical his-
> tory of each child on file cards. She was the police depart-
> ment: she regularly whacked backsides with a coat hanger, as
> well as with a ruler. She was the religion teacher: she tried to
> take at least some of the kids to church every day and after
> Sunday service she quizzed them about the sermon. She was
> the school system: she hired tennis, golf, swimming, skiing,
> and skating instructors and gave tests at mealtimes. Above all
> she taught responsibility (quoting St. Luke, "To whom much
> has been given, much will be required") and the supreme
> importance of winning ("No matter what you do, you should
> try to be first").

Rose wanted, as she said herself, God and religion to be a daily part of the children's lives. She also encouraged frugality, starting pocket money at five years of age at a rate of ten cents a week, with modest increments at each succeeding birthday. She neither felt deprived nor complained about her enormous household responsibilities. As she recalled in her autobiography, *A Time to Remember*: "I looked on child rearing not only as a work of love and duty, but as a profession that was fully as interesting and challenging as any honorable profession in the world, and one that demanded the best I could bring to it." And later, explaining her mission, so to speak: "What greater aspiration and challenge are there for a mother than the hope of raising a great son or daughter?"

In keeping with the tenets of the Catholic Church she discouraged expression of emotion, a reflection of her own state of repression and personal insecurity, all well disguised so as not to portray any sign of weakness. She could not have, if she had tried twice as hard, erased the mark of Joseph Patrick Kennedy. He was too large and strong a character not to leave his brand on his children, his errant ways on his sons in particular. By this stage Joe had purchased a Rolls-Royce and hired a chauffeur to drive it. He networked tirelessly, was a member of a number of clubs, and donated to charities. He was also beginning to make some serious moves in Hollywood.

Cari Beauchamp, author of *Joseph P. Kennedy Presents: His Hollywood Years*, describes the financier who stormed the celluloid citadel in 1926 and made both an indelible impression and a fortune before marching back out three years later:

> He strides confidently into a room wearing "the most wonderful smile that seemed to light up his entire face impressing everyone he met with his warm handshake and friendly volubility." His vibrant energy fuels a head turning charisma that commands attention. "You felt not just that you were the only one in the room that mattered," recalls Joan Fontaine, "but the only one in the world." With bright blue eyes behind

wire-rimmed glasses, a frequent laugh and a tendency to slap his thigh when amused, he is strikingly different from the typical Wall Street banker or studio mogul.

The first thing that the man who Louella Parsons, the famous gossip columnist, would describe as "the Napoleon of the movies" did was form his own team of lieutenants to help him make money from movies. The group, headed by Eddie Moore, included Ted O'Leary, another loyalist, EB Derr, an accountant who had worked at Fore River, Charlie Sullivan, who thought and spoke only in figures, and another graduate of the Fore River company, Pat Scollard. These men worked for and answered only to Kennedy, no matter what production entity was acquired. They called him "The Boss," and he referred to them as "The Gang."

Joe had a simple-enough financial plan: spot a distressed production company, buy it as cheaply as possible, and then build it up. He promised his investors that he could cut costs in half without affecting the quality of the movies, a classic slash-and-burn policy that left many employees out of work. Every cent spent on a film was tracked and reported on a weekly basis. He foresaw the future on the acting front and did not approve of the contract system but instead preferred hiring cast other than the star on a film-to-film basis.

With the backing of Guy Currier he acquired a struggling studio, FBO, and quickly established a new system of slimlined production and vastly improved marketing and distribution. Quality was irrelevant as long as the film made money. His style attracted media attention, and he became as adept at manipulating the entertainment journalists as he had been with their financial counterparts. In his short time in Hollywood he garnered more publicity than the rest of the movie moguls put together. A hundred films would ultimately carry the caption "Joseph P. Kennedy Presents . . ."

But none of the press headlines or movie titles could match the ego trip that was fulfilled by a business and sexual relationship with Gloria Swanson. But as Hollywood's premier female star was to discover, even she was expendable. She had shot to stardom in the early 1920s and was one of the world's most sought-after actresses. She and Kennedy began a torrid and high-profile affair, which Joe would shamelessly exploit by inserting a clause in a deal with her production company that she would be responsible for any loss incurred by their grand project, *Queen Kelly*. The movie, which was never released, cost her $800,000. In her autobiography, *Swanson on Swanson*, the actress recalled Joe crying over the failure of the film largely contributed to by the director Erich von Stroheim, who was notoriously profligate with studio budgets. It was not the first high-profile business arrangement Kennedy made in which one side of an apparent partnership would pick up the costs and the relationship would end in tears.

It was a time of great flux and change for the movie industry as the introduction of talkies revolutionized the business. There were huge implications for the studios, who now had to build soundstages to replace the silent format. They also had to introduce soundproofing and synchronization, and new equipment in all the theatres. Kennedy had seen the writing on the wall and formed business partnership with David Sarnoff of RCA, whose company was responsible for the transfer to sound and bought an interest in the FBO studio for $500,000. He embarked on a trail of acquisitions, approaching Edward F. Albee of the vaudeville theatre owning company and offering him $4.2 million for his stake. The idea was to add a large number of theatres to the distribution chain. After a first refusal, Albee agreed as long as he was kept on as president of the new company. Shortly after assuming the Chairman and chief executive role, Kennedy froze out Albee, who eventually left. Kennedy and his gang now had control of two major movie companies.

Such was Kennedy's growing reputation that he was asked by the struggling Pathé studio to come on board as a special adviser and help the company out of trouble. He became their effective chief executive by demanding sole decision-making authority. Within just a few months he was running three major movie companies: FBO,

KAO, and Pathé, and earning a salary of $2,000 a week from each, an annual total of over $300,000, as well as a treasure chest of stock options in all three. He also ran Gloria Productions, Swanson's production company vehicle.

It was mid-1928 and a number of investors in FBO approached Guy Currier with concerns, worried that Kennedy was losing the run of himself in business and disgracing himself in his private life. Since he had backed Kennedy in the quest for ownership of FBO, Currier had stayed in the wings while his protégé occupied center stage. He assured the investors that all would be fine, unless, he said, Joe was starting to believe his own publicity. It would become quickly apparent that this is exactly what was happening.

Kennedy and The Gang appeared to have the Midas touch, so much so that they were approached by Irving Rossheim to wave their magic financial wand at First National, a studio business that owned a lot four or five times bigger than FBO's. The Boss was offered the special adviser role with control of the company, a salary of $3,000 a week, and an option to buy 25 percent of the stock and 10 percent of profits for three years. It was a great deal, and it put Joe in the unique position of running four Hollywood companies. All he had to do was keep calm and make his impact without tearing up the foundations of the studio. But the elixir of power had its effect, and Kennedy now proved, in the most negative fashion, that he really did believe in his own publicity. He approached the task at First National with the subtlety of a battering ram.

In the interim he had not honored the spirit of the agreement with RCA for the supply of sound facilities to the studios. David Sarnoff was both incredulous and angry to discover that his company was being billed for the supply of sound services instead of the other way around. It was eventually sorted out, but the RCA chief could no longer trust his supposed partner in the venture, and set out to do what he could to reduce Kennedy's influence at Pathé.

Guy Currier also wanted to cash in his investment in FBO but the quick and savage financial and staff cuts at First National had created discontent, from the smallest department right up to board level. Cari Beauchamp describes the atmosphere in *Joseph P. Kennedy Presents: His Hollywood Years*:

> Since the official announcement of Kennedy's signing with First National board members' phones had been ringing with calls from directors and producers at the Burbank Studio unhappy with the conditions Joe's "reforms" had created. It was impossible to believe that he could slash costs by 50 percent with "no sacrifice in quality." With so many cuts already made and reportedly in the offing, they were without the support system that had attracted them to First National in the first place. The number of heads that had rolled troubled them, reducing overhead was one thing, and all-out slaughter was something else again. Fear was omni-present, with Alexander Korda coming straight out and calling Kennedy's leadership a reign of terror.

Kennedy was unmoved, and at a meeting with two members of National's board he showed no sign of compromise. He told the Board it was his intention to run the company on his own terms and then departed for a holiday in Europe. Rossheim and his board members, fearful for the long-term damage Kennedy's approach would do to their company, decided to fire him. The press release, however, announced that the separation was by "mutual consent." Joe's whirlwind time at Hollywood was effectively over, but by now he was now a very rich man.

In October of 1928 he began the unwinding of his movie assets in a series of master business strokes, which included the handling of the merger of KAO with RCA, with David Sarnoff leading the new company called RKO. Kennedy received a fee of $150,000 and then cashed in his stock options by first swapping seventy-five thousand shares of KAO stock for an option on seventy-five thousand of RKO at $21 a share. He then, with others, pulled the stock pool rabbit out of the hat, waiting while the share price rose to $50, then cashing in, making a profit of approximately $2 million.

Guy Currier got his wish when he, and his now-former business partner, cashed in their FBO assets for $5 million. Kennedy then disposed of his interest in Pathé and Gloria Productions. To the uninitiated, it appeared that, through the First National experience, Hollywood had found Kennedy and his gang out and sent them packing. But it was far more personal than that. David Sarnoff and Guy Currier were central figures in Kennedy's success in the movie business, and through his ruthless self-interest he had lost their trust. For the very same reason he lost a huge future opportunity at First National, a business eventually taken over by Warner Brothers. There is no doubt that had he played Rossheim and his board differently he could have potentially become the undisputed King of Hollywood. But while he left that particular crown behind, his treasury was richer by between $6 million and $7 million, and at the same time he proved a prescient point: a Kennedy with the right Irish team could conquer all before him.

Chapter 4: Shadow of a Gunman

———————◆———————

THE TEMPERANCE LOBBY may have won the battle to get Prohibition introduced in the United States, but in doing so it created a monster even more frightening than any fictional child of Frankenstein. The huge financial rewards associated with the distribution of illegal liquor gave the loosely structured organization known as Cosa Nostra, or the Mafia, an opportunity to flourish. The Mafia had, of course, been in existence well before the ban on the manufacture and distribution of alcohol, but the vacuum which Prohibition created offered power and riches the gangsters could have only dreamed of in advance. The plague that ensued spread the Mob's murderous and evil influence into the large urban centers, blighting them with crime of all sorts: racketeering, extortion, illegal gambling, drinking, prostitution, extreme violence, and political, legal, civil, and police corruption.

The most notorious outfit was the Chicago organization, characterized in the first instance by the gargantuan figure Al Capone and later dominated by powerful figures who would play dangerous and influential roles in the interlinking story of Frank Sinatra and John Kennedy. The genesis of the Windy City Mob was marked by turf war murders, which spiraled alongside the profits realized by bootlegging operations. Under Capone's regime, witness intimidation and corruption of city hall officials and the police department ensured that the activities of Chicago's Mafia were virtually untouched and their perpetrators remained immune from prosecution. In this era, and in Capone's gang in particular, the structure of the modern Mafia was laid down. The boss controlled the heads of the divisions through a series of subordinates selected to control the various levels of the outfit, and any betrayal, or even a whiff of it, was dealt with by summary execution.

Having failed to prosecute Capone successfully for any criminal activity, the authorities finally caught him for tax evasion and he was locked up in 1932 for eleven years. His successor Frank Nitti was usurped by his underboss Paul Ricca, who would rule the outfit for the next four decades as it widened into a multistate conglomerate spreading to Milwaukee, Kansas City, Los Angeles, Hollywood, and other parts of California with "business interests" that would include gambling, extortion, labor racketeering, loan sharking, and the drug trade.

Throughout Joe Kennedy's tenure in Hollywood, the Los Angeles crime syndicate prospered, as did their counterparts nationwide, from the alcoholic fruits of the Prohibition tree. Alberto Marco seized control of the organization in the 1920s and set up an operation partnered by the City Hall Gang. This ironically named group was made up of a corrupt political alliance led by Kent Kane Parrot and Charles H. Crawford, who between them controlled city hall bosses, the press, and top law enforcement officials.

The duo had backed a prosecutor and candidate for mayor, George Cryer, who won the election on an anticorruption ticket and was to rule the city from 1921 to 1929. He was effectively a ventriloquist's dummy, with the voice and strings provided by Parrot and Crawford, allowing them to run not just the city government but also the LA Police Department. The partnership with Marco ran the businesses of bootlegging, prostitution, and illegal gambling without fear of investigation or prosecution.

The corruption became so blatant that the press began to refer to Parrot as the de facto mayor, while Crawford was pulling in over half a million dollars a year from prostitution-related activities. In time, there was a backlash against the city hall machine, forcing Cryer to announce he would not run for reelection. The partnership further crumbled when Marco was convicted for assault with a deadly weapon. All of this activity was being watched by Joseph "Iron Man" Ardizzone, who ran successful bootlegging, gambling, and extortion operations in Southern California. Just like Kennedy in Hollywood, he identified consolidation as the way forward and saw adding the LA franchise to his existing power base as a solid commercial move.

Two of his associates, Jack Dragna and John Roselli, were ordered to move in on Crawford's bootlegging operation. Other Mob competitors were eliminated and in 1928, Marco's lieutenant, August Palumbo, was murdered by Dominic Di Ciolla for refusing a merger with another gang, and the killer promptly took over the bootlegging business. When he got too big for his boots, he was eliminated in 1931, as was Tony Buccola, head of the Matranga crime family, a year earlier. Ardizzone was now in control of Los Angeles, but before long he was in dispute with the National Syndicate on the East Coast, and in the same year that he assumed the crown, he "disappeared" and was never seen again.

Jack Dragna took over and, possessed of more diplomatic sense than his departed predecessors, bowed to the interests of the National Syndicate, whose primary objective at the time was to gain control of the labor unions in Hollywood and thus be in pole position to extort the studios and independent production companies. Dragna had an acute sense of survival, even if he was not the brightest of the bosses, knowing only too well that if he did not pay his dues to the East then he might as well dig his own grave. In any event, John Roselli was the outfit's eyes and ears in California and LA, and nothing that happened in the territory went unreported to Chicago headquarters. Handsome, dapper, and slippery as an eel, he would go on to occupy a high and trusted position at the height of the organization's power. He would also pop in and out of Frank Sinatra's life for the next four decades.

While Frank had secured his early gigs through the patronage of his mother and her powerful friends, his first real break was to be entirely of his own doing and a testament to the talent-spotting prowess Harry James. James was a colorful character and a brilliant musician and bandleader who hailed from an extraordinary background that would not have been out of place in a novel. He was born in 1916 to circus performers Everette Robert James, who was the Big Top's bandleader, and his wife, Marybelle, a trapeze artist and aerialist, whose feature act was lifting five hundred pounds with her teeth suspended above the ring. The circus traveled all over the country, and, from a very early age, Harry had adjusted remarkably well to the peripatetic existence of the circus folk, showing a natural flair for performance.

His first outing with the circus band was at four years of age, keeping beat on a snare drum. Two years later, with tutoring from his father, he was playing the trumpet, and at twelve he was leader of the second band in the Christy Brothers Circus. That familiar billing "the youngest in the world" was used to describe his youthful band leadership, probably with more justification than when the term was used to describe Joe Kennedy's bank presidency. After years on the road, the family settled in Beaumont, Texas, where thirteen-year-old Harry abandoned any pretense at schooling and played trumpet in local dance bands.

In 1935 he joined the well-known Ben Pollack Orchestra and a year later was signed to Benny Goodman's band. Poaching musicians was a common enough practice at the time, but when Tommy Dorsey tried to lure James away from Goodman, he refused. He had been earning $75 a week, and Goodman doubled his wage. But money wasn't enough to satisfy his ambition. He wanted to front his own outfit, and when he announced to Goodman that he was leaving to form the Harry James Orchestra, the not-inconsiderable matter of his contract was standing right in the way. Goodman agreed to release him and offered him financial assistance. But Benny's help was anything but altruistic. The money he gave James to help him realize his ambition was a loan that burdened him with the agreement to hand Goodman over one third of his net earnings for ten years.

The Harry James Orchestra hit the road in January 1939, and the extraordinary trumpet playing of its talented leader gave it an identity, which stood apart from other bands. Harry also knew what he wanted his musicians to play and got the best out of them by his brevity and directness of expression. There was no bullying or belting the lectern. He was a character, a hard boozer, a womanizer, and an all-around fun guy. With qualities like these, he and Frank Sinatra were made for each other. Their first meeting happened after Harry's wife, Louise, heard a live, late-night broadcast from the Rustic Cabin, and her enthusiasm for the young singer prompted him to check Sinatra out at the venue.

Still licking his wounds after the Hoboken Four debacle, Frank was working with the Harold Arden band as well as waiting tables at the Rustic Cabin. The minute James heard him sing he was bowled over, instantly recognizing his talent and the appeal that he would have to his audience. The meeting had its difficulties, however. Sinatra was delighted with the possibility that he might join a band with a growing reputation and leave his co-career as a waiter behind. He was less enthused at James's suggestion that he change his name to Frank Satin. If the bandleader had tried he could not have come up with a worse moniker. What was it supposed to mean? A reflection of the quality of the voice? It was vomit inducing, and Frank said as much, before leaving Harry at the table sucking air. James wanted to hire Frank too much to make an issue of it, and with his name intact, Sinatra signed a one-year contract at $75 a week.

His debut was for a weeklong engagement at the Hippodrome in Baltimore on June 30, 1939. He was brimming with confidence, something that left James slightly bemused as he remarked in an interview with *Downbeat* magazine: "He considers himself the greatest vocalist in the business. Get that! No one ever heard of him. He's never had a hit record. He looks like a wet rag but he says he's the greatest."

History was in the making, but it was not immediately obvious. Beside James, Sinatra looked like an ingenue, because the bandleader looked at least a decade his senior. While his vocal style was not yet the finished product, Harry James had seen the future while the critics were stuck in the quicksand of their own self-importance. George Simon of *Metronome* could muster only faint praise: "The pleasing vocals of Frank Sinatra whose easy phrasing is especially commendable." The critics were underwhelmed.

The lukewarm response by the media did not shake Harry James's faith or conviction, and he would later recall how different Sinatra was from the rest of the pack: "When Frank joined the band he was always thinking of lyrics, the melody was secondary. If it was a delicate or pretty word he would try to phrase it with a prettier, softer type of voice . . . the feeling for words is just beautiful. He could sing the wrong melody and it would still be pretty."

James was a great leader, creating a drive and sense of deep camaraderie among his band members, but as is often the way with those possessed of great creativity, he was a lousy accountant. Despite the perceived success, the orchestra was losing over $1,000 a week, and the tour bus was being pursued by owner Greyhound for unpaid bills. The extant Goodman contract was also choking him, and he eventually secured a loan of $20,000 to buy him out (over $300,000 in 2016 money). It may not have seemed cheap at the time when James's ship was sinking, but when the tide began to rise, as was about to happen, Goodman would be the loser.

In late 1939, Sinatra was approached by Tommy Dorsey. Jack Leonard, who had sung with Dorsey's band for a long time, was about to leave to pursue a solo career. Dorsey's manager set up a meeting, offering Frank a contract doubling his wages. At this stage, Sinatra was just past the halfway point of the current contract and, acknowledging the faith Harry had placed in him, was understandably nervous about approaching him for a release. In a gesture that demonstrated the innate decency of the man, James told Frank to take the deal, called his manager for Frank's contract, and tore it up.

On January 26, 1940 Sinatra played his last gig with the Harry James Orchestra in Buffalo, New York. He was genuinely upset. He had great affection for the band and held its leader in great esteem. His subsequent description of the parting would have made a fantastic closing film scene to that particular episode in the young singer's career: "The bus pulled out with the rest of the guys after midnight. I'd said goodbye to them all and it was snowing. I remember there was no one around and I stood there with my suitcase in the snow and watched the taillights of the bus disappear. Then the tears started and I tried to run after the bus. There was such spirit and enthusiasm, I hated leaving it."

Harry James's generosity would bring its own reward as he was on the cusp of making a fortune, but not before things became even worse for him. At the end of 1940, Columbia dropped the band and transferred it to a Mickey-mouse smaller label. When Manie Sacks, a Columbia executive who would feature later in Frank's life, was promoted to top dog he saw the potential in the band and promptly re-signed it to the major label.

Now signed with Tommy Dorsey on a three-year contract at $150 a week, Sinatra was discovering that his new boss was a horse of a very different color to James. Trombone was his instrument of choice, and his profession was in the blood; his father Thomas Francis and his brother Jimmy were leaders of their own respective bands. Tommy was a natural predator, and taking musicians from his rivals was his specialty. If a vocalist or musician came on his radar he would do anything, by fair or foul means, to get hold of them. He was a perfectionist, a trait that inevitably comes with a price. He even shared a few characteristics with his new vocalist—mood swings and an explosive temper.

Despite the potential for a volatile relationship, it was a great career move for Sinatra. Dorsey, with his band, was a veritable hit machine and, since signing with RCA Victor, had clocked up four top-ten hits in 1935 before achieving a national radio profile the following year. Within the band setup, the young singer would also encounter two men who would have a great influence on his future—Dorsey's main arranger, Axel Stordahl, and its then-third trombonist, Nelson Riddle. Sinatra had developed a close but complex relationship with the bandleader. Despite an age difference of just ten years, Frank looked on Dorsey as a mentor and father figure from whom he was bound to learn a lot and who liked him enough to invite him to be godfather to his daughter Nancy, who was born in June 1940.

It is well recognized in the entertainment business that one of two occurrences can split a creative partnership: failure or success. The latter came to Sinatra with Dorsey in double-quick time when "I'll Never Smile Again" hit the number-one spot in the charts in July 1940 and remained there for twelve weeks. The effect was that the audiences who had previously turned up to see the Tommy Dorsey Orchestra were now clamoring to see the band's star vocalist, who in spite of being skinny with jug ears was, because of his voice, having a big impact on the females on the dance floor.

In October of that year, the band moved to Hollywood to open a new dance venue, the Palladium, with a residency at night, and to spend the daytime making a film, *Las Vegas Nights* at Paramount Studios. Sinatra also found time to have a number of flings, including one with starlet Alora Gooding. The brief time he spent at home, when off the road, was becoming more and more unpleasant. Nancy, somewhat justifiably and with the unerring instinct of a wronged woman, was beginning to suspect the reasons for Frank's lack of contact while on the road, and screaming and roaring sessions were commonplace.

Throughout 1941 Sinatra's profile continued on its upward trajectory and, in May of that year, he was named top band vocalist by *Billboard* magazine and, by the year's end, had overtaken Bing Crosby, topping the *Downbeat* poll and bringing an end to his older idol's six-year run at the top of the chart. Sinatra should have been over the moon by this turn of career fortune—he was now widely considered to be the best band singer in the country. It had the opposite effect, however, fuelling his ambition to be a solo artist and to be his own boss. He now insisted on recording solo songs, and Dorsey agreed, appointing Axel Stordahl as arranger and conductor.

When he listened to the recorded playback of the first session, which included the songs "Night and Day," "The Night We Called It a Day," "The Song Is You," and "Lamplight's Serenade," Sinatra started talking to everyone in the studio about a solo career. The lyricist Sammy Cahn tried to dissuade him of the notion, pointing out that he was already a star with the band and that risk could easily lead to career suicide. He pussyfooted around for a while before eventually broaching the subject with Dorsey. It was totally unlike the James experience, as Sinatra would later recall:

> When I went to leave Tommy made it impossible. I remember it was in the month of September in Washington, DC, I went into the dressing room and told Tommy that I wanted to leave the orchestra and he kind of smiled. "What for?" he said. "You know you are doing great with the band; we got a lot of arrangements for you." I said, "I understand, but I just want to go out on my own." He said, "I don't think so." I said, "Okay, but I'm going to leave." He said, "You've got a contract." I said, "I had a contract with Harry but Harry took the contract, tore it up, and wished me good luck." And I added, "I'll give you one year's notice; this time next year I'm leaving."

In boxing parlance, it was round one to Dorsey, who knew he had his opponent on the ropes without really having had to try. Sinatra instinctively knew the rest of the contest would be bloody, with both fighters standing their ground. This is exactly how it turned out when the crunch came the following year. Sinatra was not going to back down this time, but because of the contract he had signed, he faced paying Dorsey nearly half of his career earnings if he walked out. There were only ten months left on the contract, but the financial fallout for Sinatra if he left could be considerable.

But the interval between the first conversation and having to wait another year had driven Sinatra from desire and ambition to consuming obsession. There were a lot of other good band singers who could at any time make the same sort of break he was considering, including Bob Ebery and Perry Como. As far as Frank was concerned, they were all lining up to take the crown as the number-one singer in America. He believed that crown would belong to him once he made the move, and he had to make the move now.

Dorsey, for his part, knew exactly how valuable Sinatra had become to the band and wanted to exploit every last second left on the contract, both in the studio and on the road. He had a lot to lose in the present but not in the future, so he could afford to play hardball. He had a star and he wanted to hold on to him, and, being the predator he was, he had no compunction in raiding other bands for talent but could not stand any of his talent leaving without his say so. The whole episode of Frank's threatened departure was becoming nasty and was causing unnecessary grief to both parties. Frank, for his part, would never, over his lifetime, forget the bandleader's intransigence.

What happened next is a tale of mystery or perhaps imagination, depending on which version one wants to take on board. One story is that Dolly asked a New Jersey Mafia syndicate boss to intervene, and Willie Moretti was the chosen negotiator with the unlikely scenario that he visited Dorsey and pulled a gun and put it into his mouth. The other was that the deal was negotiated between the lawyers of both parties without the intervention of a gunman. The story achieved mythical status when in a scene in the 1970 movie *The Godfather*, a movie director, Jack Woltz, who refuses to cast singer Johnny Fontane in a movie at the request of Don Corleone, wakes up to find the head of his prize stallion in the bed beside him. Whether the Fontane character, and his problems, is based on Sinatra and whether Willie Moretti made Tommy Dorsey a Cosa Nostra–style offer he couldn't refuse, remains unknown.

In her biography of Sinatra, *His Way*, Kitty Kelley chronicles what seems to be a credible version:

In August 1943 Frank's lawyer Henry Jaffe flew to Los Angeles to meet with Dorsey's lawyer N. Joseph Ross to try to settle the matter. In the end, MCA the agency representing Dorsey and courting Sinatra, made Dorsey a $60,000 offer that he accepted. To obtain Frank as a client, the agency paid Dorsey $35,000 while Sinatra paid $25,000, which he borrowed from Manie Sacks as an advance against his royalties from Columbia Records. MCA agreed that until 1948 it would split its commissions with GAC, the agency that Frank had signed with after he left the Dorsey band.

Given the status of Sinatra at the time and his undoubted potential recognized by Sacks, it would not appear to be a great result for Dorsey. But in time both of the main protagonists would have their say and would not provide any better insight into the truth of the matter. Sinatra said, confirming Kitty Kelley's version, "And that's how I got out of the Dorsey contract. No gangster called on anyone. Son of a bitch, I've been with that thing for so many years." Dorsey had a different version in an interview when he said, "I was visited by Willie Moretti and a couple of his guys. Willie fingered a gun and told me he was glad to hear I was letting Frank out of my deal. I took the hint."

Who to believe? It is a hard question to answer, and hard facts, needed to confirm the truth, are missing.

One certain thing was that there would be a shadow of a gunman for the rest of Sinatra's career.

Chapter 5: An American Dream

———————◆———————

B Y 1929 JOSEPH P. Kennedy had fulfilled his ambition far beyond his wildest dreams, at least where money-making was concerned. Before the Wall Street crash of October 1929, his net worth was in the region of $10 million. Despite an almost obsessive fear of losing that fortune, he was one of the lucky few that not only survived intact but also came out $1 million ahead. Within three years he would lay the foundation for another fortune by acquiring the import agency for liquor brands such as Haig Scotch, Dewar's Scotch, Gordon's Gin, and Ronrico Rum. The importation venture was not hindered by the presence of James Roosevelt, son of Franklin D. Roosevelt, now the governor of New York, soon to be the thirty-second president of the United States.

Kennedy's foresight ensured that he had bonded warehouses full of his alcoholic brands in time to profit from the repeal of the Prohibition Act in 1933. When he came to sell the company, Somerset Importers, over a decade later, he would make $8 million from an initial investment of just over $100,000. Against the backdrop of the worst depression the country had ever experienced, he had set up trust funds for his children, guaranteeing their financial security for life. He owned no less than three mansions: one in Bronxville outside New York on five acres; a second, the holiday home he had bought in Hyannis Port, Cape Cod, with fifteen rooms, nine bathrooms, a tennis court, and two acres of lawn; and a third, with six bedrooms, on North Ocean Boulevard in Palm Beach, Florida. These properties had a combined worth of close to a million dollars.

When historian James Truslow Adams coined the phrase "the American Dream" in his 1931 book, *Epic of America*, he could easily have used Joe Kennedy as a perfect example of a person who was beginning to live it. "It is not a dream of motor cars and high wages merely, but a dream of social order in which each man and each woman shall be able to attain the fullest stature of which they are innately capable, and be recognized by others for what they are, regardless of the fortuitous circumstances of birth or position."

The concept, as enunciated by Truslow, had been in existence since the early days of the American settlement with poor immigrants eking out a living on the sparse soil and dreaming of better things for the next generation, just as the Kennedy ancestors had on their poor holding in South East Ireland. In that ancestral mind the dream is a consequence of deprivation just as much as it is an aspiration. Social mobility is also at the heart of the American Dream. But despite his millions, barriers to his social mobility continued to provide the stumbling block for the Kennedy empire builder.

Joe Kennedy was fully aware of the fact that his status did not reflect his wealth or achievement. In the eyes of the blue-blooded financial aristocracy, he was an East Boston Catholic, and there was no room at the top table for a person of such lowly background. The fact that he could buy and sell most of them was neither here nor there; lineage was what counted and he didn't have it. In 1925 F. Scott Fitzgerald had explored the theme in *The Great Gatsby*, highlighting the obsession of a certain section of society with wealth and status. In the book, the central character, Jay Gatsby, emerges from a childhood of poverty to become fabulously wealthy, with a huge mansion, expensive cars, a swimming pool, and all the trappings of wealth. On the surface, he is the very essence of the American dream. His mansion on West Egg is bigger and more spectacular than his old-money neighbors in East Egg, but such obvious display of wealth and his extraordinary parties fail to impress them.

In Kennedy's case, the old money had no intention of admitting the new money to their circle, and like Gatsby's, Kennedy's wealth was regarded with added toxicity as it was wrongly assumed that it came from bootlegging. Both men have vast wealth but lack what they most crave, social status and acceptability. The novel was written in the midst of an economic boom and was a critical and commercial failure but would, in time, become a literary classic. There was no happy ending, and Gatsby's dream ends in a nightmare with his violent death. As author Lawrence R. Samuel puts it in his book *The American Dream: A Cultural History*:

"For each and every American Dream there is an American nightmare. This evil twin is always lurking in the shadows when the country is going through interesting times as the Chinese curse goes."

There was no sign of a nightmare in Joe Kennedy's life, and he had made a decision in relation to the matter of rejection by the blue bloods. If he could not join them, he could certainly climb above them, and the most obvious and effective ladder would be politics.

The political mood in the United States of the early 1930s was almost exclusively dominated by the economy. The country was paralyzed by the awful effects of the Great Depression, with unemployment standing at nearly 24 percent and the economy shrinking. Republican President Herbert Hoover, who was seeking to be reelected for a second term, had refused to implement deficit spending and financial stimulus to tackle the crisis. Instead he had appealed to rugged individualism, a concept appropriate to the days of the frontier but entirely foreign to men and women who were unemployed, starving, and robbed of all hope.

When Roosevelt announced his candidacy for the presidency, Joe offered his money, and his considerable organizational skills, to help him win the Democratic nomination. He called in a major favor, getting his friend William Randolph Hearst and his hugely influential press titles to endorse Roosevelt for the nomination. Kennedy was appointed as presidential campaign executive, his main job being to help unseat Hoover. He need not have worried. There was, in effect, no contest, and Roosevelt won a landslide victory with the Electoral College tally 472–59; the states carried 42–6; the popular vote 22,821,277–15,761,254, translating to a margin of 57.4 percent to 39.7 percent.

Roosevelt offered Americans hope with his central policy platform, the New Deal: relief for the unemployed and the poor, recovery of the economy to normal levels, and reform of the financial system to prevent a repeat of the 1929 Wall Street crash. Joe Kennedy confidently anticipated that as a valued member of the top echelon of Roosevelt's campaign team, he would get the call to be appointed to the president's cabinet and, given his financial acumen, would be offered the post of secretary of the treasury. But to his horror and acute disappointment, a Republican industrialist, William H. Woodin, was given the job, and Joe got no call to fill any other role. He arranged a meeting with the president and, after some chitchat, was promised nothing.

Roosevelt had some solid logic for passing over Kennedy for a place in his cabinet. The widespread practice of manipulating the unregulated market had led to the 1929 crash in the first place, and Joe had proved to be a master at stock dealing. The new president had vowed to clean up the practice as part of his financial reform. He had another appointment in mind for Kennedy, one that would effectively turn the poacher into a gamekeeper. Roosevelt's logic was simple and ingenious: Who knew the corrupt stock market practices better than anyone? Who, but Joe Kennedy, would be better at cleaning them up?

In 1934 he appointed Joe chairman of the newly formed Securities and Exchange Commission (SEC). He would now be running the club he had formerly been excluded from as an East Boston Catholic and would have a hugely important and influential role in the administration of a Protestant president. He was now in a position to spread fear and loathing among his former enemies. It was a task he embraced with the punctilious approach of a fanatical public servant, utilizing the talents he had displayed while making his fortune but without any sense of bad or corrupt practice.

But the news of the appointment caused much surprise and negative comments. One New Deal liberal likened it to "setting a wolf to guard a flock of sheep." Wall Street critic John T. Flynn, in his *New Republic* column, did not let balance interfere with outrage, declaring, "It is impossible. It could not happen." When someone tackled Roosevelt wondering why he had employed someone like Joe, the reply was swift and to the point, emphasizing the reason for the appointment: "Takes one to catch one."

Kennedy impressed the president with a work ethic that saw him in the SEC from dawn to dusk, forgoing the distractions of Washington social life. He returned to see his family at weekends in Bronxville, Palm Beach, or Hyannis Port but kept in touch with his children during the working week by telegram and letter, issuing advice, counsel, and encouragement to the boys. At Choate, an elite boarding school in Connecticut, seventeen-year-old Jack Kennedy had become popular with his classmates and an enthusiast at tennis, baseball, football, and golf. Apart from history and English, however, he did not extend himself in an academic sense, with the headmaster noting he had "a clever individualist mind . . . not a fully enthusiastic pupil in the academic sense."

His father was on the case in a letter, making the point but not with any sledgehammer effect:

Now Jack, I don't want to give the impression I am a nagger, for goodness knows I think that is the worst thing any parent can be and I also feel that you know that if I didn't really feel you had the goods I would be most charitable in my attitude towards your failings. After long experience in sizing up people I definitely know you have the goods and can go a long way. It is very difficult to make up fundamentals that you have neglected when you were very young and that is why I

am urging you to do the best you can. I am not expecting too
much and that is why I am urging you to do the best you can
and I will not be disappointed if you don't turn out to be a
real genius but I think you can be a really worthwhile citizen
with good judgment and understanding.

At the SEC, Joe instinctively knew that his new role as a public servant was to regulate and, in some cases, remove some of the practices on Wall Street that had made him and many others rich. He
knew that if the United States were to prosper, he would have to help
restore the health of the capital markets. The monthly average value
of new securities had collapsed from $849,000 in 1929 to $59,000 in
1933. It was a balancing act, which he managed with a sense of diplomacy, something completely foreign to his normal business.

   Although his contract was for five years, his own view was that he
was in it for the short haul. His mission, as he saw it, was to establish
the Commission and then leave it in capable hands. One particular
legacy he eventually left was the employment by the SEC of young,
talented lawyers and accountants from immigrant backgrounds who
would later be tasked to oversee the largely WASP-dominated investment firms. Another was the regular filing of information by firms to
the SEC for public consumption, dissolving the golden circle access
and giving the ordinary investor a clearer picture when it came to
making investments.

   Joe resigned after two years but was subsequently appointed to
the Maritime Commission and as an adviser to the president. But
these worthy public service involvements did not consume anything
like the time at the SEC, giving him more opportunity to interact
with his family. Speaking of his conversion to the world of politics
years later, he said, "I wanted power. I thought that money would give
me power, only to discover that it was politics not money that really
gave a man power."

   Joe performed his jobs brilliantly, at the same time winning the
friendship and appreciation of Roosevelt, confirming to him the path

to be chosen by the next generation of the Kennedy Clan. There and then Kennedy sowed the seeds of Camelot. He had found a way to rout the Brahmins and take the American Dream to a higher level, with the aspiration and real possibility that of one of his sons might one day run for the presidency.

Kennedy also knew that in business, politics, or sport, winning was the only goal; nobody remembers the also-rans, a philosophy both he and Rose would repeat over and over again to their children. The summers in Hyannis Port were run like a mild form of boot camp run by Joe when he was around and when Rose was on one of her frequent European trips. There was room for all sorts of achievement even in leisure time. It was not enough to go swimming in the pool; for Joe it was an opportunity to create all sorts of competitions. Eunice Kennedy would later recall her father's oft-repeated mantra in those summers: "Daddy was always very competitive. The thing he kept telling us was that coming in second was just no good. The important thing was to win—don't come in second or third—that doesn't count—but win, win, win."

There was little need for their father's encouragement for frantic competition to exist between Jack Kennedy and his older brother, Joe Junior. The rivalry between them would often lead to fist fights. Joe was not only two years older but, physically, much better built, and he inevitably got the better of Jack. For his part, the younger brother, whatever the punishment, would simply never give up. On one particular afternoon during a bicycle race involving a contest in which the participants raced in opposite directions to get to the winning point, a head-on collision occurred between the two, which resulted in Jack requiring twenty-eight stitches. Later there was some unproven speculation that Joe deliberately crashed into Jack when it looked as if the younger was going to win.

The Kennedy Clan: Dynasty and Disaster 1848–1984, by John H. Davis, is a monumental and interesting chronicle of the family, though it's somewhat blighted by an ill-concealed bias against the subject of the tome and Joe Senior in particular. This is probably inspired by the fact that the biographer was a cousin of the Bouviers, who would later marry into the family. Davis observes that Joe Kennedy was, in many ways, an open book, but one full of contradictions; he had a capacity for great love and affection for his family but, equally, he committed the systematic betrayal of the mother of his children. In business he possessed a capacity for great building as well as great destruction of lives and livelihoods sacrificed to the bottom line. In his book, Davis poses the question "What gave Joe Kennedy the nearly maniacal urge to win and have his children win?" He proffers this answer:

> I believe the urge stemmed from a radical personal insecurity with roots stretching all the way back to Dunganstown, Co. Wexford. Joe Kennedy came from a despised and conquered people. Brutalized by the British, the Irish, were, in turn exploited and snubbed by America's Protestant ruling class upon their emigration to the United States. Joe Kennedy was painfully conscious of a social inferiority all his life. . . . He had taken it on the chin at Harvard and Cohasset and at many other places. And he was determined that his children were not going to get the same treatment.

In spite of his fondness for hyperbole, the author provides a plausible explanation for the Kennedy patriarch's obsession with winning and his huge efforts to pass this tenet on to his children. The problem with the Napoleon complex is that victory can so easily be turned to defeat just as success is always shadowed by failure. The other underlying fault identified by Davis is a bit overcooked but contains a salient truth: remove the social barriers, and it becomes obvious that Joe Kennedy was tortured by a deep-rooted insecurity and the constant fear that his fortune and, therefore, his children's future, would be taken away.

Within a few years that fact was to be proven in the most hairraising and destructive manner and would end any personal political ambitions that Joe Kennedy harbored for himself.

In the summer of 1936 Jack Kennedy graduated from Choate and was accepted to attend Princeton University. Arriving at the college with Kirk LeMoyne "Lem" Billings, whom he had met at Choate and who would remain a lifetime friend, Jack appeared happy, but decided after a couple of months that the New Jersey Ivy League institution was not for him and applied for a place at Harvard. His desire to leave Princeton was compounded by a bout of severe gastroenteritis, which left him hospitalized in December of that year. Joe Junior was already well established at Harvard, making it much easier for Jack to fit in.

Joe Senior, replying to a communication from the dean of freshmen at Harvard, dated August 28, 1936, was, in his letter, very frank about his view of his second son's academic shortcomings: "Jack has a very brilliant mind for the things in which he is interested but is careless and lacks application in those in which he is not interested."

Jack reflected in Harvard his high school approach to subjects and confirmed his father's assessment. He excelled at subjects that caught his interest, like history and government, and got no more than average grades in the rest. He consistently ranked in Group IV and showed no signs of rising higher. He was a member of student groups and engaged in sport, but with no great distinction. Joe Junior, on the other hand, excelled academically (in a class which included Arthur M. Schlesinger, who would go on to win a Pulitzer Prize and become Special Assistant to JFK as president, and Theodore White, who would also win a Pulitzer Prize as biographer to Kennedy). It appeared to all that Joe Junior was not just the senior member of the family but in every sense the heir apparent.

Roosevelt won the 1936 presidential election with the most emphatic victory in over a century, carrying forty-six of the forty-eight states with over 60 percent of the popular vote. Joe Kennedy's continuing support and his undoubted success at the SEC and, later, the Maritime Commission, had put him in a strong position for a more prestigious post this time around. The president admired Kennedy's capability as a businessman and was appreciative of Joe's

unwavering support of FDR's eldest son, James, whose entrepreneur-
ial activities he had backed. He was exceptionally wary, however, of
Kennedy's political ambitions and his behind-the-scenes chicanery,
both of which could, at the very least, do damage to FDR's chances
of winning a third term in 1940. There's no doubt that, despite his
more-than-controversial business dealings, his Catholicism, and the
polarizing nature of his forceful personality, Joe Kennedy still had
a hankering for high office. Roosevelt knew that to turn Kennedy
against him would be unwise, dangerous even, so a scenario where
Joe would continue to feel loved while at the same time removing
him from the pitch would be ideal.

The death of the ambassador to the Court of St. James, Robert
Worth Bingham, provided the opportunity FDR had been looking for. Roosevelt offered it to Kennedy in the knowledge that the
delicious irony of an East Boston Catholic of immigrant Irish stock
returning to Great Britain as United States ambassador would appeal
to the vengeful side of Joe's personality. He was right. Joe found no
contradiction or discomfort in his immigrant ancestry. It was a political appointment, however, that both would live to regret.

Ambassador Kennedy and his children, with the exception of Joe
Junior and Jack, who were at Harvard, moved to London in March
1938. The London elite were somewhat amused by the Kennedy
desire to seek public profile in the media. The practice might have
been appropriate to a businessman and mogul, but it was frowned
upon among the members of the diplomatic corps, where reserve
and discretion were *de rigueur*. While the new American ambassador
may have been very well versed in the politics of his native country,
he had very little knowledge of international politics. It was the worst
possible time for such professional deficit as Hitler banged the drums
of war in Europe.

For Jack, his father's posting had inspired an interest in world
politics and current affairs, and after a summer visit to his family
in England he was even further convinced that his espousal of history and government was the path to follow. Both he and Joe Junior

received regular communications from the ambassador, outlining the conflicts and tensions emanating from Hitler's Germany. As Jack absorbed as much information as he could about these developments, Ambassador Kennedy was not only reading the Nazi signals incorrectly, he was also making facile and incorrect assumptions about the outcome of any future conflict and communicating them to the president.

He did not grasp the pervasive evil of the Nazi culture even after the invasions of Czechoslovakia and the Anschluss, or annexing of Austria. Worse still, he was entirely defeatist about the chances of Britain defending a German onslaught even with the help of the United States. Among the ambassador's outrageous assertions was that Hitler was some kind of genius, his turning of the German economy proving this, and that his diplomatic skills far outweighed those of his British counterparts. After the first invasion, which was inevitable according to Kennedy, there would be a negotiated settlement within sixty days. This stance alienated the British political and diplomatic establishment and rapidly became an embarrassment to Roosevelt. FDR resorted to ordering his ambassador to deliver sealed communications to the British without letting him know the contents, a sure sign that Joe had lost the trust in the president. Kennedy, like British Prime Minister Neville Chamberlain, was an appeaser, and all sympathy and patience for appeasers came to an end on September 1, 1939, when German troops marched into Poland.

The writing was clearly on the wall for Joe Kennedy. Various theories have been posited as to why, in the face of the mounting criticism, he held out for so long in a position of non-intervention, something totally at odds with Roosevelt's desire to provide vital military aid. It has been said that he was afraid of losing his fortune, and also his sons, to the war and had put self-interest before his patriotic duty. He had played a shrewd hand as chairman of the SEC, but this had been achieved by his own correct reading of the task and uncharacteristic diplomacy when carrying it out. That modus operandi deserted him entirely when he needed it most in Britain, and the net result was that he had permanently alienated Roosevelt, the very man who had helped him realize his political ambition. It is hard to believe that such a canny and clever man had allowed himself to be so out of step with his president and his countrymen.

While on a trip back home, the president summoned his ambassador to his estate in Hyde Park, New York. The content of the conversation that took place is not known, but an educated guess can be made. Kennedy's position of appeasement was an insult to both the British people and, worse still, to the Jewish communities in Europe, and in direct opposition to the president's policy. In John H. Davis's account, at an early break in the conversation, Roosevelt told his wife, Eleanor, "I never want to see that son of a bitch as long as I live." Kennedy was supposed to stay for the weekend, but he was sent packing immediately. Joe Kennedy's political ambitions had imploded as a result of his arrogance, stupidity, and big mouth, and he had nobody but himself to blame. The reason why can be speculative, but probably resides in his psyche or, perhaps, in the simple explanation that he had just gotten too big for his boots.

He had demonstrated the same ego traits in Hollywood and had gotten away with it, but he had not listened to his own much-earlier assessment that Roosevelt was a far better horse trader than he could ever be. If he had been motivated partially by the desire to keep his two elder sons out of the possibility of being involved in war, he would be proved to be completely, and tragically, wrong.

After three years' service Kennedy resigned his role as ambassador in the fall of 1940. Just over a year later on the morning of Sunday December 7, 1941, Japan launched a concerted attack on American military and naval bases in the South Pacific, including Hawaii, Guam, Midway, Wake, and the Philippines, destroying the Pacific fleet in Pearl Harbor and the air force on the ground. At the same time, Japanese ground forces invaded Malay, Thailand, and the Philippines and sank the British battleships *Repulse* and *Prince of Wales*.

As the United States declared war on Japan, Joe Junior was train-ing to fly military planes, and Jack was an ensign in the navy. Their father sent a telegram to the president offering his services: "Mr. President, in this crisis all Americans are with you. Name the battle post. I'm yours to command. Joe Kennedy."

There is no doubt that he did this with the best of intentions. In the heat of a national crisis, when his considerable organizational ability could have been used to good effect, he was ignored. While other former political enemies of the president reacted in the same fashion and their offers were accepted, Joe Kennedy was treated like a pariah. Further humiliation was heaped on him when he received a communication confirming the receipt of his wire and then silence.

This was a dark hour for Kennedy. The respectability, which the ambassadorship had bestowed on his family, had come to a shud-dering halt, and the president had cast him aside. All the wealth, the homes, the women, meant nothing without the power and influ-ence, which really mattered to him. In some sense, Joe Kennedy may always have suspected that his past and, perhaps, his enemies would have gotten in the way of him achieving real success in the political arena, but in this particular instance the fault was entirely his. His dreams now lay in ruins. But there was worse to come.

* * *

For Frank Sinatra, however, the war was somebody else's inconven-ience. In fact, if anything, it was an opportunity. Ineligible to serve in the military and classified 4-F ("Registrant not acceptable for mili-tary service"), he made himself available for troop entertainment tours while continuing to build his solo career after his departure from the Tommy Dorsey Orchestra. He had more than fulfilled his own American Dream by passing the top echelon of singers such as Dick Haymes (now with Dorsey), Perry Como, Bob Eberley, and Bing Crosby to become the most popular singer in the country. His main support came from the "bobby soxers," the nationwide army of young, predominantly teenage, female fans, many of whom were obsessed with Frank. The fanatical devotion of these fans would be repeated two decades later by the Beatlemania phenomenon that accompanied the Beatles, but Sinatramania was the original of that particular species.

For those fans and their older female counterparts, who idolized Sinatra in a more understated fashion, it was his voice and not his looks that captivated them. His extraordinary and improving vocal talent was the instrument of their seduction. Sinatra made each member of his rapidly growing fan club feel that he was singing to her, and her alone, with lyrics that were equally exclusive.

Like the Beatles, Frank was not the object of sexual adoration but represented the triumph of the ordinary—a kid from a poor neighborhood, who had defied the limitations of his status and family background to become rich and famous using nothing more complicated than the simple act of singing. He would soon occupy the collective imagination on the silver screen by extending his status to become a Hollywood star. The fact that he did not possess matinee idol looks only served to increase his appeal. In fact, Sinatra appeared more special precisely because he was not the conventional glamour boy or man. He remarked at the time that this phenomenon was not "a sex thing," as he put it, but another sort of mutual love: "Every time I sing a song, I make love to them. I'm a boudoir singer."

Inevitably, the relationship between Frank and his adoring female fans would spawn male resentment. The young men, lovers, husbands, and fathers were overseas serving their country, fighting the Axis of Evil—Germany and Japan—while Sinatra was making millions of dollars and occupying the romantic minds of their wives and girlfriends, on both stage and screen. There was nothing wholesome about the relationship with the fans because, as the men knew well, Sinatra was a sex fiend and a wife cheater in whose company no beautiful woman was safe. The World War II GI was, at best, ambivalent about Sinatra. In truth, the majority resented or hated him deeply, perceiving him as the embodiment of the stay-at-home, draft-avoiding predator. This was compounded by his scrawny, non-macho physique.

This attitude was copper fastened by the incredible fact that unlike other entertainers, who risked their lives during the war to play to the troops, Sinatra waited until after the war was over to travel with Phil Silvers and others to the Mediterranean theatre. He was too busy during the war making money and bedding women. He was also becoming more involved in Hollywood.

His movie debut in 1943 was a cameo part as himself in *Reveille with Beverley*, starring Larry Parks, a low-budget Columbia production made for the tiny sum of $40,000. The film was a huge commercial success, taking over $2 million at the box office. His first featured role followed in the musical film based on the Broadway hit *Higher and Higher*, written by Gladys Hurlbut and Joshua Logan and also starring Michele Morgan and Jack Haley. The RKO movie received mixed reviews on the East Coast, but ecstatic reviews on the West Coast, *The Hollywood Reporter* noting: "The cinema captures an innate shyness in the singer who has uniquely become an idol. . . . People who have never understood his appeal to swooning fans, have even resented him, will have no trouble in buying the guy they meet on the screen here."

The guy on the screen was the guy next door: natural, relaxed, and never forcing any aspect of performance, moving with ease from dialogue to song. Sinatra was again playing himself, which the producers correctly guessed would boost the box office. The movie, which was made with a far bigger budget than his debut, turned in a tidy profit, again bringing in over $2 million at the box office.

The *Los Angeles Times* acknowledged his performance: "He plays himself in *Higher and Higher*, appears more at ease than we expected, and should find a place as a film personality with careful choice of subjects. Crosby did, didn't he?"

The film went on general release at the start of January 1944, and with two box office hits Frank Sinatra's film career had begun auspiciously. At twenty-eight years of age he was now at the top of his game and the future radiated nothing but brightness. The making of an entertainment legend seemed a racing certainty.

* * *

In the South Pacific another future idol had also made his name, this time on active service. Nine months previously, on the night of April 1, 1943, Lieutenant John F. Kennedy was in charge of a Torpedo Patrol boat PT109, when, out of the blue, it was mowed down by a Japanese destroyer near the Solomon Islands, killing two of the crew and seriously injuring the remaining nine. Despite his injuries, Kennedy showed calmness, courage, and extraordinary leadership qualities in guiding his injured comrades to shore, including one unconscious man whom he pulled to safety by his life jacket strap. He showed further ingenuity after landing on Plum Pudding Island when, after being stranded for four days, he sent a message via island natives in a coconut to the nearby military post, ensuring the rescue of he and his crew. In recognition of his efforts, Jack Kennedy would be awarded the Purple Cross and the Naval Medal for bravery and returned home as a war hero.

But there would be tragedy as well as triumph for the Kennedys. On August 12, 1944, Lieutenant Joseph Kennedy Jr. and his copilot, Lieutenant John Willy, took off in their BQ-8 aircraft packed with twenty-one thousand pounds of Torpex explosive from their base at RAF Fersfield, sixteen miles southwest of Norwich in Norfolk, England, as a part of a secret mission known as Operation Aphrodite. The aircraft was heading to a destination in Northern France, and the plan involved the pilots bailing out over the Channel, allowing the plane to be guided by remote control to its target. On its first remote-controlled turn, Joe removed the safety pin and radioed in the agreed code word. Just two minutes later over northeast Kent, the plane was blown apart when the explosives somehow ignited. The bodies of the crew were never found. Joe Junior was posthumously awarded the Navy Cross, the Distinguished Flying Cross, and the Air Medal.

The Kennedy clan had two war heroes. Joe Senior encouraged his remaining children to admire and envy their dead brother because Joe had made the ultimate sacrifice by dying for his country. Jack Fitzgerald Kennedy was now the heir apparent to the political ambitions of his father. One prince had passed on to a greater reward, but another stood in line.

Chapter 6: Frankie Goes to Havana

———————————◆———————————

Lucky Luciano cast his cockeyed gaze across the bay and the sea, the surface dappled with Caribbean winter sunshine. The pleasurable aroma of the finest Cuban cigar, courtesy of his local *patrón*, Fulgencia Batista, drifted a pleasurable trail across the living room of the penthouse suite, the most well-appointed and expensive in the Hotel Nacional. This was a historic hotel located on the Malecon in the middle of Vedado, Havana, in Cuba. Standing on Tagana Hill, a few meters from the sea, it offered a magnificent view of the harbor and the city.

The hotel had hosted, and would host, many famous figures including the actors Johnny Weissmuller, Tyrone Power, Errol Flynn, Marlon Brando, John Wayne, and Marlene Dietrich among others. This guest was just as famous, but for all the wrong reasons. He was a murderous psychopath who would do anything to maintain his power but, at the same time, possessed talents that would have made him a successful tycoon in any legitimate business environment. However, legitimate business was not the path he had chosen, much to his later regret.

Charles Luciano wasn't an Italian American mobster, he was an actual Italian mobster. He was born Salvatore Lucania on November 24, 1897 in Lercara Friddi, a small town southwest of the Sicilian capital of Palermo. Luciano's parents had immigrated to the United States when he was ten. He'd risen to the top of the organized crime tree through a combination of greed and sheer ruthlessness. The nickname "Lucky" allegedly derived from the fact that he had survived a savage beating as a young man and cheated death, despite having his throat slashed.

Sitting opposite Lucky was his longtime business partner and Mafia accountant, Meyer Lansky. The Jewish mobster was an accepted part of the Cosa Nostra fabric, having earned his position as a friend and associate of both Luciano and another senior crime figure, the man they were currently discussing, the notorious Bugsy Siegel. Lansky and Ben "Bugsy" Siegel, who was also Jewish, had grown up together in Brooklyn and had a long history of criminal involvement. The poker-faced Lansky, who rarely displayed the slightest emotion, was visibly upset. While Luciano had never seen this side of him, he might have detected a tear in the corner of his eyes. They had sent innumerable men to their graves with just the flick of an eyelid.

But even the cruelest of the cruel, like Lucky, could concede that this was different. For the first time in their long association Lansky had let the personal interfere in the matter of business.

Luciano took a few slugs of champagne as he listened to a long memory-studded plea for the life of Meyer's oldest and most trusted partner in crime, an association that stretched back to their teen-age days in the bootlegging trade. "He saved my life at least three times. I wouldn't be sitting here only for him," begged Lansky. Lucky shrugged his shoulders: "I totally understand, but the past was the past and the present and future is the problem," he said. "Give some people power and responsibility they can't handle and they lose the run of themselves, worse still if they won't admit it and stupidly try to defend their crazy position."

Luciano ranted on: "In Hollywood he lost the fucking run of himself, thought he was somebody he wasn't, borrowed money all over the place, never paid a dollar back and cost us all." Standing up to reinforce his point, Lucky continued: "That kike, your fucking friend, was put there to screw the moguls, not every two-bit starlet that came his way. He's knockin' around with the likes of Tony Curtis and Frank

Sinatra and he thinks 'I have to have what they got.' So he borrows it from them and us, what the fuck? . . ." Then Luciano started screaming: "We send him to Las Vegas to concentrate his mind, to make money for us . . . and the bastard goes crazy on that Flamingo project and we are all, you included, left hanging for six million dollars. It can't go on, can't go on . . . just one thing to do and let someone else clean up the mess."

Lansky listened in silence shaking his head, and, putting his hand to his forehead, he made one last plea, not impassioned—he had gone beyond that. "Ok," said Luciano, "I'll see what I can do . . . but the Flamingo will have to come right, and quickly." Lansky agreed and they shook hands. He'd just plucked his childhood friend from the jaws of death.

It was February 1947 and despite the intensity of that meeting things were distinctly looking up for Luciano, the most powerful figure in the Mafia. Less than nine years previously, though, his world had fallen apart.

In the 1930s, Lucky Luciano had revolutionized the Mob from a disparate, fractious organization more focused on killing than making money, into a national corporate machine. The syndicate, as it was officially known, was operated by two dozen crime bosses who controlled bootlegging, numbers, drugs, prostitution, the waterfront, unions, food markets, and a host of other illegal, although in some cases quasi-legal, business activities across the United States. Their ultimate decision-making body, known as the commission, was effectively a criminal board of directors on which they all sat. The expanding web had swallowed numerous significant legitimate businesses all over the country and extended its corrupt hold on politicians, judges, and police officers.

Luciano had a brilliant business brain and an extraordinary talent for organization. He was also fond of the good life and rented a large suite in the Waldorf Astoria Hotel in New York. Sartorial elegance was a vital part of his image: tailor-made suits and handmade shoes, and a beautiful young woman always on his arm. But he had a vicious, ugly side, learned from many years of streetwise survival where the strong thrived and the weak were crushed, as one of his girlfriends, the Hollywood starlet Thelma Todd, found out. Luciano had a fractious relationship with the actress, subjecting her to beatings, getting her hooked on amphetamines, and, on one occasion, forcing a bottle of Dom Perignon down her throat when she refused to share a drink while she was on the wagon. On the morning of December 16, 1935, her maid had found her body slumped over the wheel of her Lincoln convertible in the garage of her Los Angeles house. Her death was adjudged by the coroner to be suicide from carbon monoxide poisoning. There was no note or testimony of suicidal intentions at the inquest, which also failed to account for a broken nose, bruises around the throat, and two cracked ribs, which under the circumstances were hardly self-inflicted.

It was the beginning of a bad year all around for the gangland boss. Thomas E. Dewey, a dogged district attorney who would later become governor of New York and a two-time presidential candidate in the 1940s, was appointed New York's special prosecutor. Having had significant success a few years previously, with the prosecution of the bootlegger Waxey Gordon, Dewey had earned the nickname "the Gangbuster." His mission now was to clamp down on the myriad rackets run by mobsters and he decided to go straight to the top by concentrating on people like Luciano with a vengeance. In a sensational trial, Lucky was charged with "pandering" and multiple counts of organizing prostitution and was found guilty, and in June of 1936 was sentenced to thirty to fifty years, heralding the end of the road for the then-thirty-nine-year-old criminal in the prime of his life and at the top of the criminal tree.

What Dewey didn't know was that he, in fact, owed his life to the man he had just put away. His first target as prosecutor had been Dutch Schultz, the German Jewish mobster who provided the only real competition to the Italian "families" of the time, but mainly worked hand-in-glove with them. When Dewey brought him to trial, but failed to have him convicted, he let Schultz know that he was preparing a new file of charges and was determined to see him put inside.

Schultz decided to order a hit on Dewey and had the exact location selected—a telephone box near the prosecutor's home, where he rang in every morning before traveling to the office. As per the rules, the planned killing had to receive the imprimatur of the top Mob bosses, ultimately Luciano. He in turn conferred with the commission and a decision was arrived at to refuse permission on the grounds that the murder of such a high-profile public official would bring consequences for the syndicate that could cause large financial losses and fatally affect future plans.

As an insurance policy against any maverick action by Dutch, Luciano had Schultz and three of his associates murdered. One of the gunmen who carried out that contract was Bugsy Siegel.

Then in a scenario that would foreshadow another bizarre collaboration between a government agency and a criminal organization a quarter of a century later, the jailed Luciano was given a break. In the middle of World War II, US military and naval intelligence officers approached labor racketeer Joseph Lanza and Meyer Lansky with a proposal for Luciano. The men controlled the port and docks along the East Coast and their workers through the unions, which were, in turn, effectively controlled by the Mob. In the wake of the Japanese attack on Pearl Harbor there was huge concern about potential and actual Nazi infiltration and sabotage of the ports, so a deal was offered whereby Luciano's cooperation, and that of his associates, would lead to a pardon at the end of the war and deportation for him to Italy as a free man. Lucky agreed, and the result was that dockworkers tied to Mafia-controlled unions, fishermen, and criminals, both high and low, became the ground observers for US intelligence agencies.

When the time came to have the bargain honored, in a further twist of fate, it was none other than the newly elected New York Governor Thomas Dewey who was calling the official shots. He could not renege on the pardon but he extracted his pound of the mobster's flesh by granting it conditional on Luciano never setting foot on US soil again. In February 1946, after a lavish party aboard a liner, Luciano set sail for Italy, first staying in his home patch of Lercara, later moving to Palermo, Naples, and Rome, eventually returning to Naples. He could have opted to settle there comfortably for the rest of his life but he was too young, at just shy of fifty years of age, to retire. In any event he missed the cut and thrust of Mafia business and even more so the power of his status. He was a king in exile and what use was his crown if he could not rule in the land where he once reigned? Toward the end of 1946 and under his real name of Salvatore Lucania, he secured two Italian passports and with the appropriate visas, traveled to Caracas, Venezuela, Mexico City, and finally Havana, where the Mob operated with impunity.

Havana was the closest to a homecoming he could get. A couple of months earlier he had ordered Lansky to convene a commission conference with "delegates" from all over the United States, the biggest since 1929. The "meeting" began on February 10, 1947 with twenty-two crime bosses traveling to pay homage to the exiled boss and to discuss a business agenda that was drawn up to secure the fortunes of the Mafia for generations to come. Among the guests was a large contingent from New York, including Frank Costello, who had filled in for Luciano during his exile, and Willie Moretti, Frank Sinatra's mentor and unofficial godfather. Tampa, New Orleans, and Buffalo were represented, as was Chicago, by Anthony Accardo and Sam Giancana. All of the invitees brought Luciano a "present" of an envelope stuffed with cash. When the envelopes were opened at dinner on the first night, the amount totaled over $200,000.

Lucky was delighted with the welcome and the fact that the gathering was prepared to secure his position at the top of the Mafia hierarchy by naming him as *capo di tutti capi* or "boss of all bosses." But the news that gave him a source of special delight was that Frank Sinatra would be coming over to hang out with the greatest gathering of the most notorious mobsters in the history of organized crime in America. Havana was not only a hot spot of mobster-controlled gambling, racetracks, entertainment, and prostitution under the protection of corrupt government officials, who made a fortune from their cut of the activities, but also a huge tourist destination for Americans, and Frank was well aware of the attractions that awaited him.

How Sinatra thought that he could visit and hang around with America's biggest gangsters without notice from either the media or the FBI, who had been on his case for three years, is hard to fathom. By now the bureau was convinced he was a major Communist sympathizer and certain sections of the press were beginning to agree. There had been widespread and persistent rumors that he had paid a lot of money to dodge the draft. More than once he had been accused of having what an FBI informant, later referred to as, a "hoodlum complex."

Even worse still was the company in which he arrived. Sinatra flew into Havana on February 11 with Joe Fischetti and his brother Rocco, who had been cousins and members of Al Capone's Chicago gang. He had spent the previous night with them in the Florida mansion owned by Luciano. The Fischetti brothers were bringing Luciano's share of earnings from the country he was barred from in several pieces of luggage. The estimated total of this cash drop was $2 million, and Frank carried his share of the loot as he stepped off the plane.

The first port of call was a visit to Luciano at the Nacional. Lucky greeted Frank like an old friend and clearly the mobster loved the singer's company. They were spotted at a number of venues and functions including a casino, racetrack, and nightclub. Not surprisingly, there was a member of the press happening to visit this haven of excess at the very same time. The society writer had observed Sinatra at the casino in the company of Luciano on two consecutive nights and at the racetrack on one of the days. Meanwhile, the Federal Bureau of Narcotics had two informants, a liftboy and a telephone operator, watching the comings and goings from Luciano's suite on the eighth floor and Sinatra's on the seventh.

While Sinatra was enjoying the nightlife of Havana, the delegates were conducting serious business by day. Since Luciano's deportation,

Frank Costello had been acting head of the family. Tensions had been building between the caretaker boss and the Genovese faction, with Vito, the head of that family, making no secret of his ambition to take over as head of the syndicate. Luciano cleverly resurrected the *capo di tutti capi* position and secured the backing of another heavy hitter, Alberto Anastasia, who, feeling his waterfront operations were under threat by Genovese, was anxious to block him.

It was political détente to avoid a potential bloodbath. The commission agreed, and Luciano, now the supreme boss, got Anastasia and Genovese to shake hands in front of all. Then the equally, if not far more, important business of the drugs trade was discussed. Some of the bosses present objected to the trade on the ground that it was dangerous as it drew too much law enforcement and media attention. This view, however, was not shared by the majority who saw it as a way to replace the vast profits the syndicate had made from liquor during the prohibition years.

Luciano had a long track record in the drugs business dating back nine years when, after the murder of Arnold Rothstein (allegedly by Dutch Schultz), he and another Jewish associate, Louis Buchalter, had taken over the murdered gangster's large narcotics importation trade. In the previous decade the syndicate had begun importing drugs from Asia and South America to Cuba, and from there into Florida. The Havana-based gambling, entertainment, and prostitution activities and the corrupt partnership with the Government, its equally corrupt President Batista in particular, provided the catalyst to make Cuba the major holding area for distribution to the United States and Canada.

Now the commission agreed that the shipments would be landed at Mob-controlled ports along the southern coast, mainly New Orleans in the state of Louisiana and Tampa in Florida. The major families would take charge of each territory: the Luciano (later Genovese) and Mangano (later Gambino) families had New York, New Orleans was in the possession of the Marcello family, led by Carlos Marcello, and in Tampa the Trafficante mob led by Santo

Trafficante Jr. was in charge. The foundations were being laid for the biggest global drugs organization in history.

The last item on the agenda for the delegates to consider was the future of Bugsy Siegel. The syndicate had put Siegel in charge of building the Flamingo Hotel in Las Vegas, which had run into all kinds of difficulties, with major delays and a massive construction cost overrun from an original $1.5 million to $6 million. The suspicion was that Siegel, with the help of his lover Virginia Hill, had been skimming off funds to the tune of $600,000. The vote was to kill Siegel, and the contract was agreed upon.

But Luciano, using the leverage of his newly reinforced status as *capo di tutti capi*, asked for a stay of the execution to see if the hotel could perform, and its virtually untenable multimillion-dollar debt be paid. The syndicate agreed a temporary reprieve. Meyer Lansky's plea to Luciano had succeeded—for the moment.

Meanwhile, Sinatra was coming to the end of his stay, totally unaware that he was even on the radar of the media and the FBI. As far as he was concerned he was an accidental tourist who just happened to stumble into a number of Italian Americans like himself, and into a bit of social fun. People generally dislike admitting they are wrong, and Frank would certainly have fitted that category, but one thing he could not possibly be called was naive. He was about to face a rude awakening, as was his host.

Within a week, Scripps Howard journalist Robert Ruark, a hard-living, drinking Hemingway wannabe whose column was syndicated to over one hundred newspapers, ran an exclusive on the singer's Havana trip with a typically provocative headline:

"Sinatra is playing with the strangest people these days."

The dateline was Havana, February 20, and Ruark wrote:

It is probably my wistful old worldliness cropping up again, but I am frankly puzzled as to why Frank Sinatra, the lean thrush and fetish of millions, chooses to spend his vacation in the company of notorious convicted vice operators and

assorted hoodlums from Miami's plush gutters. This curious desire to cavort among the scum is possibly permissible
among citizens who are not peddling sermons to the nation's
youth, and may even be allowed a mealy-mouthed celebrity,
if he is smart enough to confine his social tolerance to the
hotel room. But Mr. Sinatra, the self-confessed savior of the
country's small fry, by virtue of his lectures on clean living
and love-thy-neighbor, his movie shorts on tolerance, and his
frequent dabblings into the do-good department of politics,
seems to be setting a peculiar example for his pimply, shriek-
ing slaves who are alleged to regard him with the same awe as
a practicing Mohammedan for the prophet.

The FBI agents were assiduous followers of syndicated columns, and
there was more grist for their mill when other columnists jumped
on the bandwagon. Hearst writers Westbrook Regler of the *New York
Journal-American* and Lee Mortimer of the *New York Daily Mirror*,
both of whom had been attacking Sinatra for being a draft dodger
and Communist sympathizer, now gleefully put the boot in, com-
menting specifically on the low end company Frank was keeping.

Within a week of Ruark's article being published, the first of the
FBI's files on Sinatra had been compiled. The four-page document
had, interestingly, only three paragraphs on Frank's mob connections
and twenty about alleged associations with subversive or Communist
groups, reflecting the current obsession of the agency's director, J.
Edgar Hoover. Draft dodger, proven or unproven, but equated with
coward, Communist sympathies or mere suspicion, and carousing
with the most dangerous and powerful criminals in America could
hardly endear Sinatra to the ultraconservative director who would
wait in the long grass for fourteen years before he pounced.

Sinatra's sense of self-preservation from powerful enemies,
mainly the press, was clearly not too finely tuned at the time, if it
ever was. His Havana jaunt had put him in the firing line of powerful hacks. He should have taken his medicine and run. He also

underestimated those with whom he was dealing and their power. Both Ruark and Mortimer were tough, hardened newsmen with a highly developed sense of their own self-importance when it came to their craft.

Ruark's column would eventually be syndicated to 160 publications. Mortimer occupied a lofty position in *The New York Daily Mirror*, where he forged a close association with the editor Jack Lait and was a highly prized reporter and critic and had a long-running Broadway column. By 1939, he even had his own radio program. These were two guys to avoid in person if at all possible, especially when you were already on their slating menu. All the more so when Sinatra's response to their latest criticism was laughable given both the facts and the evidence. "I was brought up to shake a man's hand when I am introduced to him without investigating his past. Any report that I fraternized with goons or racketeers is a vicious lie," he said. He told gossip columnist Hedda Hopper that he had dropped by a casino in Havana one night and was asked if he would mind meeting somebody and had shaken the hands of a few guys. These were staggering statements to make when, in the first instance, they were blatantly untrue. Photographic evidence, which emerged later, would prove that it was Sinatra who was peddling the lie.

A couple of weeks after returning from Havana, Frank spotted Lee Mortimer and his date at Ciro's restaurant in Los Angeles and followed them outside. The most recent jibe had appeared in a Mortimer film review in which he named the actor as Frank "Lucky" Sinatra. It started with a verbal altercation before Sinatra punched Mortimer but delivered a far bigger one to himself when the pack of already slavering media hounds tore him limb from limb in the aftermath. How dare a mobster's minion, a pinko, a draft dodger, attack a member of the free press, was the tone of virtually all the pieces.

Sinatra was arrested the following morning and accused of battery, handing the hacks open shooting season on a plate. Kay Kino, Mortimer's date, said she saw Sinatra throw the first punch before somebody grabbed the journalist and held him, allowing Frank to hit him again. Photographer Nat Dallinger, widely regarded as Hollywood's first paparazzo, who was there also, corroborated the account. The FBI, in the usual fashion, followed this episode with glee, collecting all the media reports and contacting Mortimer to see if they could help him connect Sinatra with subversive groups. The columnist was far more interested in his Mob connections as a joint author, with his editor, of a series of best-selling crime books, so there the potential collaboration with the FBI ended. The episode concluded with Sinatra paying out $9,000 in compensation to Mortimer, not an inconsiderable sum at the time, but the humiliation and adverse media attention was far more costly.

The incident also brought unsolicited and unwanted attention onto the syndicate. The media furor surrounding the assault had alerted the authorities to the renewed presence of Luciano in Cuba and the brazen act of holding court with a "conference" just ninety miles from the country from which he had been deported. With typical arrogance, the Godfather had assumed that his connections with Batista and others, and the revenue from the Havana operation, would ensure that he could oversee the plans to make the island a vast drugs warehouse, from which he could operate with impunity.

Lucky clearly underestimated the determination of the United States law enforcers to have him out of the way. Within weeks the authorities threatened the withdrawal of essential medical supplies if the Cuban government did not agree to deport him on a permanent basis. They complied rapidly, and the architect of the modern Mafia, the *capo di tutti capi*, was on his way back to Italy.

Meanwhile, despite another plea from Lansky, Bugsy Siegel's luck finally ran out. While a re-launch of the Flamingo had proved moderately successful, the future under Bugsy's control looked uncertain. The liability of his presence in the Mob was further underlined when he refused to report his California "earnings," namely his skimmed cash, saying he would return loans in his "own good time." His imminent execution was becoming well known in Mob circles. His girlfriend, Virginia Hill, had slept with a slew of top mobsters including

Joe Epstein in Chicago, Moe Dalitz of Detroit, Joe Adonis in New York, and Tony Accardo of Chicago. She was held, relatively speaking, in high regard by all of them because she knew how to keep her mouth shut about business and talk at length about nothing. But the relationship was incredibly volatile, fuelled by jealousy, other affairs, and Siegel's propensity for violence, which often left Hill battered and bruised. This angered other mobster ex-lovers, particularly Moe Dalitz, another Jewish associate of Lansky, who threatened to kill Bugsy. He was quietly told not to bother; it was already being looked after.

The planned hit was reinstated with Lansky's reluctant approval. On the evening of June 20, 1947 after a meal out with some friends, Siegel returned to the house Hill rented in Beverly Hills. As he relaxed in the living room, a man with a powerful army carbine took aim through an open window and blasted off nine shots. Three hit Siegel, two in the head and neck, causing one of his eyes to eject and land twelve feet away. Half of his once-handsome face was blown off. Twenty minutes later, two of Lansky's associates, Gus Greenham and Moe Sedway, walked into the Flamingo and took over. One of a crowd of mourners who visited Hill's house the following day to pay his respects was none other than Frank Sinatra.

Three years later Frank's career had gone into free fall, perhaps by the cyclical nature of the entertainment business no more immune to gravity than the rest of the earth. He propelled the fading light of his professional life further into personal darkness when he embarked on a very public and scandalous affair with Ava Gardner, ruining his marriage to Nancy. Even his voice was beginning to crack. With a supreme sense of hypocrisy, since Mafia bosses would screw any woman in sight, Willie Morretti dispatched a telegram to Sinatra when he heard the news of the split from Nancy:

"I am very much surprised what I have been reading in the newspapers between you and your darling wife. Remember you have a decent wife and children. You should be very happy regards to all. Willie Moore."

Sinatra would much later reflect on the man he was then and would continue to be by saying that he had lived a life of violent emotional contradiction with an over-acute capacity for sadness and elation. He was also desperate for some sort of decent recognition and a form of respectability that his profession and associations denied. In all he was reaching out for something, the potential consequences of which, as with his trip to Havana, deserted him.

The FBI was proving as hard to shake off as the papers. Sinatra had become aware that the bureau had been keeping a keen eye on him, particularly since the Havana conference. Despite the feigned arrogance of his dismissal of them as a concern, Sinatra knew the negative impact public knowledge of continued FBI interest in him could have. In late summer he made contact with the agency through an intermediary. On September 7 of that year, FBI Assistant Director J. P. Mohr wrote a memo to Deputy Director Clyde Tolson:

> (Redacted) called to my office today after having endeavored to arrange an appointment to see the Director . . . to contact the Director with regard to a proposition Sinatra had in mind. (Redacted) stated that Sinatra feels he can do something good for his country under the direction of the FBI . . . by going wherever the Bureau decides and contacting any of the people from whom he might be able to obtain information.

Tolson wrote a line at the bottom of the memo:

"We want nothing to do with him."

Director J. Edgar Hoover added, "I agree."

It seems incredibly hard to fathom what was going on in Sinatra's mind to offer himself as an informant or go-between for the FBI and to offer to pass on information, the only currency of which would be found in his Mob connections. The implications of being found acting that way are too horrifying to contemplate. Admirers or not, Lucky and his associates would not have had one second of hesitation in feeding him to the fish. The fact that the FBI was having none of it must have been a further humiliation, as they had used, and were using, men of far more dubious character than Frank to tout information.

It is also certain that Hoover was well aware of another oncoming train that would give Frank more grief than the evidence of this memo would suggest he could bear.

Evidence of Sinatra's nascent trips into the underworld were emerging at the Senate committee on organized crime, headed by Estes Kefauver, the man who would eventually beat Jack Kennedy to take the democratic vice-presidential nomination in 1956. Sinatra's Havana trip was exposed to the committee by a package of photographs showing him consorting with the major figures who had run the convention, including one photo of him with his arm around Luciano on the balcony of the Hotel Nacional. There were many other incriminating images of him consorting in various venues with the assembled mob. So much for being introduced to "somebody" in a casino.

The committee's lawyer, Joseph Nellis, wanted to question Sinatra in public along with Costello, Lansky, and others, a move which would probably have finished Frank's career there and then, had it happened. Instead Sinatra's lawyer suggested he would answer questions in private and agreed to a meeting with Nellis in a law office in Rockefeller Center, Manhattan, at 4 a.m. on the morning of March 1, 1951, a time when there would be no possibility of the press finding out. When Frank arrived, having been dragged out of bed for the occasion, he was extremely nervous and, looking the worse for wear, chain smoked all throughout the interview. Despite weak explanations and the demeanor of a man who had a lot to hide, Sinatra emerged relatively unscathed. Nellis was in possession of very incriminating evidence and his interviewee responded with weak explanations. But he appears to have given Frank a very easy ride.

He began by going through some routine introductions, scarcely paying attention to names. He asked Sinatra if he knew Lucky

Luciano. Frank responded by saying that if he had heard his name he wouldn't have associated it with the notorious underworld figure. The fact that Sinatra's grandfather was born in the same village as Lucky obviously escaped the brief of his interrogator. On the subject of the meeting of the two men, Frank reiterated his previous claim that they had been briefly introduced in a hotel restaurant. After this innocent encounter he had just gone back to his hotel room, Frank stated. On the subject of the money drop to Lucky, Sinatra pleaded total ignorance. Asking about the suitcase he'd carried off the plane, Nellis claimed the FBI believed he'd been carrying hundreds of thousands of dollars in his bag for Luciano. Sinatra said that it contained art supplies, his "razor and crayons." One of Sinatra's lesser-known hobbies was sketching. When it came to meeting Mob guys it was all a matter, Sinatra insisted, of "hello and goodbye" and for some reason beyond credulity, Nellis and his boss accepted that there was no good reason why Frank Sinatra should be interviewed in public. He was off the hook.

Within three years, his career would be back on track and he would have made an extraordinary comeback to the top of the entertainment tree. Anxious then, as always, to expunge the view that the American public still believed he was a draft dodger, Frank then offered his services to entertain the troops engaged in the Korean war. His offer was rejected.

Two years later he offered again and was turned down. Hoover and the FBI were watching with interest. A September 1954 memo contained details of a meeting between Sinatra and three army generals to discuss the denial of clearance for Korea. General E. Kastner pointed out that "a serious questions exists with Mr. Sinatra's sympathies in respect to Communism." Frank replied that he despised Communism and would be going to the attorney general to clear his name.

This was Sinatra's last formal, and ultimately rejected, attempt to be accepted by the establishment. Within a short few months and by dint of circumstance, he would become a part of it by accident and association. A family tie to his Rat Pack act would hook him onto the rising political star of the Kennedy family of Boston and, in particular, John Kennedy, who was blazing a trail that was planned to end at the White House.

As a postscript to the Havana events and his perceived association with the Mob, and to give further lie to Sinatra's denials about his relationship with Lucky, several years later when the Naples police searched Lucky Luciano's house, they found a gold cigarette case with the inscription "To my dear pal Lucky from his friend Frank Sinatra." His frequent denials of his connections were beginning to wear very thin indeed and his career was going in the same direction. The shadow of Havana showed no signs of fading; rather, it would come back to haunt him.

Chapter 7: Kennedy's Irish Mafia

———————◆———————

As the second World War drew to a close, Joe Kennedy's appeasement "antics," as they were seen in the United States, had left him outside the center of the Democratic Party and his own dreams of high political office, however fanciful, lay in tatters. With his namesake and eldest son now dead as a result of a war, which he had spoken so vigorously against, Kennedy now invested his energies and his considerable wealth in the political advancement of his second.

Many important elements need to be in place before an aspiring candidate can run for office: his or her inherent attractiveness and capability, the monetary muscle required to finance a campaign, and somewhere advantageous to run. Jack had plenty of the first two, and Joe had unlimited amounts of cash. The problem was finding a suitable district where Irish roots would be an advantage and where Catholicism would not be the opposite. Early on the congressional seat of the Massachusetts Eleventh Congressional District was identified as a possibility. The last three representatives had been of Irish extraction and the district was progressively favoring this particular demographic, as hard working descendants of immigrants, with their fortunes improving, moved south of the city. Located on the south side of Boston, bordering the Kennedy home neighborhood of Brookline, the district consisted of Cambridge, Somerville, East Boston, the North End, and Brighton. It also covered the waterfront area of Charlestown, an area regarded as extremely pro-Irish, and east Boston, the neighborhood in which Joe grew up. But a problem stood in the way of clearing the field for Jack.

The incumbent, the legendary James Michael Curley, was a powerhouse of state politics, having served three terms as Mayor of Boston (succeeding Honey Fitz for his first term in 1914), a term as governor of the state and a previous term in Congress earlier in the century. It seems somewhat odd that Curley might eschew the national stage for a return to state politics, but the local power which the mayor's office offered had always been a draw for Curley; as a congressman he had no budgetary control, and in the mid-1940s he appeared anxious to restore his local reputation, whic had suffered as a result of a number of scandals. The lure of Joe Kennedy's money, which almost certainly changed hands even if only for electoral support purposes, and the fact that he would, at the very least, be storing up some favors with the Kennedys and, indeed, Honey Fitz, an old adversary, probably tipped the balance. In any event Curley announced he would not seek reelection to Congress. Having been elected Governor of Massachusetts, another Irish American, Maurice Tobin, had vacated the mayor's office leaving John E. Kerrigan as the acting mayor. Kerrigan was no match for Curley and the wily campaigner was back in city hall for a fourth term as mayor.

When he returned from the war a job as a journalist was arranged for Jack at *The New York Journal-American*, a newspaper owned by Joe's friend William Randolph Hearst. He wrote widely on political topics and covered the British general election of 1945, which saw the mighty war leader and Kennedy hero, Winston Churchill, electorally dumped, in the most unceremonious manner, in favor of the left leaning Clement Atlee. By the end of that year he was ensconced in Eleventh district politics and had begun to promote himself and his candidacy throughout the wider Boston area. It's somewhat difficult to believe today, given all that has happened to the family in the intervening seventy years, that the Kennedy name was relatively unknown in Boston at the time. PJ Kennedy had died in 1929 and the main political power of the previous fifty years had been achieved in the name of the Fitzgeralds.

Both Jack and his father knew that they would need to harness the political goodwill built up over generations on both sides of the family in order to get the young candidate on the first step of the political ladder. To turn that goodwill into votes, Kennedy needed a team, and Joe, with the ever-present assistance of Eddie Moore, began to assemble a group of operatives, who would provide the sort of expertise they knew it took to construct a political campaign. Whether it was deliberate or by coincidence, the key figures that emerged as the backbone of Jack's team around this time had two main characteristics: they were unswervingly loyal to Kennedy and the wider family, and they were Irish. They would all, almost without exception, remain with Jack for the greater part of the next two decades and share in the extraordinary highs and tragic lows of his political and personal life. As Lawrence O'Brien III would later remark about this extraordinary group of men who became known as Kennedy's Irish Mafia, "They were there at the beginning, and they were there at the end."

Joe Kane, old man Kennedy's cousin, was first to join. A veteran of many local political battles in Boston, he was instrumental in bringing some of the early team together, and his no-nonsense approach to understanding the Eleventh Congressional District, and what it would take to deliver a seat there, meant the campaign wasn't lumbered with time wasters. His early selection of Bill Sutton, a returning soldier who had worked on two previous elections in the district and had a deep "on-the-ground" understanding of the electorate, was important because of his knowledge, but significant also because of one recommendation he would make. Sutton, quoted by Kenny O'Donnell in the book *Johnny We Hardly Knew Ye*, says, "I told him (Jack) he should try to get Dave Powers because Dave knew every voter in Charlestown by his first name. Dave and I used to sell papers together in the Charlestown Navy Yard, so that was ten thousand people Dave knew to start with."

Powers wasn't interested in Sutton's approach and so Jack decided to give it a try himself. On the evening of January 21, 1946 he showed up to the top floor apartment at 88 Ferrin Street in Charlestown, where Dave was staying with his widowed older sister and her eight children. Jack stuck out his hand and said, "My name is Jack Kennedy and I'm a candidate for Congress." The two struck up an immediate rapport and thus began one of the most important and significant relationships of Jack Kennedy's life. Dave would stick by Jack through thick and thin and while most others would come and go over the coming years, Powers would remain Kennedy's closest friend until the end. Within a couple of weeks Dave was the local Kennedy man, renting a vacant premises on Main Street as the Kennedy for Congress Charlestown HQ and collecting the $50 a month from Eddie Moore to pay the rent.

This somewhat haphazard approach to volunteer or staff recruitment yielded some of the most effective and loyal members of the team. Through John Dowd, a friend of Joe's who ran a Boston advertising agency, Jack was introduced to John Galvin, the firm's public relations director, who supervised the drafting of press releases and speeches. He in turn brought a school and college friend of his named Mark Dalton into the group. How Dalton met Jack is symptomatic of the chaos that existed in the early days of the 1946 campaign for Congress. Dalton had recently been discharged from the Navy and had set up his own law practice: "I was sitting there alone with the desk and the books and wondering what I was going to do, and the phone rang and the call was from John Galvin." Galvin explained that Kennedy was in his office and that he was going to announce his candidacy in a radio speech that evening. Galvin knew that Dalton had experience in both politics and writing, having worked for a local democratic politician called Paul Dever. "Could you give us a hand on this speech?" Galvin asked. "I'd be glad to," replied Dalton. Powers later claimed that Dalton became Kennedy's most-trusted and most-influential political adviser and that he "listened more to Mark than to anyone else" over the next six years. Apart from his political experience, Dalton brought a keen intellect to the table and took an interest in the detail of matters such as labor laws, housing, taxation, and other subjects, the details of which bored Jack.

As the Kennedy organization became more structured, key operatives began to take responsibility for individual regions of the district in the same way that Dave Powers was the point man in Charlestown. In Somerville, the man was Ted Reardon, a roommate of Joe Junior's at Harvard and a close family friend, who would become Jack's congressional assistant. In Cambridge, it was John Droney, and Billy Kelly in East Boston. The central campaign headquarters was the Bellevue Hotel on Beacon Street, where Honey Fitz was living in retirement and Jack lived for the first months of the campaign, before moving to a rented apartment at 122 Bowdoin Street, just around the corner. Friends and volunteers generally entered the campaign by way of a visit to the hotel to meet and get the "once over" from Joe.

Jack also collected old friends to lend a hand, although it became clear that many of them were joining, not just out of a sense of loyalty, but because they genuinely believed in him. Paul "Red" Fay, who had served in Jack's unit on PT109 during the war, came from his California home and stayed at the Bellevue for two months. His Choate friend Lem Billings postponed his postgraduate studies in order to see the campaign out.

Kennedy's youthful vigor meant that he could endure a longer day than most of his older rivals, as Dave Powers recalled: "I'd get him out of bed at the Bellevue Hotel at around six thirty in the morning and we'd rush over the bridge to Charlestown. He would stand outside the Charlestown Navy Yard from seven to eight, shaking thousands of workmen's hands as they went in to their jobs." After a day of walking, canvassing, and shaking hands, the day would inevitably end in a house in the district where there would be a rally or political forum: "We would arrange with young girls, schoolteachers or telephone operators or nurses, to invite their friends to a party at their house to meet Jack." The undoubted success among the female voters was taken to a new level by Rose and her daughters when they hosted a series of teas, designed to introduce Jack to the more mature female voters. People turned up in the hundreds for a chance to meet Joe and Rose as well as their handsome, eligible son. The undoubted success of the initiative, which some of the campaign team were flat against, on the grounds that it all seemed too "effeminate" in the tough Eleventh district, delivered even more female support than Jack's inherent charms were undoubtedly yielding. It was also clear that this new pace was being driven by the nucleus of key operators who were now working with Kennedy on a daily basis and who had replaced, to a large extent, many of the older political veterans who hung around the Bellevue with Joe or Honey Fitz.

The hard work, the vitality of the campaign, and the thousands of dollars spent—either on legitimate items by the volunteer team or on less legitimate ones by Eddie Moore on Joe's behalf—paid off, and Kennedy's first outing as a candidate was a spectacular success. Having won the primary in some style, achieving twice the vote of his nearest challenger, he swept to victory in the election, overwhelming his Republican opponent, Lester Bowen, by 71.87 percent to 27.05 percent. He took his seat as a freshman congressman on January 3, 1947.

It was clear from the outset that John Fitzgerald Kennedy was going to be his own man when it came to political decision-making. He also saw the cronyism of the old-school politicians as counterproductive to his interest in getting things done. To Jack they operated as a club, with their well-being often coming before those of their constituents, and he purposely eschewed powerful figures such as John McCormack, the king of the Twelfth District and leader of the Massachusetts Democrats. Despite this and his failure to go along with his fellow Democratic congressmen on a number of issues, Kennedy was reelected unopposed in 1948 and destroyed his republican challenger, Vincent Celeste, with over 80 percent of the vote in 1950. There is no doubt that Jack could have remained in Congress indefinitely and effortlessly, as McCormack did for over forty years, but he had already laid plans for a statewide campaign with his eyes on the Senate for 1952.

Despite his enormous popularity as a congressman in his own district, the jump from a Congressional candidate to one for the Senate was a huge one, even for someone with all of the requisite skills of a new era politician such as Kennedy. Massachusetts might have been among the smallest states geographically, but the 1950 census ranked it as the ninth most populous in the United States, with a population of over 4.6 million people. To garner votes right across the state from the western part of Berkshire County, which borders New York State, to Provincetown at the tip of Cape Cod, Kennedy would have to appeal to a wide diversity of voters. He also faced another major obstacle. Henry Cabot Lodge Jr., the incumbent, who was fifteen years older than Kennedy, appeared impossible to beat. Lodge had an impressive record as a politician and a war hero, having given up his seat to fight in World War II, easily regaining his seat on his return with nearly 60 percent of the vote, and reentering the Senate on the same day in 1947 that Jack first sat in Congress.

But Lodge made two mistakes as he eyed reelection. In late 1951 he was instrumental in persuading Dwight Eisenhower to seek the Republican nomination for president against Senator Robert Taft of Ohio. Having done so, he became Eisenhower's campaign manager and, in doing so, neglected his own Senate campaign. His second mistake was to underestimate the Kennedy appeal and the well-oiled political machine that had been gathering around the thirty-four-year-old. Since the congressional contest of 1946, Powers, Reardon, and Dalton had been pivotal to Jack's electoral success, and Dave, in particular, had been central to the running of his personal life. Now three new faces were to enroll in the group, who would become more important in time—with the notable exception of Powers—than any of the others: Kenny O'Donnell, Larry O'Brien, and the candidate's younger brother.

In February of 1952, Kenneth P. O'Donnell, who, as a young man, had helped out on the 1946 campaign, joined the team full time, compliments of a call from Bobby, who knew he wanted to get into the business of politics. Kenny had demonstrated a strong political nous and fierce, uncompromising loyalty to both Kennedy brothers. O'Donnell was a football teammate at Harvard when he met Bobby, and the two had hit it off immediately. Kenny was from Worcester, about fifty miles west of Boston. Steeped in the Irish American Catholic tradition, his father, Cleo, was the football coach at the College of the Holy Cross and later its director of sports, and Kenny was a star player himself, eventually becoming the starting quarterback on the Harvard football team in 1947. O'Donnell was tenacious, progressive, and, in time, a ruthless organizer, who immediately made his instinctive feel for politics noticed in the Kennedy organization. Sharing an office with Mark Dalton, who had assumed the role of campaign manager, he began to learn more about the campaign for Senate as well as to spot the roadblocks, which were holding up the ability of the workers on the ground to make more progress.

When the organization began to move into a higher gear after Kennedy's announcement of his candidacy in April, these blockages became more apparent and O'Donnell found himself at the center of a decision that would change the direction of the campaign. Citing unmanageable interference from Joe Kennedy and his older political cronies, Dalton resigned. Kenny immediately turned to Bobby as the only person he believed could, as he put it "control the old man," but Bobby's answer was simple: "Don't drag me into it." He was dragged into it, however, and within days Bobby had assumed the role of campaign manager. Despite what could have been construed as feigned disinterest, Bobby launched himself into the role with gusto, adding the element of decisiveness, which had been lacking up to that point. As O'Donnell remembered, "There was no more lack of administrative authority. When you wanted something done, Bobby would say go ahead and do it and it was done, period."

Despite all of this new professionalism, there was a sense that younger members of the team, like Bobby and Kenny, who had assumed positions of pivotal importance, were, in many ways, learning on the job. If Joe Kennedy and his sons were agreed on anything, it was that the Kennedy organization needed more experienced professional help, and that help came in the form of Larry O'Brien. At thirty-five, the same age as Jack Kennedy, he was already a political veteran, having been recruited by his father, at just eleven, to serve as a volunteer in the 1928 presidential campaign in his home area of Springfield in Western Massachusetts, where O'Brien senior was a local leader of the Democratic Party. Young Larry had worked closely with the local Springfield congressman, Foster Furcolo, since 1942 and had learned the ins and outs of local political machinery. Accounts differ as to whether he became available to the Kennedy team after a falling out with Furcolo or whether Furcolo fell out with him because he joined Jack's entourage. Either way, he soon became an invaluable insider who, with his understanding of campaign structure, communications, and the developing science of polling, complemented the skills that the others in the Irish Mafia brought to the table.

By the autumn of 1952, the campaign was in high gear, and Jack's weeks and months of touring the state and meeting people were paying dividends. While there was an air of confidence in the Kennedy camp, there was still a sense that Eisenhower's strength in the presidential race, the vote for which would be held on the same day as the Senate election, would help carry his good friend Lodge over the line. When the votes were counted on November 5, Eisenhower won the presidency by a landslide, with 55 percent of the popular vote. In Massachusetts's Senate election, where the new president achieved over 54 percent, his strength failed to deliver for Lodge, with Jack winning with 51.4 percent of the vote.

It was more than a validation of Kennedy's popularity as an attractive, progressive candidate for a new generation. His win demonstrated that the old order could be changed and that people with limited experience could succeed in politics, and indeed, in political management. Central to the success, though, was the team that surrounded the candidate, and central to that team was its Irishness and its unswerving loyalty to Jack Kennedy.

Jack had also brought another key asset onto the team. In May of 1951 he'd been introduced to Jacqueline Bouvier at the home of his friends Charlie and Martha Bartlett. The Bartletts had figured that the two would get on and that proved to be the case. Urbane, charming, attractive, and sophisticated, Jackie was an ideal addition to Jack's profile, despite the reservations of his sisters because she was not too interested in the "rough and tumble" of the Kennedy outdoor lifestyle.

Joe, however, approved of the match. There were rumors that, in an attempt to create the perfect political package for his son, Joe had approached Jack Kelly, the Olympic rowing champion and father of the movie star Grace Kelly, about marriage to his daughter, and that money had been discussed. Joe apparently had been rebuffed, and Grace went on to marry Prince Rainier of Monaco in 1956, with a $2 million dowry from her father. Joe knew that Jackie had some dubious relatives, including her father, the notorious gambler and womanizer, John Vernou "Black Jack" Bouvier, but, then, he was in no position to lecture on the subject of skeletons in the cupboard.

The wedding took place in Newport, Rhode Island, on September 12, 1953. and was the society event of the year. Joe ensured it received the widest coverage possible in the society columns of the national newspapers and magazines. Over six hundred guests, including political, business, and social figures, packed St. Mary's Church where the archbishop of Boston performed the ceremony, which included a special blessing from the pope. The couple honeymooned in Los Angeles, in the Beverly Hills mansion owned by William Randolph Hearst—ironically, the house where years later Francis Ford Coppola would shoot the famous horse's head scene for *The Godfather*.

* * *

As Jack's personal life was all sweetness and light, Sinatra's was disintegrating. His marriage to Nancy, which had been teetering on the brink as a result of his numerous extramarital liaisons, was now very firmly over. His lack of fidelity, allied to his penchant for nightclubs, alcohol, and showgirls should have taught him that marriage was something to be avoided, for the moment anyway. Instead he flung himself headlong into the most tempestuous relationship of his life, with the one woman who would prove more than his equal.

Chapter 8: Sinatra in the Garden of Ava

———————◆———————

AVA GARDNER WAS born on Christmas Eve 1922 near the farming community of Smithfield, North Carolina, a small town south of Raleigh, the state's second-biggest city, to the youngest of seven children of a poor tobacco sharecropper, Jonas Bailey Gardner, and his wife, Mollie. Ava's mother was gregarious, warm, and ambitious while her father was shy, introspective, and a man of few words. He was a hard worker but it was nearly impossible for him to make a proper living, and the family, after losing their house, faced a period of long-term homelessness.

As things became desperate, Mollie, who would eventually become the main breadwinner, landed a job as a cook and housekeeper at a dormitory for teachers near Brogden School close to Durham, about fifty miles north of Smithfield. The position was reasonably paid and also provided accommodation for the family. It was an opportunity that Mollie embraced with great skill and energy and she remained at the Teacherage, as it was known, for a number of years. When cuts in funding at the board of education forced the closure of the facility, Mollie moved the family farther north to Newport News, Virginia. Her next position, managing a boarding house for ship workers, landed the Gardners in a rather different, and rougher, setting than the Brogden institution. The metropolitan setting meant that there were girls from more affluent backgrounds in the local school, something that just emphasized for young Ava the poverty of her background, and the clothes and the style accessories that Mollie could not afford for her daughter.

Ava had developed into a beautiful and striking teenager and it was her mother, rather than her father, who kept a close watch on any interaction with the opposite sex. Whilst protective and consistent in her warnings to Ava about keeping her virginity until marriage, Mollie never had a frank discussion with her youngest daughter about the facts of life. As a result, Ava felt extremely awkward when the subject of sex was discussed among her friends and was unnaturally wary about dating and boys.

Jonas had never properly adapted to life in Virginia and was, without doubt, hugely uncomfortable with the fact that his wife had become the effective head of the household. The fact that he could not properly provide for his family was totally at odds with his traditionalist rural values. His health began to deteriorate and he developed a wracking cough, the result of years of smoking tobacco leaf.

It was the height of the Depression, and there was no money in the Gardner household for proper medical attention or a hospital stay. Mollie did her best to nurse him but his condition worsened and he died in the winter of 1937. The family, and Mollie in particular, was devastated. Jonas may not have been a great breadwinner, but he was a decent man who never got the breaks in life to realize his own modest ambition of providing a roof over the heads of his wife and children.

The boarding house was then redolent of loss and grief, and Mollie could not wait to get away from it and the bustling city, to the peace of the rural setting that she had grown up in and was now appreciating more than ever. In the summer of the following year she got the break she needed. Hearing of a vacancy in a job identical to the one in Brogden, she applied and was accepted, and the family moved once again, this time back to North Carolina and a place called Rock Ridge.

Ava attended Rock Ridge High School and graduated in 1939 without showing any interest in academic achievement, or any other form of achievement for that matter. If she had done anything in the last year of her formal education, it was to turn the heads of the senior boys, who could not but notice her stunning good looks. After graduating, it appeared, as with so many young women of her generation, that she was destined for secretarial training at a commercial college. She certainly displayed little aptitude for acting or any love for the silver screen. Whatever anxiety she may have harbored about her future was well hidden under a cool exterior. To those who met her in those days she did not appear to have any extravagant dreams, but her sister Beatrice made up for what ambition she lacked for herself. Nineteen years her senior, Bappie, as Beatrice was known, had, after an early marriage and divorce, ended up working as a sales assistant at department store in New York City. Attractive and outgoing, she soon met a new man, Larry Tarr, who ran a photographic studio.

When Ava arrived to visit Bappie in Manhattan, Larry was bowled over by her looks and took a number of shots of her, one of which he put in the studio window. The thought of modeling or any form of glamorous lifestyle never crossed Ava's mind, but life in the big city had certainly made its impact. She returned to North Carolina in 1940, and, enrolling at secretarial school, decided that she would develop the skills necessary to provide her with a passport to a life in New York or Washington.

There was another passport hanging inside the window of Tarr's studio but it would take time to get stamped. Fate intervened one day in 1941 when Barney Duhan, a lowly clerk from the legal department of Loews, stopped outside the studio. His attention was drawn to the photograph of the beautiful young teenager that Larry had stuck in the window.

Loews was the international and national cinema and theatre chain owner and major investor and distributor for MGM, and Barney often glamorized his lowly position by posing as an unofficial talent "scout" for the company. The real purpose of his scouting was to get his paws on as many lovely young women as he could. He had realized that the mere mention of the Rolls-Royce of Hollywood studios was usually enough to engage star-struck teenage girls in conversation. What happened after that generally depended on what they were willing to trade in order to advance the relationship and how much influence they believed Barney really had.

According to one account, Duhan scurried to the nearest pay phone and rang Tarrs. He gave his name, and that of his employer, and said that he was interested in the girl in the photograph. Other reports say he walked into the studio looking for Ava's phone number and, when rebuffed by the receptionist, said that somebody should send her portfolio to MGM. One way or another, Duhan's personal mission failed, but Bappie got the message, and she and Tarr put together a package of the photos he had taken, which they then delivered to the MGM offices in Times Square. Bappie was subsequently contacted with the message that the film studio was interested in meeting Ava and conducting a screen test.

The test was supervised and shot by Al Altman, head of the New York talent department. Recognizing that her Southern drawl would be virtually incomprehensible to the executives on the West Coast, he decided on a simple, largely silent recording which involved little other than the eighteen-year-old Ava carrying a vase of flowers to a table, placing it and then turning from a few different angles toward the camera. After a few repetitions with medium and close-ups, Altman wrapped the filming. Although he was as struck by her beauty as anyone who met her, Altman did not hold out much hope that Ava would be signed, or even considered. That was, possibly, the first and only time in his highly successful talent spotting career that he was wrong. Having viewed the test, studio boss Louis B. Mayer sent Altman a telegram:

SHE CAN'T SING. SHE CAN'T ACT. SHE'S TERRIFIC.

Within a week she was invited to sign a standard seven-year contract and traveled to Hollywood with Bappie as her chaperone. To deal with the southern drawl, she was assigned to an elocution teacher and, for the next five years, would play bit and walk-on parts and be the subject of many publicity and in-house photographic shoots to promote the studio. If her early movie career didn't amount to much, she certainly experienced a lot of drama off screen. In 1942, at nineteen years of age, and still a virgin, she married one of Hollywood's biggest stars, the serial adulterer and sex addict Mickey Rooney. Having continuously rejected his initial advances and well aware of his reputation, Ava realized that Rooney wasn't giving up. She eventually gave in to the well-paid little man with a sex drive that defied his height.

News of the engagement prompted Louis B. Mayer to call the couple in to his office to attempt to dissuade them from a course of action which he perceived might damage the huge money-making operation that was the Hardy series, in which Rooney was the star. Even when the usual Mayer tactic of the carrot was replaced by a baseball bat, to his eternal credit, Rooney refused to budge, something which must have impressed the $50-a-week contract actress, if only because he was willing to destroy his relationship with the most powerful mogul in Hollywood for the sake of her hand. All the studio grooming and elocution lessons could not change the fact that Ava was, after all, a simple gal from North Carolina.

At the outset it appeared that her fiancé was motivated by true love. Mayer made an offer that the studio would take care of the wedding arrangements, something that was willingly accepted by the happy couple. This was motivated by Mayer's strategy to keep the event as low key as possible, and everything, including the wedding ceremony and the honeymoon, remained under the control of Mayer's underlings.

The wedding took place in Ballard, California on January 10, 1942. MGM booked the couple into the Del Monte Hotel near Pebble Beach for the start of the honeymoon. Rooney, by his own admission, got too drunk to have sex with his bride on the wedding night, and things were postponed to the following night. It appears to have worked better with less alcohol, and Ava took to lovemaking like the proverbial duck to water. Like all relatively late vocations

(and "relatively" is the crucial word), it would prove to be dangerous. Ava would almost instantly develop an insatiable appetite for
sex and would use it in the future in the most destructive manner.

As the newlyweds began their married life, it was clear that this
was not a union of equals. Rooney's career was at its height, and he
was committed to a minimum of four pictures a year. His wife's movie
career, on the other hand, was progressing at snail's pace. Drinking
and fighting followed, exacerbated by Rooney's inability to keep his
pants on outside the family home. As Ava was to say herself, "He went
through the ladies like a hot knife through fudge." The writing was on
the wall almost immediately, and the marriage disintegrated rapidly.
After one particularly nasty bust up, Ava left, and, despite the constant pleas from her husband, she refused to relent, and the marriage
was over.

Her next marriage would prove just as disastrous as her first and
she could not have chosen a worse second candidate. Artie Shaw, the
devilishly handsome bandleader, changed wives as frequently as he
did orchestras and his own musical tastes—he would notch up no
less than eight spouses in a long lifetime, as well as a number of other
high profile liaisons. He was dapper, well dressed, and a pseudo-
intellectual and control freak, his massive ego fueled by his huge
success as Benny Goodman's main competitor. Ava had divorced
Rooney and was free when she met Shaw at a party in 1943. He had
divorced from actress Lana Turner after just four months together,
and was back on the circuit (Turner herself would go on to have
seven more husbands). He impressed her hugely, not just because he
was a mega music star of the time but also because of his apparently
high intellect. Her career at MGM was still going nowhere, so she
spent a lot of time on the road with Artie, traveling with the band
and boozing late into the night with them.

The couple married on October 17, 1945, his fifth marriage, and
it would last until the following year. Shaw was a nasty narcissist,
described by his own son as a deeply unhappy man, unable to give
or receive love. He wanted his wives like Lana and Ava to act like

traditional housemaids, roles he must have known they could never play. He treated Ava like dirt in front of others, and, not for the first time, she took solace in the bottle. The more she loved him the more he hurt her and forced her into psychoanalysis, a fad that he had taken up.

What would rescue her from her doomed marriage was work. A decent role would prove her talent and, at the very least, would improve her self-esteem. The opportunity came in the shape of an Ernest Hemingway story called *The Killers*. The short story, first published almost two decades before, tells the story of a visit to a small town outside Chicago by two laconic, wisecracking hit men, hired to kill a down-and-out boxer called "The Swede." Despite being warned, the target refuses to run and accepts his fate.

Former reporter and independent producer Mark Hellinger purchased the rights to the story, and the project was backed by Universal. Hellinger hired Tony Veiller and John Huston to write the screenplay, which was written in late 1945 and early 1946, with production slated to begin in April. Hellinger was determined to avoid casting big names, and apart from Edmond O'Brien, who had had some previous success, the two main parts were played by Ava, cast as the queen of betrayal, Kitty Collins, and a young Burt Lancaster as the Swede, in his big-screen debut. Universal undertook a huge marketing job in advance of the New York opening on August 28, and the film hit the ground running, breaking box office records at the Winter Garden and receiving superb reviews. Ava's performance, as the beautiful, duplicitous Kitty, made her an overnight star, her character becoming one of the great femme fatale roles in cinema history.

For Ava, the triumph of *The Killers* was dampened by the collapse of her marriage to Shaw, but there was compensation to be found in being an integral part of a film that was not only a critical and commercial success but also nominated for four Academy Awards. She may have been justifiably disillusioned with love but her career had taken off in the most dramatic fashion imaginable. With work to concentrate on and given her miserable track record, it would have been logical for her to avoid intense relationships in general, and marriage in particular. To be fair, she did manage to do so for the next two years, until she appeared on Frank Sinatra's radar.

Ava and Frank had met before and she had not liked his self-centered attitude and arrogance. Timing is always of the essence in the matter of success or failure of a relationship, and in this instance the timing could not have been worse. They met again in the latter half of 1949 at a party at producer Daryl F. Zanuck's house in Palm Springs. Frank hit on her immediately and she rebuffed him, reminding him that he was married. Frank assured her that the marriage was on the rocks and he was living separately from Nancy and his kids. Had she taken into account any lesson she may have learned from her failed marriages, Ava should have run away from Sinatra and kept running. Instead, when he offered her a lift, she took it.

With a few bottles of liquor and two .38 revolvers in the glove compartment, they drove to the desert and, like a couple of crazed teenagers, they shot up the street lights of a small town and should have ended up getting arrested. In the station the local cops, instead of arresting them, were star struck in the presence of two Hollywood stars and offered to drive them home. They were further impressed when Frank rang his publicist in Los Angeles, who asked the cops to name a price to drop any charges they might be intending to proffer, later chartering a private plane and arriving with a suitcase full of cash. This was the inauspicious beginning of a ghastly, toxic relationship that would make Ava's previous marriages look like advertisements for family values.

To make matters worse, Sinatra's star appeared to be in terminal decline while Ava's was rising rapidly in the opposite direction. Despite his assurances at Zanuck's party, there was nothing permanent, in hard fact or writing, about Frank's separation from his wife except in his own mind, and to complicate matters, he had three young children. Leaving aside external personal pressure, there were mutual character traits that combined to set off the alarm bells. The couple provided a mirror image of each other: hot headed, passionate,

unstable, addicted to sex, with a fondness for high drama, the big gesture, and alcohol to excess. They were possessive and prone to jealous
rage and had a consistent propensity to bring out the worst traits in
each other, both in private and in public. There was strong chemistry
between Sinatra and Gardner but it was both volatile and toxic.

The external commercial pressures on Sinatra were also considerable. His screaming bobby sox fans had grown up and moved on
to more serious pursuits in their lives, leading to a large drop in his
record sales and an absence of his recordings in the jukeboxes. In
the year he got together with Ava he dropped out of the top echelon
of the *Downbeat* poll after dominating it for the previous six years.
This time he could only manage sixth place behind, among others,
Frankie Lane, Bing Crosby, and Mel Torme.

The previous year the Howard Hughes and RKO produced film,
Double Dynamite, in which he had starred opposite Jane Russell and
Groucho Marx, and been shelved and would be a critical and commercial flop when released three years later. The rumor was doing the
rounds that MGM was going to drop him. Sinatra did have a five-year
contract at $250,000 a year with CBS Television for *The Frank Sinatra
Show.* However the critical reaction was lukewarm, with struggling rat-
ings and a lot of negativity within the higher echelons of the network.

In contrast, Ava was in huge demand, and while her lover was
being cast into the entertainment wilderness, she starred in no
less than ten films, including *Show Boat, Lone Star, The Snows of
Kilimanjaro,* and *Mogambo.* The couple had tried to keep their affair
low key, but by early 1950 it was proving more and more difficult.
After attending the funeral of his friend and press agent, George
Evans, Frank went to Houston with Ava for a hotel opening. That
evening they attended a dinner at an Italian restaurant hosted by
the mayor and when a photographer approached the table Sinatra
threatened him. He left without the picture but the incident was
reported the next day in *The Houston Post* and immediately picked
up by the wires and relayed all over America. Somewhat predictably
the scribes sharpened their swords and aimed for the jugular.

The opportunity for blanket typographical bombing of Sinatra was given fresh impetus when Nancy made a statement, either poignantly or deliberately, on Valentine's Day announcing that her relationship with Frank had become unbearable. She announced she was separating from him and had instructed her lawyer to work out a property settlement. Although he was not to be dissuaded from the path that he had chosen with Ava, he needed the huge media attention created by Nancy like a hole in the head. If he had had a less fractious relationship with the press, the reaction might have been a little more muted, but the hacks got stuck in and he was cast in the role of a merciless adulterer who had abandoned his wife and young family for a real life femme fatale who had already seen off two marriages. That she might have been the victim in her previous relationships would not protect her from the newly adopted position of prudery by the press.

There was more to come when Frank was staying at the Hampshire House Hotel in Manhattan prior to an engagement in the Copacabana Club. Put out when Ava attended a party thrown by Artie Shaw at his home, Sinatra flew into one of the many jealous rages that would characterize their relationship. He caused chaos at the hotel when, after ringing Ava at the party, he told her that he was going to kill himself and she heard gunshots on the other end of the line. When the police got to the room the evidence had been covered up, and Sinatra was lying on the bed as if nothing had happened. There were several other versions of the story including one that Ava had just gone to see Shaw to talk about her problems with Sinatra and the mobsters he was hanging out with. She then returned to the hotel, where she was sharing a room with Bappie, and the telephone rang with the same result.

In her memoir, *Ava,* she wrote that when she picked up the phone in her room, he said he was going to kill himself:

> Then there was this tremendous bang in my ear and I knew
> it was a revolver shot. My whole mind sort of exploded in a

great wave of panic, terror, and shocked disbelief. Oh, God! Oh, God! I threw down the phone and raced across the living room and into Frank's room. I didn't know what to expect to find—a body? And there was a body lying on the bed. Oh, God was he dead? I threw myself on it saying, 'Frank, Frank,' . . . And the face with a rather pale little smile turned toward me and the voice said, 'Oh, hello.'

This account has a ring of truth about it but it is somewhat obscured by an indulgent, as opposed to inquiring, ghostwriter and reads more like a movie script. The scene ends, according to this version, with Ava forgivingly holding him close. It would get worse and worse, but the two lovers stuck together like obsessive clams, and marriage would only compound the felony that lay at the heart of the union. It was like a merry-go-round of emotional torture—fight, scream, make love, make up, a constant and vicious circle. And both would use infidelity as a stick to beat the other.

Ava went to Spain to start work on *Pandora and the Flying Dutchman* as MGM, her employer, was making the first moves to dump Sinatra from a contract that still had a year to run. Another source of insecurity and suffering for Frank was the ongoing negotiations with Nancy about the financial terms of their separation. The problem for Sinatra was that for all the opprobrium that had been heaped on him about the affair there was no mention of divorce, which his wife had ample grounds to pursue.

If getting Ava to Spain for *Pandora and the Flying Dutchman* had been employed as a tactic to drive a wedge between Frank and Ava, it worked. The location for the film in Tossa Del Mar, Catalonia, was spectacular, and made for the romantic but doomed theme of the film. The bullfighter Mario Cabre, at thirty-four in the twilight of a modest career in the ring, played a love interest of the central character, Pandora, an American nightclub singer and femme fatale, played by Ava. During filming the script became a reality and the handsome matador and the Hollywood star had a brief fling, which was most likely just a one-night stand. They were, however, spotted around the fishing village holding hands in the aftermath. Cabre, the most flattered of the couple and more than likely smitten, shot his mouth off to the local press, swearing his undying love.

The international papers picked up the story, and the result for Sinatra was more than a wedge and closer to a stake through his heart. While it was clear that all Ava wanted was sex for a night it was also part of the pattern of the relationship. She later admitted that she went with other men just to punish Frank, and with Cabre it was matter of her being drunk and finding him attractive. For the matador, who also fancied himself as a poet, it was a feeling that persisted even after Sinatra arrived at the location and he was cast aside. He would go on to write a book of poems about what became an infatuation with Ava, which he launched at the Spanish Institute in London in the summer of the same year. The poems were full of longing and melancholy, the result, as he put it in one line, of the feelings of a "lacerated lover." Ava, for her part, would later be dismissive of the experience and the smitten bullfighter: "Mario was handsome and macho as only a Latin knows how to be, but he was also brash, conceited, noisy, and totally convinced he was the only man for me."

He would continue to be remembered for much longer by Frank, who brought the whole sordid episode up time and time again in the many loud drunken arguments that would follow. On one occasion during a drunken spree in the Cal Nevada resort, the bullfighter's name was invoked yet again by Sinatra and Ava admitted, for the first time, that she had slept with him. Refusing to drop the subject, Frank went on and on until she left and went home to Los Angeles. He then took an overdose, and his friends, staying with him at the time, begged her to come back.

Everyone around the couple walked on eggshells, in a constant state of alert, dreading the next explosion or ghastly row. But when Nancy eventually enacted her divorce from Frank on November 7, 1951, he married Ava at the home of the brother of his old friend and record collaborator, Manie Sacks. The marriage did not arrest

Sinatra's free-falling career, however. The following year, 1952, would prove to be his worst ever. The divorce from Nancy had cleaned him out financially, and as Ava's fortunes continued to improve he became a sort of kept man, a status that he would resent and hate and one that would add further fuel to the flames of their relationship. This troubled love affair, combined with the other pressures had a debilitating effect on Frank. He had lost a lot of weight he could ill afford, his hair was beginning to recede, and his face reflected the lines of his pain. He looked a decade and a half older than his bride. To cap it all, *Meet Danny Wilson* bombed and was taken off the screens quickly, and in April CBS pulled the plug on *The Frank Sinatra Show*.

* * *

By June he had neither a record company deal nor representation of a talent agency and his contract with MGM had long gone. His club engagements drew poor houses. In contrast his wife would soon be offered a new movie contract worth $1 million for a dozen films. It was Ava who kept him going during this period, telling him that it would take just one good part to bring him out of the darkness and back into the light. He too was convinced that was all that was needed and she vowed to help him in spite of all the dreadful things that happened between them.

Having been lent to Twentieth Century Fox for a big role in Hemingway's *The Snows of Kilimanjaro*, which was to be shot in Kenya, Ava was urged by Sinatra to turn it down to be with him for some planned concerts in New York. While it had the potential to be career suicide for her, she agreed, but she did meet the director and had her scenes scheduled to be shot all together, which meant a shorter period for her involvement. This was a real indication of the depressed spirit and chronic insecurity that had taken hold of Sinatra at the time. He saw the reflection of rock bottom and it induced a sense of desperation. Ava, for her part, selflessly tried to get a clause written into her contract for a project that would star her husband, but this would amount to nothing. Nobody wanted Sinatra, period.

As the bust-ups and the fights and the break-ups continued, Ava landed the lead female role opposite Clark Gable and a cast that included Grace Kelly and Donald Sinden in *Mogambo,* a remake of the 1932 film *Red Dust,* which had also featured Gable and Jean Harlow. The veteran John Ford was hired to direct and the film was scheduled to shoot in a number of locations in Africa including the Congo, Uganda, and the Kenyan Rift Valley, with interiors in Pinewood Studios in London. Ava had continued to canvass for Sinatra, who was touting for the part of Maggio in a forthcoming screen version of *From Here to Eternity.* She made a pitch to Harry Cohn the Columbia Pictures mogul at a dinner party hosted by himself and his wife at his home. While Cohn was not averse to the idea, he had Eli Wallach in mind for the part. The matter was left open for the moment.

Sinatra was convinced that this was the opportunity and he told Cohn the part of Maggio could have been written for him. In the interim he flew to Nairobi with Ava in advance of the start of filming of *Mogambo.* The plan was to stay for the duration of the shoot, as he had nothing else to do. Hanging around while set-ups are being done is bad enough for the actors. For Sinatra, with no part to play, it was torture. Mercifully for the couple, Frank got a call from Cohn to go to California for a screen test. The deal was that he would have pay his own travel expenses and Ava was only too delighted to oblige. While he was away she had sex with a number of the crew, including a location manager and big-game hunter named Bunny Allen. In November she discovered she was pregnant and with the help of the production company flew to London for an abortion. Frank had no idea what was going on. He and the public were told her trip was for the treatment of a tropical infection.

Frank returned to Africa for Christmas and then went back to the United States while Ava finished the shoot in Africa before she traveled to London for the interiors at the end of January 1953. It was a new year and a new dawn when Frank got the news that he had landed the part of Maggio. Ava's performance in *Mogambo* was nominated for an Academy Award for Best Actress in a leading role.

It appeared that life was on the up for the troubled couple. Frank was back with what would surely prove to be a resounding bang.

A young Frank Sinatra. Circa 1917.

Headshot of Frank Sinatra. Circa 1943.

Frank Sinatra and arranger Axel Stordahl (top right). Liederkrantz Hall, New York City, 1947.

(William P. Gottlieb)

Frank Sinatra. Liederkrantz Hall, New York City, 1947.

(William P. Gottlieb)

Former First Lady Eleanor Roosevelt and Frank Sinatra. Los Angeles, California, 1947.

(Franklin D. Roosevelt Library)

Frank Sinatra on the set of The Frank Sinatra Show. The photograph was on the cover of *Metronome* magazine, 1950.

(Metronome magazine)

Image of Frank Sinatra from *TV Radio Mirror* magazine, 1957.

(Macfadden Publications)

Frank Sinatra in the studio. Circa 1960s.

John F. Kennedy poses with Dunker the dachshund during his tour of Europe. The Hague, Netherlands, 1937.

(John F. Kennedy Presidential Library and Museums)

John F. Kennedy during his time at Harvard University. 1939.

(John F. Kennedy Presidential Library and Museum)

John F. Kennedy as a junior grade
lieutenant (LTJG). 1942.

(Frank Turgeon Jr.)

View of the extended East Front of the Capitol Building, where
the inauguration of President John F. Kennedy was held. President
Kennedy is in the center, delivering his inaugural address; Vice
President Lyndon B. Johnson, other officials, and guests sit behind
him. Capitol Building, Washington, DC, 1961.

(U.S. Army Signal Corps)

President John F. Kennedy and First Lady Jacqueline Kennedy arrive at the National Guard Armory for President Kennedy's Inaugural Ball. White House Secret Service agent Gerald "Jerry" A. Behn follows the president and first lady. National Guard Armory, Washington, DC, 1961.

(Abbie Rowe)

President John F. Kennedy and his party watch from a balcony as Secretary of the Interior Stewart Lee Udall and his wife, Erma Lee Udall, enter the hall of the National Guard Armory. With Kennedy are First Lady Jacqueline Kennedy, Vice President Lyndon B. Johnson and Lady Bird Johnson, and Kennedy's parents, Rose Fitzgerald Kennedy and Joseph P. Kennedy Sr. Inaugural Ball, National Guard Armory, Washington, DC, 1961.

(Abbie Rowe)

President John F. Kennedy looks up from his seat in the balcony of the National Guard Armory during the Inaugural Ball. National Guard Armory, Washington, DC, 1961.

(Abbie Rowe)

President John F. Kennedy delivers remarks via telephone to the American Veterans of World War II Convention in New York City. White House, Washington, DC, 1962.

(Abbie Rowe)

President John F. Kennedy signs bills to combat crime and racketeering. Looking on (left to right) are: Senator Kenneth Keating of New York; FBI Director J. Edgar Hoover; Attorney General Robert F. Kennedy; Chief of the Legislation and Special Projects Section of the Criminal Division in the Department of Justice Harold Koffsky; Deputy Chief of the Legislation and Special Projects Section of the Criminal Division Edward Joyce; and Chief Counsel of the Senate Judiciary Committee Jerry Adlerman. White House, Washington, DC, 1962.

(Abbie Rowe)

President John F. Kennedy in the Fish Room of the White House preparing to deliver remarks for a public service film entitled *Voting on November 6*. White House, Washington, DC, 1962.

(Cecil Stoughton)

President John F. Kennedy meets with FBI Director J. Edgar Hoover and Attorney General Robert F. Kennedy. White House, Washington, DC, 1962.

(Abbie Rowe)

President John F. Kennedy with singer Julie London at a White House Correspondents' Association Dinner. Sheraton Park Hotel, Washington, DC, 1961.

(Abbie Rowe)

President John F. Kennedy with actress Dorothy Provine at a White House Correspondents' Association Dinner. Actor Ralph Bellamy stands behind Kennedy. Sheraton Park Hotel, Washington, DC, 1961.

(Abbie Rowe)

President John F. Kennedy and Frank Sinatra outside the Sands Hotel. Las Vegas, Nevada, 1961.

(AFP)

Attorney General Robert F. Kennedy, Marilyn Monroe, President John F. Kennedy, and Arthur Schlesinger Jr. at a birthday party held for Kennedy's forty-fifth birthday. Apartment of Arthur Krim, New York City, 1962.

(Cecil Stoughton)

President John F. Kennedy and Attorney General Robert F. Kennedy in the West Wing Colonnade of the White House, outside the Oval Office. White House, Washington, DC, 1962.

(Cecil Stoughton)

Attorney General Robert F. Kennedy speaking to a crowd about racial equality. Outside the Justice Department, Washington, DC, 1963.

(Warren Leffler)

President John F. Kennedy minutes before his assassination. Also in the presidential limousine are Jacqueline Kennedy, Texas Governor John Connally, and his wife, Nellie. Main Street, Dallas, Texas, 1963.

(Walt Cisco, Dallas Morning News)

Attorney General Robert F. Kennedy speaking to the Platform Committee. Washington, DC, 1964.

(Warren Leffler)

Portrait of Harry James, Coca-Cola radio show rehearsal, New York City.

(William Gottlieb)

Jimmy Durante and Louis B. Mayer during an award dinner at Mount Sinai Men's Club. Los Angeles, California, 1948.

(Los Angeles Times)

Press photo of Louis B. Mayer and Lorena Danker shortly after their marriage. 1948.

A photograph of screen siren Ava Gardner, featured in the Japanese magazine *Eiga no Tomo*, 1953.

(Eiga no Tomo)

FBI Director J. Edgar Hoover in the Oval Office. White House, Washington, DC, 1967.

(Yoichi Okamoto)

Chapter 9: Kennedy Steals the Show

——————◆——————

IT WAS NOT designed as a dress rehearsal, but that is what the Democratic Party Convention of 1956 turned into for Jack Kennedy. The primary purpose of the event, held in the sweltering heat of a Chicago August, was for the delegates to choose the party's nomination for the presidential election to be held the following November. The leading candidate and ante-post favorite was Adlai Stevenson, who, despite being beaten by Dwight Eisenhower in the election of 1952, looked like he would be running against the incumbent again. With other high-profile candidates like New York Governor Averell Harriman and Senators Lyndon Johnson and Stuart Stymington in the mix, Kennedy appeared to be destined to play a minor part in the proceedings.

The normal protocol of the convention dictated that the presidential candidate, once chosen, then nominated his vice-presidential running mate. In deciding not to re-nominate Alabama's Senator John Sparkman, his running mate from 1952, Stevenson opened the position to a free vote by the convention, an opportunity that the Kennedy camp would seize with impressive aplomb. In advance of the event, however, Jack had been at pains to make public the fact that he was not seeking the nomination, a position that was widely expected anyway, for strategic electoral reasons, to go to a candidate from the South.

It became clear, however, to anyone in the media who bothered to notice, that it was a case of the senator protesting too much, because days in advance of the vote the Kennedy storm troopers—made up of Bobby, O'Donnell, O'Brien, and Jack's speechwriter, Ted Sorensen—had set up camp in the Palmer House Hotel. Jackie and other members of the senator's direct family, including his sisters Eunice and Jean, had also arrived in Chicago, not something a disinterested convention attendee would have arranged or, indeed, inflicted on his closest relatives. Jack had also, somewhat ambivalently, made it clear that if Stevenson selected him, he would not turn him down, so, from the outside, the picture was confusing. But seasoned observers felt that a Kennedy candidacy for vice-president was a most unlikely scenario. His profile was still relatively low nationally, and his Catholicism was generally regarded as a distinct disadvantage outside his home state.

While it made no political sense, the young and vibrant cabal that was the Kennedy camp was preparing for some eventuality, however remote. Whatever transpired, Jack wanted Bobby on the floor of the convention to gather intelligence and canvass support on his behalf but found him denied an official place as a delegate. He approached Thomas "Tip" O'Neill, the man who had succeeded to his congressional seat when he had been elected to the Senate in 1952. O'Neill, who was in charge of naming four delegates, had selected three local politicians for his district and kept the remaining one for himself. Three decades later, the man who would distinguish himself as speaker of the house and as one of the United States' most prominent Irish Americans, recalled in his memoir what happened next: "I'm sorry Jack but I have already notified the delegates. And I told him who I had picked."

Kennedy would not budge and told O'Neill that his brother was a brilliant politician, the smartest one he had ever known. "You know lightning may strike at that convention and I could end up on the ticket with Stevenson. I'd really like my brother on the floor, as a delegate so he could work for me." O'Neill relented and gave his own delegate ticket to Bobby, a gesture for which he received no thanks.

When he mentioned it in passing to Joe Kennedy he was hardly surprised at his response, but also never forgot his reply: "Tip, let me tell you something. Never expect any appreciation from my boys. These kids had so much done for them by other people, they just assume that it's coming to them."

It could hardly have escaped a canny politician like Tip O'Neill that the chief architect of such an attitude was, in fact, Joe Kennedy himself. Who else was responsible for giving them such a sense of entitlement? But what emerges from O'Neill's account is that the Kennedy camp, in spite of all the odds, was in a state of high preparation for the possibility of success in the vice-presidential competition.

There was clearly another agenda—to make sure, whatever the outcome, that Jack would make a big impact on the convention delegates, the Democratic Party, and of course the media. The brothers, and their associates, were highly media savvy, something they did not lick off the stones, but were taking the manipulation of the press to more sophisticated heights than their father could ever imagine. They were only too aware that the convention was receiving coverage on radio, television, and in the press all over America, a golden opportunity to upgrade Kennedy from the local to the national stage.

Within the party he was already becoming well known and well regarded. His book, *Profiles in Courage*, which detailed acts of bravery and integrity by eight US senators in history, had been published to positive reviews earlier in the year. Before the keynote speech by Tennessee Governor Frank Clement opening the convention, the delegates had been shown a twenty-minute film on the history of the party produced by Dore Schary, the president of MGM. Jack, who had recorded the voice-over in Los Angeles the previous month, narrated the film. To cap all of this, Stevenson offered Jack the opportunity to make the speech nominating him as the Democratic candidate, the most high-profile and widely covered part of the whole convention.

The Kennedy team tore up the first draft of the speech, which had been scripted by Arthur Schlesinger Jr. and journalist John Barlow, and Jack and Ted Sorensen got to work, burning the midnight oil, to fashion their own version. Their intention was to provide another platform for the growing image of the speaker—young, energetic, and highly articulate. Joe Kennedy, meanwhile, was on holiday in the South of France but remained in close contact with his sons and their team.

Having swept in after the first ballot, Stevenson then left the choice of his running mate to the convention delegates, giving the main contenders, Estes Kefauver, Hubert Humphrey, Albert Gore, and, to the surprise of all, Jack Kennedy, about twelve hours to complete their canvass. The surprise decision energized the convention as the candidates literally dived into a frenzied lobbying process involving telegrams, telephone calls, and personal representations of all sorts.

The first call for the Kennedy camp was a to a phone in a rented villa in Val sur Mer on the French Riviera. Joe Kennedy had already expressed his opinion about the matter of his son running on the vice-presidential ticket. His concerns were straightforward. Like every race he had run in his own life he did not believe in running for second place. He had also assessed that Stevenson would almost certainly be defeated by Eisenhower and feared the damage that any association with the ticket might do to his son's future political prospects.

His negativity did not, however, prevent him from making numerous calls to influential members of the party to support his son's candidacy or from encouraging the Kennedy camp to operate at full tilt. But the aggressive nature of the canvass and the youth of the candidate intimidated many in the higher echelons of the party with Jack frequently referred to as a whippersnapper, reflecting the age topography of the politics of the time. Jack Kennedy, at thirty-nine and on the verge of early middle age, was young when compared to the patricians at the top table of the Democratic Party.

The work reaped early rewards in the first two ballots, with Kennedy coming a close second to Kefauver. The senator from Tennessee pulled away, however, in the third and final ballot, winning the nomination by 755.5 to 589. Failing, in the heat of the battle, to appreciate the larger picture, Jack found it difficult to hide his disappointment. Nonetheless, he got up to the podium and made a gracious speech, urging unanimous support for his victorious opponent to a huge ovation from the delegates.

Dave Powers expressed the view thus: "He lost so gracefully, that from then on, he looked like the all-American boy. He made more friends losing. The world loves a loser and he was the ideal loser that day."

From nowhere he had gained widespread and positive publicity, a big plus for his popularity and for his youthful image. He now represented the change that the Democratic Party would find irresistible and within a matter of months the whippersnapper's day would come. When the dust had settled he was more realistic and positive about the experience, saying, "In twenty-four hours' work we almost won the second spot. If we work for four years, we can pick up all the marbles."

* * *

The Stevenson-Kefauver presidential ticket of 1956 would prove to be a disaster. In November of that year they lost the Electoral College vote by 457 to 73, the states 41 to 7, and the popular vote 57.4 percent to 42 percent. Had Jack Kennedy been part of the campaign it is arguable that his national political future would have been all but finished, severely handicapped at best. But instead the two Democratic candidates were consigned to political oblivion, and the road to the White House opened up to the senator whose name, because of the huge role he had played at the convention, was now so familiar.

Frank Sinatra watched the whole political pantomime from the wings, literally. As a supporter of Stevenson, he had been asked by the organizers to sing the national anthem for the delegates and he, like millions of others, had been both impressed and energized by the role played by the young senator from Massachusetts. Frank's connections with the party stretched back to his mother Dolly's work for the local Democratic organization in Hoboken. In an interview with poet Walter Lowenfells in the *Daily Worker* just over a decade before he had referred to the early influence of his mother: "I was brought up in a tenement in a very poor neighborhood. My mother is what you would call a progressive. She decided she didn't want to be just a housekeeper and studied nursing and is now a nursing graduate. She was always interested in conditions outside her own house."

The year before that interview, 1944, Frank had sent a letter to President Franklin D. Roosevelt, who had invited him to tea in the White House, an experience that had a profound effect on him, as would finding himself in the presence of Jack Kennedy twelve years later at the Chicago convention. FDR had asked him about his voice and its effect on his female fans, something that took Sinatra by surprise, as he explained afterward: "I was a little stunned when I stood alongside him. I thought, here is the greatest guy alive today and here's a little guy from Hoboken shaking hands with him. He knows about everything, even my racket."

He was so impressed that he donated $5,000 dollars to the party's campaign coffers, the beginning of an ongoing relationship with the Democratic cause for many years to come. His political sympathies, however, took a sharp turn to the left in the immediate aftermath of the end of the Second World War, something that placed him firmly on the radar of J. Edgar Hoover, who opened a file on him, something he was doing on Jack at around the same time. Apart from the connection with his father, who was obviously known to Hoover, Jack had come to the director's attention because of his fling with the Danish journalist Inga Arvad, who had become close to a number of senior Nazis during a wartime posting to Berlin. Hoover had marked her down as a possible Nazi spy and her connection with the son of a prominent American businessman and diplomat certainly warranted attention in his opinion.

At the time Sinatra had lent his name and had given financial support to a variety of left-wing causes and organizations but, much to Hoover's chagrin, had been careful not to sign up as a member of any of them. He was both vocal and public about his opposition to racial, class, and political intolerance, nowadays seen as liberal but then regarded as subversive. In 1945 he starred and sang in a ten-minute film short, produced by RKO and directed by Mervyn Le Roy, called *The House I Live In,* a dramatized plea for ethnic and religious tolerance for all classes and creeds. Prominent leftist composer, Earl Robinson, wrote the title song and the script was the work of screen-writer Albert Maltz who had close ties to the Communist Party. The film received the acclaim it deserved and Sinatra was given a special Honorary Academy Award for his performance.

Not even Sinatra might have expected, other than in liberal social, artistic, and political circles, plaudits for his progressive stance on matters which had potential to harm his career. He had, of course, experienced intolerance in Hoboken as a kid of Italian immi-grants, and he had spoken of it many times during his career and would do so in the future. Not everybody saw things Sinatra's way. The right-wing press used his progressive stance as more ammuni-tion for attack, excoriating him for his Mob ties. Hearst Publications' Lee Mortimer criticized him for veering to the "port side," a rather dainty way of calling him a leftie, calling *The House I Live In* a "class struggle or foreignisms posing as entertainment." Maltz would later be blacklisted and jailed for refusing to cooperate with the House Un-American Activities Committee, and while Robinson escaped this fate, his income would dramatically diminish because of his political associations.

In 1948 Sinatra campaigned for the reelection of Harry S. Truman and for Adlai Stevenson in his first failed presidential bid in 1952. It appeared that, in the matter of politics, his association with organized crime and his infamously loose morals provided neither a barrier to his support of senior politicians nor an impediment to their eager acceptance of it. But what, apart from acceptability and, perhaps, respectability, could account for Sinatra's intense interest in, and desire to be a part of, the world of politics? He was as in awe of the leaders of that world as his fans were of him. He had also come to realize that however wealthy and successful a star of screen and musical stage he might become, he could never have the same power or privilege of a star on the national political stage. He expressed that sentiment when addressing a rally of Roosevelt-Truman supporters during the 1944 presidential campaign: "Some people say I may hurt my career taking sides in a political campaign and I say to them to hell with this career. Government is more important."

In an excellent essay for the *Virginia Quarterly Review*, Michael Nelson, professor of political science at Rhodes College put forward this proposition:

"Sinatra's hope was that political involvement would cause the public to associate him with statesmen rather than mobsters, with public service rather than hedonism, and with dignity rather than volatility."

Right after the convention, Jack flew to the Riviera to join his father at the rented villa for a period of rest and recuperation. At the same time, a pregnant Jackie was at her mother and stepfather's mansion on the Auchincloss estate near Newport, Rhode Island. She had already suffered one miscarriage and was, understandably, nervous and apprehensive about the pregnancy. If her husband shared the concern he wasn't showing it and his actions appeared to testify to this. After a brief visit with his father, and joined by Senator George Smathers, he left Antibes on a yacht for a Mediterranean trip taking in the islands of Capri and Elba. The men were joined by a group of young women and remained out of telephone contact for five days.

On August 23, her mother rushed Jackie, beset with severe stomach cramps, to Newport Hospital where she underwent an emergency Caesarean operation, delivering a stillborn child. With no means of contacting her cavorting husband, it fell to Bobby to inform him of the infant's fate. When Jack finally rang home he appeared more put out by the fact that his sunny holiday might be interrupted than by the death of the child, and it was only at the insistence of Smathers, advising him that his political future might be comprised, that he returned home three days after receiving the news.

While some sort of moral compass was necessary in politics, Jack Kennedy was aware that the real crime would be if he was caught, so his constant womanizing continued unabated in spite of the risks. The biggest risk was, in fact, the possibility of his disintegrating marriage ending in divorce, which, because of his Catholicism, would scupper any realistic chance of winning the presidential nomination, not to mention an election. For Jack though, his behavior was simply a case of history repeating itself. His sense of entitlement (which had been mentioned to Tip O'Neill) and the example set by his father in the matter of sex outside the marital home, placed Jackie in the exact same position Rose had occupied in the past. It was well known in political circles that the marriage was in trouble, but when there was no definite separation or divorce on the horizon, a persistent rumor did the rounds of Washington, suggesting that Joe Kennedy had intervened and paid a million dollars to Jackie for her to remain in the role of devoted politician's wife.

While not leading to tolerance, Jackie's own family experience certainly led to a degree of ambivalence when it came to marital infidelity. Her father, Black Jack Bouvier, was possessed of a fatal penchant for slow horses, fast women, and volatile stocks. His spectacular matinee idol looks and dark complexion attracted women in droves and he hunted them down with intensity, disposing of them just as ruthlessly. His wife Janet refused to tolerate his behavior, suing for divorce on the grounds of his serial adultery. That might have been fine had it been kept in the family, so to speak, but the salacious details of Black Jack's sexual adventures were leaked to the *New York Daily Mirror* which, on January 26, 1940, splashed the details and the names of the women cited in the divorce papers all over front and inside pages. The story was, of course, picked up by the wire services and republished all over the country.

As a relatively shy and private young woman, Jackie had found the washing of the family linen in public both humiliating and intolerable. Both she and her sister Lee had craved a normal family life but it had been denied to them in the most spectacular fashion. It was highly unlikely, therefore, that as a senator's wife, Jackie would want to put herself through such public humiliation again. Whatever she felt about Jack's philanderings, it was far more preferable to suffer it in private than to live it out in the spotlight of the media.

Her father had also managed to squander the family fortune and had put his two daughters in the position of having no money of their own, making them almost exclusively financially reliant on their spouses. This fact may have aided the provenance of the story about Joe's million-dollar "bribe." John H. Davis rubbished the story in his book *The Kennedy Clan* and, given his closeness to the Bouvier family, was in the best possible position to assess the veracity of the story: "The rumor has never been proved true and there is strong evidence that it is false, for Jack Bouvier's personal secretary John Ficke told me that after Bouvier died and his estate was being settled, Jacqueline was terribly anxious to receive her legacy of $79,700 and kept bothering him for it."

When Black Jack, by now a chronic alcoholic drinking alone in his New York apartment, succumbed to the deterioration of his body on August 3, 1957, Jack was very supportive to his wife and flew to New York from Washington to help with the funeral arrangements. He also ensured that a fulsome obituary was published in the *New York Times*.

May 1957 saw a significant boost to Kennedy's profile when *Profiles in Courage* won the Pulitzer Prize in the biography category, receiving widespread national media coverage. The young man of action in the service of his country at war was now also a man of letters, a superb public speaker, and a rising political figure. Suddenly the elders of the political establishment, most of whom had been born in the previous century, began to look creak-jointed and decidedly out of touch. As media speculation about the presidential prospects of the young senator escalated, Jack continued to deny any such ambitions.

He was in huge demand for speaking engagements all over the country, and, with Ted Sorensen at his side, he fulfilled as many as one a day for weeks on end. Here was an example of a concerted campaign with no immediate goal, but with the overall aim of maintaining and building Jack's profile on the national stage. Behind the scenes Joe was both pulling political strings and prevailing on his extensive media contacts in preparation for the battle ahead. As his biographer Richard Whalen put it in his book, *The Founding Father*, "a publicity build-up unprecedented in U.S. political history."

His influence was also obvious in Jack's careful courting of southern politicians while keeping faith with the Eastern liberal political establishment, a delicate balancing act Kennedy handled with a skill that indicated his increasing grasp of the art of the game. Fence sitting was part of the survival kit of any politician, and Jack received surprisingly little criticism for adopting this stance. He assiduously avoided being labeled conservative or liberal, insisting that he was first and foremost a Democrat.

Despite his reticence to make his intentions known, the bare fact of the matter was that there was, at this stage, no other obvious candidate for the forthcoming 1960 Democratic nomination for president. Estes Kefauver, who had lost in 1956 alongside Stevenson, was now in the tightening grip of alcoholism. Lyndon Johnson, at this point, was showing no interest, and those who had hinted that they might run, like California Governor Pat Brown, Stuart Stymington, and, somewhat incredibly, Adlai Stevenson, did not hold the same appeal as Kennedy.

Jack's good year was rounded off in November when he was present for the birth of his daughter, Caroline. She was christened in St. Patrick's Cathedral with a large attendance from both sides of the family. It proved a joyful event for the Irish Mafia because the baptism attracted huge media coverage, which they did not discourage, as it cemented, in the public's mind, the view of Kennedy as a devoted family man, an ideal image for a presidential candidate. Caroline's birth had opened up a whole untapped avenue of media opportunity.

One obstacle lay in the way of the next step to the White House: the following year's Senate elections, which would provide the final platform for the bid for the presidential nomination. Kennedy's team had already agreed that reelection would not be the deciding factor, but rather the size of the majority Jack might win by. His Republican opponent was Vincente Celeste, a Boston lawyer who displayed the weakness of his position in the race by emphasizing Kennedy's wealth and privilege, while at the same time, bemoaning his own disadvantage, thereby diluting his credibility. The Kennedy machine, operating in overdrive, delivered such a punishing that Joe had to inquire of the team if they were trying to kill Celeste. Jack was so energized that, in one day, he delivered fifteen speeches in the same number of towns.

He also continued to make trips and speeches outside the state, the logic being that a continued national profile would amplify the support in Massachusetts. It was a high-risk strategy but it worked. On polling day, November 5, 1958, the early indications of a landslide were spot on, with the margin of victory beyond even Joe's expectations, justifying his estimated $1.5 million backing of the campaign. Kennedy received a popular vote of 1,362,926 to Celeste's 488,318, representing a margin of 73.2 percent to 26.3 percent, a massive increase on the 1952 result. Now Jack wasn't just a politician, he was a political superstar. The collective eyes of the Kennedy camp were now firmly focused on the White House.

Chapter 10: The Jack Pack

———————◆———————

Frank sinatra had a problem with Peter Lawford. That problem stretched back to 1953, despite the fact that they knew each
other well for at least six years before, and had appeared in a number
of films together. It was difficult enough to fall out with a guy like
Peter, and for Sinatra it was doubly difficult because, in many ways,
they were two of a kind. They shared common traits, and appetites
for sex, booze, night life, and, of course, their mutual career paths in
the entertainment business. They had also both felt the long-term
effects of domineering and somewhat cruel mothers and both even
had physical defects. Lawford's was as a consequence of an accident
with a plate glass window, which left him with a claw-like right hand,
and, like Sinatra's ear and scar, had kept him out of the war.

The bust-up between the two happened in the year that Frank's
fraught relationship with Ava Gardner finally hit the rocks. In the
wake of her MGM publicist making a public statement on the end of
the marriage, Sinatra went into an emotional meltdown and crawled
like he had never crawled before, to no avail. As far as the second Mrs.
Sinatra was concerned, it was over, and she displayed a determined
and cool resolve in avoiding any temptation to change her mind.
Frank, on the other hand, was distraught, hurting with a murderous
jealousy at the thought that any other man might replace him on her
arm or, perish the thought, in her bed.

Then, a short time later, the notorious gossip columnist Louella Parsons penned a piece in her column that reported that Ava and Lawford had been seen together in a well-known Hollywood restaurant. The redoubtable gossipmonger also put two and two together to get five, largely on the basis that Peter was a notorious womanizer, and Ava's form well known. In truth, Ava had invited both Lawford and his business manager, Milt Ebbins, to meet with herself and Bappie on a purely social basis. Sinatra went ballistic, rang his imagined rival, and while screaming and ranting told him he would arrange to have his legs broken, a threat the frightened Lawford took very seriously, given his knowledge of Frank's supposed Mob connections.

Eventually, through various interventions and pleadings, Sinatra was disabused of the notion that Lawford had replaced him, but whatever small suspicion may have lingered prompted him not to speak to Peter for five years. It was clear to many who had ended up on the wrong side of Frank that the result was usually permanent banishment. Lawford would not reside there forever, for the strangest, or perhaps the most obvious, of reasons.

The British-born actor was somewhat worthy of Sinatra's suspicion because of his track record for bedding stars and starlets including Lana Turner, Rita Hayworth, Judy Garland, Anne Baxter, and June Allyson as well as being a regular visitor to Hollywood bordellos. In addition there were rumors that he was bisexual. When he had first signed to MGM, the story had done the rounds that his mother had approached studio head Louis B. Meyer to ask him to put her on the MGM payroll as her son's assistant. When Meyer refused she claimed Lawford needed to be "supervised" because he was a homosexual. An actor of modest talent, Peter made the best of his B-movie lead roles and as an A-movie support player, his good looks and charm providing his main appeal. This made him a social and party animal who loved the beach life and would turn up to the opening of an envelope.

He finally settled down when he married Patricia Kennedy, Joe and Rose's sixth child, in April 1954. Joe Kennedy, who was aware of Lawford's reputation through his Hollywood connections, naturally viewed his daughter's choice with some skepticism and drew up a pre-nuptial agreement, which he later withdrew when Lawford expressed himself happy to sign. While Joe wanted the best for his children, he could hardly refuse a man whose sexual behavior mirrored that of his own, and Lawford, unlike Joe, had never been married. The B-movie actor was now part of one of the most powerful dynasties in America and in an ideal position to improve both his fortune and influence. Despite this, Sinatra still did not seek him out, even when spotting him among the family group at the 1956 Democratic Convention. It would take another two years for the ice, which Sinatra had created, to be broken between them, and it happened in the most casual of fashions and by a degree of chance.

In 1957 MGM dipped into the television market for the first time with *The Thin Man*, a series based on the book by Dashiell Hammett and the successful 1934 movie of the same name. The series of seventy-two programs, made for NBC, starred Lawford as former private eye Nick Charles, who resides with his wife and their wire haired terrier, Asta, in a luxurious Park Avenue apartment. From the time the weekly half-hour drama was broadcast in September of that year it was an immediate success, and would run until August 1959.

In August 1958 Patricia Lawford was pregnant and the couple were invited to a dinner party by the actor Gary Cooper and his wife Rocky, and accepted with much trepidation. The reason was not that Peter would be working late on *The Thin Man*, but that Pat's dining companion would be none other than Sinatra. When Lawford eventually arrived, he was pleasantly surprised to find Frank in deep conversation with his wife. When Lawford slipped as unobtrusively as possible in to his seat, Frank turned to him first and after a pause back to Pat said, "You know I don't speak to your old man." They all broke up laughing, and the ice broke with it. A new era had begun in relations between Lawford and Sinatra, and ultimately with Jack Kennedy.

From the position of an avowed enemy, Lawford's marital connections had projected him and his wife into Frank's innermost circle. The friendship also developed into a business partnership with their mutual involvement in Puccini's, a restaurant in Beverley Hills, and later in a film production company, and ultimately when Lawford was invited into the Rat Pack. Frank had become so close to the Lawfords that by the time she gave birth on November 4, Pat decided to give her new baby Victoria the middle name of Frances, after *Francis* Albert Sinatra. But as much as they adored him, they also knew a lot about Frank's volcanic temper.

On New Year's Eve of that year the Lawfords were part of a private party at Romanoff's in Beverly Hills. They were seated with Sinatra, actress Natalie Wood, and her husband Robert Wagner. By now the Lawfords not only saw Frank on a weekly basis, but also spent most weekends, at his insistence, at Palm Springs, a two-hour drive from their home in Santa Monica. The Lawfords always stayed in the same bedroom and had taken to leaving some of their clothes there; such was the regularity of their visits.

As the festivities were ending at Romanoff's, Sinatra suggested they move the party to his house. When they refused, Frank went mad and stormed out of the restaurant. When Lawford called the Sinatra residence the next morning, Frank's valet answered the telephone, saying his boss was still asleep because he hadn't got to bed until 5 a.m. "Oh, Mr. Lawford. What happened last night? I better tell you that he's pissed. Really pissed off. He went to your closet and took out all the clothes that you and your wife keep here and ripped them into shreds and then threw them into the swimming pool." The valet went on to tell Lawford that Frank had at first tried to make a bonfire out of his clothes, but the fire wouldn't get going, so, frustrated, he tossed everything in the pool. The next time they met Frank, there was no mention whatsoever of the incident.

When the Lawfords weren't at Frank's, he was at their place. Peter and Pat lived in a large house on the beach in Malibu which had been formerly owned by Louis B. Mayer, and this provided the location for reciprocal visits from Sinatra and other stars, and in the near future would become a California stop-off point for a bit of fun for members of the Kennedy campaign team, including the senator.

The immediacy of such a détente, and its apparently casual nature, certainly proved a relief to Lawford but is hardly surprising against the political backdrop on which the burgeoning figure of Jack Kennedy was writ large. Although Lawford would not have been so venal to recognize it at the time, Sinatra saw an opportunity, not just simply to get close to the Kennedy camp, but to gain entry.

Frank had rubbed shoulders with the likes of Roosevelt and Truman and other Democratic high flyers but, having used him on the campaign trail, they had distanced themselves from him, largely due to his dubious connections. He may have thought that if he established a relationship much earlier with the latest Democratic presidential hopeful then he might bask longer in the political glow. But Sinatra's life, his career, his success, and his revival in the mid-1950s, was all down to his intrinsic relationship with the Cosa Nostra. He might not have been a "made man," in the manner of Mafia acceptance, but he was viewed as an Italian with connections and, while everyone was afraid of mobsters, everyone wanted to know Frank, especially the mobsters. When times were tough and venues were difficult to find, the Mob helped. The Copacabana, being the most notable, always looked after him and gave him bookings. That was Frank's Faustian pact with organized crime.

The Desert Inn, run by Moe Dalitz, also accommodated him when he first performed on the Strip in September 1951, and it did not take a rocket scientist to come to the conclusion that the Mafia controlled the vast majority of hotels, casinos, and performance venues on the Strip.

For the sake of the gaming licenses, these venues had appointed managers and stakeholders to appear on paper to effectively conceal their beneficial owners. Ever since Meyer Lansky's men had walked into the Flamingo in 1947, when Bugsy Siegel's body was still warm, that had been the case. The most spectacular example of this kind of operation was the Sands Hotel, which would become inextricably linked with Sinatra as well as a host of other star entertainers. Lansky and a number of members of the Chicago outfit, including

Tony Accardo and Sam Giancana, were among the syndicate of investors who had raised $5.5 million to build the hotel and casino. As Wilbur Clark had done at the Desert Inn, a front man was chosen by the name of Jack Freedman, a gambler and horse owner, but the project was overseen by close Lansky associates Joseph "Doc" Stacher, who was the effective boss, and Jimmy "Blue Eyes" Alo to supervise construction.

The building, designed by the Los Angeles–based architect, Wayne McAllister, was spectacular when completed. There were four two-story motel wings, each with fifty rooms surrounding the half-moon shaped pool. Inside the main building there was a great hall with a reception desk in one corner, slot machines, a bar and cocktail lounge, and in the center, roulette and craps tables. Three terrazzo stairways led to the large casino, which was lit with dimmed chandeliers. Signs pointed on to the Copa Room and restaurants.

The most striking image was provided by the roadside sign, a classic of its time.

McAllister designed it to reach fifty-six feet in height with modern script reading: "Sands," with the small subtitle underneath, "A Place In the Sun." At night, the neon glowed a haunting red. Later a rectangular sign would be added advertising the acts. The hotel and casino opened on December 15, 1952 and within six months would recoup the whole of the initial investment, indicating the extent of the unbelievable cash cow the syndicate had created. The "management" brought in the legendary showman Jack Entratter, who had been the entertainment impresario at the Copacabana, to ensure the success of the entertainment. A nonsmoker and non-drinker with an imposing physical presence, Entratter would ensure that the top acts of the entertainment world would be performing at the Sands, and that the entire operation would set the standard for the Strip. The roll call would ultimately include Sinatra, Dean Martin, Jerry Lewis, Lena Horne, Tallulah Bankhead, Tony Bennett, Marlene Dietrich, and, of course, the Rat Pack, who would make the performance space at the Copa Room the biggest draw in town.

Sinatra had been booked for the Copa Room well in advance but had to finish his contract at the Desert Inn. He was not due to make his debut at the Sands until September 1953, but in the interim the word of his performance as Maggio had spread to the Hollywood hotline and by the time he hit the Copa Room he was a big star once again. To ensure his loyalty he was given the opportunity of buying a two percent share in the hotel-casino, which he took up. Frank was now a shareholder in a Mob-controlled business, and the Sands would become his entertainment headquarters.

Five years later everything was going swimmingly between Frank and Peter. A new partnership of kind emerged between them when Peter and Pat purchased the storyline to *Ocean's Eleven,* a proposed movie, which had as its central theme a group of World War II veterans combining as a gang to rob a casino. The Lawfords had paid B-movie director Gilbert Kay $10,000 for the idea but had no real Hollywood influence to advance the project. Frank stepped in and took it over and, after securing the backing of Warner Brothers, doubled Peter's purchase price, guaranteed him a part, and cut him into a share of the gross profits. When Frank was nice, he was real nice.

* * *

Meanwhile, in the wake of his overwhelming Senate reelection result against Celeste, Jack Kennedy was once more playing coy about his intentions for about running for president in 1960. Despite the Senate success, and the very considerable impact of the handsome and highly presentable forty-one-year-old on the public consciousness, particularly after the 1956 convention, there were doubts and doubters within and without the Democratic Party. These were mainly concerned with the perceived immaturity of the possible contender. It had been just over a dozen years since Jack had entered politics, in an era in which the vast majority of world leaders were on the wrong side of sixty years of age.

Apart from the doubters there were sufficient circumstances to worry about or at the least give Jack pause for thought. First, no Catholic had ever been elected president; second, no candidate of forty-three years of age had ever been elected. While Protestant church membership in the country was double that of Catholics, there was no national anti-Catholic movement as there had been in 1928 when Al Smith had run for president. The charge of immaturity, however, would be difficult to counteract. In the world of politics, Jack was still, by any measure, a whippersnapper, and for that very reason he was not a member of the silver-haired inner circle of the Senate. Of possible less consequence, but a fact, was that no senator, Democrat or Republican, had received a nomination to run for president since 1920.

One of the Kennedy election strategy team would later remark that politics boiled down to arithmetic and at the particular juncture the figures did not seem to stack up. The inevitable temptation was to wait another four years and hope the interval might diminish the religious and age handicaps. Jack summed up the dilemma: "If I were a governor of a large state, Protestant, and 55, I could sit back and let it come to me."

The opposite argument was apparently simple: holding on might lessen the obstacles but there was no guarantee—it was now, or maybe never. That view would ultimately hold sway, but in the spring of 1959 Jack Kennedy was not entirely convinced, hence his coyness on the matter. His father was not in agreement—he had allowed his own political ambition to implode and he was not going to allow his son to miss any opportunity for any reason put forward by others. To prove the point, in July he purchased a Convair private plane, at a cost of $385,000, to provide nationwide access for the family contender.

Whatever personal doubts Jack might have had, there were obviously none in his father's mind, and in April 1959 the first meeting of the campaign team took place at Palm Beach under Joe's supervision. The team was comprised of the familiar names, including O' Donnell, O'Brien, and Dave Powers. Brother Ted was also in attendance as was sister Jean's husband, Steve Smith. Bobby and Pierre Salinger were otherwise engaged but would join later.

In truth, whatever reservations had lurked internally or externally, the campaign had merely lulled and had never really stopped.

Jack and Ted Sorensen were constantly searching for new topics, themes, and writers as they traveled extensively, writing and giving more and more speeches. By the fall, the plane, named *The Caroline*, had covered twenty-two states, with Sorensen preparing speech sections and combinations to suit the locale, culture, and considerations at each stop. Jack's image as a youthful, energetic modernizer with the common touch, despite being a member of a rich and privileged family, became the subject of a prolific number of magazine articles.

At considerable expense to Joe, the team also commissioned numerous private polls, the favorable results of which were passed on to the more sympathetic and supportive media outlets; all calculated to further amplify the image and credibility of Jack Kennedy as a future candidate for president of the United States. It was becoming abundantly clear that whoever was going to run against Jack for the nomination was in for an uphill battle. As one observer would later remark, the Kennedy organization doesn't run, it purrs and has the smooth rhythm of a delicate watch. One night in October 1959, Sorensen was chatting to Jack late one night in a hotel room in Evansville, Indiana, about the nomination when, out of the blue, Kennedy turned to him and said, "I think I can make it."

Frank Sinatra was someone who believed the very same thing and was busy, with the help of Peter Lawford, nailing his colors firmly to the Kennedy mast. He'd spent some time with Jack at the Lawford beach house during the summer of 1958 and was gradually edging closer to the center of the group of admirers who were favored enough to consider themselves in the "Jack Pack."

* * *

In a matter of a very short time Jack and Frank would be, in the first instance, party buddies, and then Sinatra would assume a more central role in the constant round of fund-raising. In the same year he was Kennedy's guest of honor at his private suite in the Mayflower Hotel in Washington, which was used to host dinner parties for favored supporters and celebrities, and there were other get-togethers when the senator was traveling through the West. In early November 1959, Sinatra attended a Kennedy fund-raiser event in Los Angeles and afterward the two ate at Puccini's, before Jack and Dave Powers stayed at Frank's Palm Springs home. While there is no doubt that a friendship, based on fun and shared interests, had developed, the mutual flattery between the hot shot political star and the international singing sensation belied the hugely selfish reasons both had for their association.

On January 2, 1960, at the Senate Caucus room in Washington, Kennedy announced his candidacy for the Democratic presidential nomination. His most likely opponents would be Pat Brown of California, Stuart Symington of Missouri, Lyndon B. Johnson of Texas, Hubert Humphrey of Minnesota, and the clearly irrepressible Adlai Stevenson. Three of the candidates, Symington, Stevenson, and Johnson, announced that they would not compete in the primaries and would instead put themselves forward based on their respective, and impressive, records. They were also relying on the perceived Democratic Party wisdom regarding Kennedy's youth and inexperience. While it was well known they would both run, Stevenson and Johnson would wait until a week before the convention, set for mid-July, to officially announce their candidacies.

Meanwhile, life for Frank Sinatra and his Rat Pack of Dean Martin, Sammy Davis Jr., Peter Lawford, and Joey Bishop was hectic. As well as their nightly show at the Sands, *Ocean's Eleven,* which had been developed into something of a home movie for Sinatra and the pack, was in production. The director, Lewis Milestone, had accommodated the Pack members in his shooting schedule to allow for the evening shows, which, much to his annoyance, were followed by the obligatory drinking sessions until dawn. As the gambling and entertainment mecca began to develop bigger and bigger resorts, Sinatra himself, and his ability to draw a high profile Hollywood crowd, put Las Vegas on the map. The syndicate that owned the Sands must have been ecstatic as a host of stars including Lucille Ball, Jack Benny, Cole Porter, Kim Novak, and Cary Grant, not only booked in to see the Rat Pack in action, but also provided acres of publicity and, consequently, more and more demand for the venue.

A series of shows titled "The Summit" aping the title of the political one taking place at the time in Paris between Dwight Eisenhower, Nikita Khrushchev, and General de Gaulle ran from January 26 until February 16, generating eighteen thousand reservation booking attempts for the Sand's two hundred rooms. For this event, Sinatra named his stage troupe the Jack Pack in honor of his friend, Senator John Kennedy, and in support of his campaign.

Apart from his interest in show business as an aid to political ambition, Jack Kennedy could now appreciate just what Frank Sinatra could do for his campaign. As "the brother-in-law" Lawford put it, "Let's just say that the Kennedys are interested in the lively arts and that Sinatra is the liveliest art of all." Dave Powers recalled that Jack also loved insider celebrity gossip, which Frank chatted freely about, and both agreed, after the stay in Palm Springs, that Sinatra was a fabulous host. He laid on his hospitality lavishly and introduced Jack to the sort of interesting, fun people he liked to spend time with. But in the early part of 1960, Sinatra would make an introduction that would become a time bomb with the capability to destroy Jack Kennedy's political career.

On February 7, 1960 Jack flew with his entourage to Las Vegas to attend the Summit, to tee up some fund-raisers, and to give a quick press conference at the Sands Hotel. That evening they had dinner at Frank's table in the Garden Room. One of the guests was a stunning twenty-five-year-old brunette by the name of Judith Campbell, who sat beside Jack during the late night show at the Copa Room and was, like the rest of the audience, mightily impressed when Sinatra introduced Kennedy from the stage as the next president of the United States.

Judith Immoor, as she was born, was the daughter of a middle-class Catholic family of Irish and German heritage. The family had moved when she was a child to Los Angeles where they set up home in Pacific Palisades, an affluent suburb on the west side of the city. Her childhood and adolescence were normal, until the age of fourteen when her mother was seriously injured in a car crash, forcing Judy to drop out of school and receive tuition at home.

Her older sister, Jacqueline, was an actress of modest talent and, using the stage name of Susan Morrow, had a short career appearing in a number of television shows, including *The Loretta Young Show, Perry Mason, Gunsmoke,* and *Bronco.* Judy was a stunningly beautiful young woman who had wanted to follow in her sister's career footsteps, but her talent did not match her looks. Instead, she ended up hanging around Hollywood sets with luminaries like Charlton Heston, Lloyd Bridges, and Debbie Reynolds.

When she was eighteen she was at a party with Robert Wagner when she met actor William Campbell. He had starred in a number of forgettable B-features (including *Love Me Tender,* in which he became the first man to sing onscreen alongside Elvis Presley). This moved the couple into Hollywood circles, and she developed some friendships, which outlived her marriage. She was introduced to Frank Sinatra in Puccini's and a few days later he invited her to go with him to Hawaii with the Lawfords, and they embarked on a brief affair that foundered when she refused to be party to a threesome with Frank and another woman. The night she met Jack, it was Ted Kennedy, accompanying his brother on the visit, who had initially made a play for her attentions. But it was his charming elder brother whom Judy immediately fell for.

She was impressed by the candidate's charisma, intelligence, and down-to-earth attitude, but showed no sign of glorying in his fame and status. For his part, he could not, aside from any carnal impulse, which was never far away, but be struck by the sensuous, beautiful young woman. He asked her to lunch the following day, an intimate meeting that took place on the patio of Sinatra's private suite. Jack took Judy's contact details and promised that they would meet up again in the near future. She may have thought it a typical empty promise but it soon transpired that the presidential hopeful was more than enthusiastic. Five days after their introduction she received a dozen red roses followed by regular phone calls. Early the following month they met at the Plaza Hotel in New York and had sex, which she would later describe as perfunctory on his part, primarily concerned with his own satisfaction. That probably should have been that, if Kennedy had been playing his political cards properly.

It may not have struck Frank Sinatra that the introduction would go beyond a one-night stand and develop into an affair. But there were circumstances attached of which Jack had no knowledge at the time and which should have tempered Sinatra in his choice of companion for Kennedy. Peter Lawford should also have been alarmed, but he appeared as gormless as Sinatra in what amounted to laying an explosive device on the Kennedy campaign rails. This was a case of poor judgment all around, which would have serious consequences down the tracks.

Chapter 11: The Road to Glory

———————◆———————

S PENDING TIME WITH Judy, however pleasurable, wasn't the most important consideration in Jack Kennedy's life in the late spring of 1960. His entire focus, and that of his team, was on the primaries. The Kennedy camp strategy was to blitz these statewide selections of delegates to the national convention, and if the results came their way then Jack could enter the cauldron of national selection of the party's candidate in mid-July in what all hoped would be an unassailable position. To take Hubert Humphrey head-on in Wisconsin, next to his home state of Minnesota, in March, and then in Protestant-dominated West Virginia, had been identified as the key priorities. The campaign team and members of the Kennedy clan literally invaded Wisconsin, prompting Humphrey to remark that he "felt like an independent merchant running against a chain store."

Although not a winner-takes-all scenario, the Wisconsin primary would provide a severe test for both candidates. While Kennedy had maintained, somewhat dramatically, that he would be out of the race if he lost, the eyes of his team were firmly fixed on the four predominantly Protestant districts. The hard-fought effort by the Kennedy camp paid dividends with victory on April 5, but it was a closer call than anticipated and did not provide an excuse to pop open the champagne.

The winning margin of 476,024 to 366,753, representing a 56 percent to 44 percent share of the vote, provided some comfort. It also gave Humphrey the confidence to stay in the contest, particularly given that the protestant districts had fallen his way. If that trend were to be replicated in West Virginia, then the Kennedy campaign would face a huge credibility gap no matter what happened in the other primaries. O'Donnell and O'Brien knew that the key question in relation to Kennedy's Catholicism, not just in the nomination battle, but the presidential campaign as a whole, could be answered in this state. Defeat for Jack here would, without doubt, derail the campaign, and lead to the prospect of a hung convention.

During the month of April the battle for West Virginia began, with Bobby and Larry O'Brien traveling to Clarksburg to meet the northern chairmen at the Stonewall Jackson Hotel. Their trip was somewhat spoiled by the fact that a recent Gallup poll had given Humphrey a 60–40 lead in the state. They then moved on to the campaign headquarters in the Kanawha Hotel in Charleston to meet the southern party chairmen. The perceived wisdom was that the religious issue, which had been assiduously avoided by the Kennedy camp, must have influenced the results of the poll. The problem would have to be faced. It was generally agreed that Jack had handled the issue well when he dealt with it front on, saying: "There is nothing in my religious faith that prevents me executing my duties of office. If I thought there was I wouldn't have taken it. If I thought there was I shouldn't be a candidate for president. I shouldn't be a senator. I shouldn't have been a congressman and I shouldn't have been taken into the service of the United States."

* * *

In a broadcast with Franklin Roosevelt Jr., who had been drafted in by Joe to help on the basis that his father had been hugely popular in the state, Kennedy was asked how his religion would affect the presidency. He replied by saying that it was a matter for the oath as it stood, to uphold the separation of church and state, and anyone who violated this oath sinned against the Constitution and God. It was also, he later declared, a matter of tolerance versus intolerance, dropping the ball into his opponent's court of publicized tolerance.

There were other more worldly forces at work, however, for Jack's campaign, largely at the instigation of his father. Joe reportedly approached Sinatra to seek the help of Sam Giancana in Illinois and, more importantly, in West Virginia. On home turf in Illinois, Giancana and his associates could deliver any amount of Chicago district votes, but West Virginia was a different matter, and would demand a bit more than orders from the boss. $50,000 was reportedly handled by Giancana associate Paul D'Amato, who dispersed the money as bribes to key election figures and to officials who could deliver votes. After the primary the FBI recorded a number of complaints about bribery and the buying of votes. A future FBI wiretap would record Giancana complaining about the lack of appreciation by Sinatra, and the Kennedys, for his help in Illinois and West Virginia.

The extent to which the Mob helped to influence the vote in West Virginia is impossible to calculate, but it was not essential, as the result would show. On election day in the state, May 10, both candidates traveled to Washington to address a Democratic Women's Group. Humphrey retuned to the state capital, Charleston, but, whether out of confidence or fear, Kennedy chose to remain in DC. Bobby was ensconced in the Kanawha Hotel ready to follow the trends and totals after the poll stations closed at 8 p.m. The first indicators or tallies began to appear at 9 p.m. and looked promising, but just after 10 p.m. it became clear that the result would not only go in Kennedy's favor, but by a very considerable margin.

When Jack and Jackie returned home from a nervous night at the movies, there was a message to ring Bobby in Charleston. This time champagne was popped and Jack headed to the airport to fly to Charleston and a primary victory of stunning proportions. Even the most optimistic member of the campaign team could not believe the West Virginia statistics. Kennedy took 236,510 to Humphrey's 151,187 votes, the margin 60.8 percent to 39.2 percent. The victorious candidate took fifty out of the state's fifty-five counties. Humphrey conceded defeat and withdrew from further campaigning for the nomination. With ten primaries in the bag, including Illinois, where he won with 65 percent of the vote, and no candidate close, Kennedy could travel to the Convention with some degree of confidence. There was still the threat of Lyndon Johnson lingering in the background, however, and the battle for delegates would continue right up to the last moment.

Judy, meanwhile, had continued to be at the beck and call of Sinatra, not for his own sexual needs, but, as with the case of Jack Kennedy, to be offered to friends or associates whom he wished to impress. It was obvious that she was taken with, and attracted to, older men of wealth and power, but unlike the Hollywood casting-couch there were no promises of opportunities for work, even of the most menial kind. A week after Kennedy had bedded her, Sinatra invited her to Miami, where he was performing a series of concerts in the Fontainebleau, and introduced to her to Sam Flood. The name was one of a number of aliases used by Sam Giancana. Frank omitted to inform her of Giancana's real identity, something she would later discover. It did not deter her, however, from getting involved in a sexual liaison just dangerous as the one she was having with Jack.

Had she known more about the man she was now also involved with, it's unlikely she would have stuck around for too long. Giancana was, as head of the Chicago Outfit, one of the most powerful mobsters in the country. Not only had he been responsible for, literally, hundreds of hits to remove rivals and to dole out punishments, but, with his extensive investments, he was the criminal king of Las Vegas. Judy quickly became added to the list of his mistresses, and he made up for his ugly physical features, which matched his mean personality, by showering her with gifts, including cash and jewelry.

While her motives, driven by a combination of naivety and a vulnerable necessity to please as a result of her low self-esteem, could be reasonably speculated upon, Sinatra's motives are less clear. He had just engineered a situation in which the most powerful figure in organized crime was sharing a woman with one of the most powerful politicians in the land. If he was pursuing respect through active association with politics at the highest level, could the possible future implications of his actions have escaped his attention? Or was he simply trying to keep his powerful allies happy all of the time?

Frank Sinatra did not lack intelligence, but he was impulsive. That said, he must have been only too keenly aware of Bobby Kennedy's deep antipathy toward Giancana and the other Mafia bosses during the McClellan hearings. As chief counsel in June of the previous year, he had examined Giancana in the most pejorative of terms, asking him if he dealt with his opponents by stuffing them in trunks. Giancana, of course, had declined to answer. When Bobby then asked him if he would tell anything about his operations or just giggle when counsel asked a question, the Fifth Amendment was again pleaded, and Bobby remarked, "I thought only little girls giggled, Mr. Giancana."

The only logical explanation to Sinatra's behavior was that he had envisaged a scenario in which both parties might, in the short term, have a mutually beneficial relationship. That turned out to be the case, but in the long run the odds were against it being anything other than huge trouble. What none of the parties to this unfolding drama knew was that this unseemly relationship had drawn the unwelcome attention of J. Edgar Hoover. The director had instructed his agents to keep the situation under close watch, and would soon introduce wiretaps into the equation. Hoover was no fan of anybody in the ménage, and a connection between any of them was anathema to his particularly skewed vision of the world, where anything that happened without his approval or control was deviant and subject to surveillance.

In March 1960, Hoover received a communication from the New Orleans bureau, which stated that an informant, with access to the Mob in the Miami area, had learned that underworld members, including Joe Fischetti and other hoodlums, were actively endeavoring to secure the nomination for Kennedy. Mention was also made of Frank Sinatra and his support of the campaign, as well as of the

songwriter, Jimmy Van Heusen, and of the Lawford financial interest in the Sands Hotel. The informant had overheard a conversation
that indicated that Kennedy was compromised by a relationship with
a woman but he was unable to give a name in the report. This was
an obvious reference to Judith Campbell. The informant also said
that *Confidential* magazine was investigating a rumor relating to a
party, which had been held in Palm Springs, with Kennedy, Sinatra,
and Lawford present. The publication was a Hollywood muckraking
tabloid with a huge circulation that employed the services of former
LAPD police officer turned notorious private eye, Fred Otash.

Otash was the reporter with *Confidential*. He had been forced to
resign after he was found to be associated with the operators of an
illegal gambling operation. *Confidential* claimed to have the affidavits
of two mulatto prostitutes in New York that implicated Sinatra and
Kennedy, citing them as clients. While the story never stood up, and
consequently remained out of print, except in the FBI files, it was
indicative of the lack of discretion on the parts of both men. Otash
was widely considered a lowlife; he consumed a quart of whisky and
four packs of cigarettes a day and he used threats, fabrication, and
blackmail to fill his columns. That either man could allow himself to
be the target of such a vile publication was pure stupidity. But Frank
and Jack were dancing a fraught tango, which could only end badly.

Kennedy's campaign team was getting real input from Sinatra
and Jack took whatever opportunity he could to use his association
with Frank, and the wider Hollywood community, to add more fairy
dust to his profile. Sinatra's ability to add real value to Jack's campaign became really evident when composer Jimmy Van Heusen and
lyricist Sammy Cahn reworked their 1959 Oscar winning hit "High
Hopes" as the theme tune to the campaign: "Everyone is voting for
Jack, 'cos he's got what all the rest lack, everyone wants to back—Jack,
Jack is on the right track, 'cos he's got High Hopes, High Hopes, nineteen sixty's the year for his High Hopes."

The song was recorded as a single, which, through rather dubious means, found its way to jukeboxes in every state of the election

trail, with financial inducements paid to venue owners to have the song on their playlist. The crisis for the campaign team was that while they were aware that Frank was both useful and supportive, his reputation for hanging out with the Mob could be seized on by rival candidates to discredit Kennedy in some way.

Sinatra's profile was damagingly heightened when *The New York Times* broke a story on March 21 that he had hired Albert Maltz, the blacklisted screenwriter, to work on a project about an army deserter in the Second World War. The subject matter of *The Execution of Private Slovik* was controversial enough, but the conservative press interpreted the whole affair as Frank collaborating with a Communist. O'Donnell and others were aware of the Maltz involvement and had asked Sinatra to delay any announcement of the fact until after the primaries were over.

But the story got out and the right-wing press tore Sinatra apart for trying to revive the career of a Communist, described by the Hearst press as an unrepentant enemy of the country. Sinatra tried to defend his position and his right to hire anyone he liked, but his stance simply compounded the felony. The Kennedy team was now getting extremely nervous about the controversy's effect on the campaign, especially after notable right-winger John Wayne weighed in, asking what Jack thought of his crony hiring such a man. The final straw was when it was suggested from the church pulpits that Kennedy being soft on Communism would be detrimental to the Catholic vote. Joe immediately grabbed the reins and, after consulting Cardinal Cushing in Boston and Cardinal Spellman in New York, both of whom who confirmed this view, rang Frank and gave him the ultimatum to choose either Maltz or the Kennedys. Sinatra did his duty, something that cost him the $75,000 fee due to the writer. He then made his decision public in a statement.

The affair prompted FBI assistant director Clyde Tolson to request a summary report of all the information held by the agency on Sinatra. This was delivered to one of his lieutenants, Alan Belmont, on March 30. One item of particular interest noted that in July of the previous year Sinatra and Dean Martin had flown to Miami from the West Coast to attend the wedding of the daughter of one Samuel M. Giancana. There were other informant reports, which confirmed the close relationship between Frank and Giancana. One report confirmed a sighting of the two on a trip to the El Rancho, Las Vegas, and another, which was even more damning: "During a search of Samuel M. Giancana by Custom Officers in Chicago, Illinois, during June 1958, the notation 'Sinatra Officer 5–4977. Home Crestview 4–2368 was found among his effects.' Crestview 4–2368 is a private number for Frank Sinatra in Los Angeles."

The file also contained a roll call of all the left wing organizations and hoodlums he had been associated with over the years. The net result was that the FBI now had a renewed general interest in Frank Sinatra and his associates, and a particular interest in his involvement with Jack Kennedy.

As the campaign rolled on the negative reaction to this latest controversy scattered behind like the election flyers. As the Irish Mafia headed for the Democratic Convention in Los Angeles, they were on a high, secure in the belief that nothing, not even the intervention of an elder democratic statesman, could stop the Kennedy juggernaut from capturing the party's nomination. A week before, former President Harry Truman had told a press conference that Kennedy was too immature for the job and should withdraw, and former First Lady Eleanor Roosevelt made a statement that he represented "the new managerial elite that had neither principles nor character." While distinctly unhelpful, there was a widespread view that they simply reflected the attitude of the old guard in the party.

The Kennedy team occupied a number of suites and rooms on the eighth floor of the Biltmore Hotel in preparation for the opening of the convention on July 11 at the Sports Arena, and ran a lavish hospitality suite to further woo the delegates. The night before the opening, Sinatra, and a host of entertainment stars attended a fund raising dinner at the Beverly Hilton Hotel where he and Judy Garland performed for the guests. A virtual army of Hollywood stars supported Kennedy onstage at the opening ceremony of the convention, including Janet Leigh, Tony Curtis, Lawford, Lee Marvin, and Edward G. Robinson, all of whom were introduced to the gathering. When Sammy Davis Jr.'s turn came, the Mississippi and Alabama delegates booed him. They all then sang the national anthem.

Despite all the controversy along the road to this moment, which was so central to his political career, Jack put Frank to the forefront of his pitch to the convention and made a huge show of his backing by the entertainment business. Many of the stars helped other members of the team work the floor, meeting and greeting the delegates. Meanwhile, over at Marion Davies' house, Joe was on the phone day and night, extracting commitments from influential delegates and making all sorts of extravagant promises. Sinatra was a regular visitor to the mansion in Beverly Hills.

On the morning of Wednesday, July 13, the day of the balloting, Dave Powers reminded Jack of his remark after the vice-presidential defeat in 1956: "Well, this is the day you have been waiting for, this is the day you will pick up all the marbles." That evening Kennedy won the party nomination for president on the first ballot. When the Wyoming delegation gave him a two-thirds majority, the target of 761 votes was exceeded, with Kennedy getting 808 and Lyndon Johnson finishing a distant second at 409. The rest of the field was well out of sight.

The following day, to the surprise of the media and members of his own team, Jack asked Johnson to be his vice-presidential running mate. When the southern vote at the convention was analyzed, Kennedy's reasons became evident. Out of the 409 southern delegates, 307 went for Johnson and only 13 for Kennedy. If he wanted to win the general election there was no doubt that he needed the support of the South. Bobby was completely against the choice and, at one point, tried to dissuade the Texan from accepting. Many years later, Evelyn Lincoln, Jack's longtime secretary, stated in an interview that she had overheard the discussion between Johnson and Bobby on the subject while she was going in and out of the room at the Biltmore. She recalled that Johnson had claimed to have information about Jack's womanizing, which had been supplied by Hoover, and used this "as a card, so to speak." Either way, Johnson was on the ticket.

That evening the Lawfords threw a victory party at their Santa Monica home, with Sinatra and the celebrity supporters and another addition, Marilyn Monroe, all raising their champagne glasses to the victorious candidate. In the late afternoon of that Friday, the Democratic presidential nominee addressed a crowd of eighty thousand in the Los Angeles Memorial Coliseum and delivered his acceptance speech. Drafted by Ted Sorensen, his remarks were aimed at uniting the party for the forthcoming election, and aimed as a salvo against the opposition and Vice-President Richard Nixon, who most pundits were predicting would win the Republican nomination in ten days' time. Kennedy aide Walt Rostow came up with the concept of the "New Frontier" to match the battle slogans of President Wilson's "New Freedom," and Roosevelt's "New Deal."

It was more of a call to election arms than an acceptance speech and a denigration of his opponent, whose "political career seemed to show charity to none and malice for all," adding, in no uncertain terms, that in his view Nixon was unfit to follow in Eisenhower's footsteps. He quoted his favorite speechmaker, Winston Churchill, to illustrate that the New Frontier was a forward vision (even with its echoes of the Wild West): "If we open a quarrel between the past and the present, we shall be in danger of losing the future," he said. It was not a set of promises but a set of challenges that "sums up not what I intend to offer to the American people but what I intend to ask of them."

The New Frontier, with ideals and aspirations from the eradication of poverty to exploring the galaxy, provided a potent and dramatic battle cry for the Democratic presidential candidate who had, for the moment, swept away the obstacles of his youth and religion. There was another side to the image that the victorious candidate had portrayed, that of a of a modern, handsome, young statesman whose intellect did not prevent him from having the common touch, all of which added to the public allure and popularity of Jack Kennedy. But in the shadows, away from the public consciousness, he was involved in an underhanded strategy and plain bribery. He was consorting not just with ordinary criminals but with notorious hoodlums and, as usual, with scores of willing young women.

Facilitating and, indeed, conducting this offstage, dangerous charade was Frank Sinatra who, no more than his now best political bud, or his brother-in-law, had any idea when the time would be right to let the curtain fall on such dark arts. And at that moment in time, with a fat Cuban cigar in his hand, a rare smile must have passed on the weasel-like features of Sam Giancana as he looked forward to a new era of freedom from federal pressure and any threat of prosecution, something he understood was to be his reward from the Kennedys. But in the wings Hoover had become even more alert, alarmed by Jack's victory and the prospect of a Kennedy presidency and what it might mean for him. And, as the campaign gathered momentum, he continued to apply pressure to his agents for more information on the offstage antics of Sinatra and the presidential candidate.

Fred Otash was also sifting through the garbage of New York life in an effort to find something, anything, to stick, as an FBI file dated July 26, 1960 shows. A nameless Hollywood prostitute told agents that Otash had contacted her earlier in the month looking for information about her participation in sex parties involving Kennedy, Lawford, Sinatra, and Sammy Davis Jr. She told him that she had no knowledge of such activities. Agents following this up met Otash in his office on July 11. He told them that somebody was making attempts to spy on Kennedy's hotel room but inferred that *Confidential* was looking for dirt on the senator for use in articles before the November election (the gumshoe was obviously hoping that Kennedy would win the nomination which, on the eleventh of July, had not yet been decided). The call girl told the agents that Otash wanted to set up Kennedy by putting a wire on her and that she had refused. The FBI would later hear one of their own wiretapped subjects discussing the senator's sexual exploits.

Meanwhile, after the convention Jack Kennedy had little time to indulge in any such exploits, but he did manage to hook up with Judy Campbell twice in August. He also traveled to Las Vegas to party with Sinatra and there were visits to the Lawfords in Santa Monica. In September, however, he faced into two months of a punishing schedule of campaigning, with an average of four hours' sleep, and an ongoing round of breakfast and lunch meetings, press conferences, campaign speeches, and travel. The campaign team had targeted New York, Pennsylvania, California, Michigan, Texas, Illinois, Ohio, New Jersey, and Massachusetts, as the nine states whose combined electoral votes could produce 237 of the 269 necessary to win the presidency, and each of these states had to be visited, and each vote attracted.

August also saw the premiere of *Ocean's Eleven* in Las Vegas, and Sinatra and the Rat Pack were out in force. The film, which received mixed reviews, was a surprising commercial success, adding considerably to the publicity around the Kennedy campaign, in which Frank was central to the organization of entertainment promotions and fund-raisers. In early September, Tony Curtis and Janet Leigh, who had been active supporters during the convention, hosted a "Key Women For Kennedy" event at their home, and on September 7 a crowd of two thousand turned up and, as well as listening to speeches, were treated to three songs from Frank, who was applauded by Ted Kennedy, the Western organizer for his brother. Frank also assembled a Hollywood group to attend the Democratic governor's ball in Newark, New Jersey, and sang for the audience. In September, he and Lawford were on location for the film *The Devil at 4 O'Clock*, and every spare moment they had away from the set, was spent campaigning. Wherever they went the emphasis was on entertainment as a key component of the canvassing process. Other high profile stars like Harry Belafonte, who appeared in one campaign television ad, helped to target African American voters, and in a host of other commercials, Lena Horne, Milton Berle, Gene Kelly, Ella Fitzgerald, and Henry Fonda all endorsed the Kennedy-Johnson ticket.

With Catholics amounting to only 26 percent of the population, religion could not disappear as an issue in the campaign and, as he had done in during the primaries, Kennedy dealt with it openly. On the campaign trail in Texas on September 12, while addressing the Greater Houston Ministerial Association in Houston, he told the audience, "I am not the Catholic candidate for President. I am the Democratic candidate for President who also happens to be Catholic. I do not speak for my Church on public matters—the Church does not speak for me." Sorensen had said that they could win or lose the election in Houston on that night, so this was an acid test. The preachers questioned him at length, but he convinced them that he would not take direction stating, "May I just say that that I do not accept the right of any ecclesiastical official to tell me what I should do in the sphere of my public responsibility." It appeared from the general reaction that Kennedy had managed to assure an audience of his most ardent critics where he stood on the matter.

On September 26, what is generally regarded as the defining moment of the campaign took place. After much negotiation, both Kennedy and Nixon had agreed to a series of four televised debates. With approximately forty million television sets in the country at that time, for both camps this innovation was regarded as something that could potentially circumvent a lot of the slogging on the campaign trail. Nobody could have predicted just how transformational the events could be nor how they would go on to shape future presidential elections.

The first debate was broadcast on September 26 from Chicago to an audience of sixty million viewers. The consensus appeared to be that Kennedy was both relaxed and well prepared, while Nixon was somewhat ill at ease. Jack had walked on set at the last minute, something that seemed to have an unsettling effect on his opponent. When measured later, the radio audience felt that Nixon had the edge while those who saw the debate on television had the opposite view. Both contestants played it tight—there was not a whiff of real aggression, controversy, or even real differences in the political analysis of each.

There was no contest between the visual; the handsome Democrat was well ahead on points on that score.

Kenny O'Donnell said later that after that debate the 1960 campaign was a completely different ball game. When the team discussed it on October 1 at Hyannis Port, the inner circle, with the exception of Jack, was enervated with optimism and renewed energy. The consensus was that next time around, Kennedy should emphasize the differences in policy between the Democrats and Republicans. The more public perception, in the visual sense, was of the good cop, bad cop variety—Nixon a bit shifty looking as opposed to the handsome, pearly toothed hero type, personified by Kennedy. In the second debate six days later, Nixon gave a much-improved performance, but the debates, including the other two, were conspicuous by their largely boring content. But all that really mattered was the reach: the combined audience over the four debates was estimated to be somewhere between 85 and 120 million.

Joe, meanwhile, keeping out of sight but not out of mind, worked assiduously behind the scenes. He met Teamsters official Harold Gibbons to soothe concerns about the Kennedy antipathy (Bobby's in particular) toward Jimmy Hoffa, and he almost certainly gave assurances to Giancana and other Mob members in regard to their support.

As Election Day approached, the consensus was that the result would be too close to call. Three of four opinion polls gave Kennedy a very slight lead but sampling experts concluded that it could go either way, with one declaring that he had never seen the lead change so many times since they had started political sampling over two decades previously. Jack Kennedy had not gotten all the marbles yet.

At 8:45 a.m. on the morning of November 8, accompanied by Jackie, Kennedy cast his vote at the West End branch of the Boston Public Library. They then left for the airport to fly to Hyannis. After she voted, Jackie looked at her husband and, referring to her voting machine, said nervously, "I hope that thing worked."

Chapter 12: The Golden Dawn of Camelot

———————◆———————

A S DAWN BROKE over Hyannis Port on the morning of November 9, 1960, it was becoming clear that John Fitzgerald Kennedy was to be the thirty-fifth president of the United States. The closest race in modern electoral history had given him a victory of just 112,827 votes. The vagaries of the Electoral College system ensured Nixon had become the first candidate in American presidential electoral history to lose an election, despite carrying a majority of the states.

Kennedy had been up most of the night with Bobby, Kenny, Dave Powers, Peter Lawford, Pierre Salinger, and most of his family. The Kennedy summerhouse, where the family had been vacationing since the late 1920s, had been converted into a makeshift election count center. On the big enclosed porch there were telephones, staffed by female operators, calling party leaders and poll watchers all over the country. In the dining room, there was an adding machine, more telephones connected to direct lines from various Democratic headquarters, and news service teletype machines. The pollster Lou Harris had set up a small office in one of the children's bedrooms, where beds and toys had been put away to make room for tables full of calculations and past election records.

Having gone to bed, uncertain about his fate, at close to 4 a.m., Jack was awakened at about 9:30 and told that he had carried Minnesota and won the election. At around 1:00 p.m., the entire family and entourage assembled to watch Nixon's press secretary concede the election. The official photographer had tried but failed to get the group to sit for a family portrait. He spoke quietly to Joe Kennedy who, agreeing it would be the only chance, announced that a photograph was to be taken. Everyone was herded into the library and Joe positioned his family for the historic shot. The famous moment in time captured the president-elect, his wife, father and mother, and siblings and their respective partners in front of the fireplace.

With Nixon having bowed to the inevitable, Kennedy and his family were now able to stage a formal acceptance at the Hyannis Port Armory.

Sinatra and his entourage, meanwhile, had watched the voting on the West Coast at the home of Tony Curtis and Janet Leigh, along with other Hollywood stars and movie people, including Bill Goetze, Billy Wilder, Milton Berle, Dick Shepherd, and others. The Curtis-Leigh home had served that evening as a focal point for many of the Hollywood Democrats who had worked for Kennedy, mostly at the behest of Frank. All evening, calls had come in about the progress of the count. The callers had included Henry Fonda in New York, Sammy Cahn in Las Vegas, Lawford in Hyannis Port, and also Sammy Davis Jr., who was performing at the Huntington Hartford Theater in Hollywood, but had given his audience updates on the election returns as they became available.

Frank was ecstatic. He'd not just made a positive and highly visible contribution to the campaign with the "High Hopes" record, he had also encouraged scores of his entertainment industry buddies to lend their support to the Kennedy effort and probably influenced hundreds of others to part with their dollars as a result of his association. Now his friend was to be commander-in-chief, and Frank had played a very tangible role in his election. In an early afternoon call to Hyannis, Sinatra connected with Salinger and, expressing his delight, made himself available to the incoming president in whatever capacity he might see fit to utilize him.

As the Kennedys and their advisers began the task of assembling the administration of the first president born in the twentieth century together, it was clear that those who had made his success happen would themselves become central to the running of the country for the next four years. O'Donnell became the president's appointments secretary, a somewhat menial title which belied the fact that in a White House without a chief of staff, Kenny was to become Jack's de facto number-one operator and the "keeper of the gate." Salinger, as expected, became press secretary, and Dave Powers was appointed "Special Assistant," a title which suggested Jack just wanted to have him around the place, much like before. Despite Kennedy's reservations about nepotism but at his father's absolute insistence, Bobby was made attorney general of the United States.

It became clear in early discussions, particularly with Bobby and O'Donnell, that replicating the formula, which had done so much to deliver JFK's victory, would be a great asset over the next four years. The Eisenhower presidency had been good for America in terms of the old warrior's conservative attitude to Communism and the increasing prosperity of the burgeoning middle classes—something his vice-president and son-in-law, Nixon, had hoped to replicate. But voters polled in late November made it quite clear that they had voted for the young Massachusetts senator because he represented change, style, glamour, and a new approach to politics. As far as Kennedy and his entourage were concerned that was exactly what they were going to get.

On December 12, Sinatra was at the Sands in Vegas when Salinger called. "Bad news Frank," said Kennedy's new press secretary jokingly, "You're not going to make the Cabinet, but the President wants you to be his secretary of entertainment." And that was exactly the role Frank would play.

It was a daunting job, however unofficial the title. And all the more so when it was decided that Sinatra would primarily be in charge of the inaugural gala to be staged on the eve of the inauguration ceremony and parade scheduled for January 20. The gala venue was to be the DC Armory, located east of the Capitol building, a mausoleum-like structure that had been constructed in 1941 as the armory headquarters and a military training facility. It was subsequently adapted to a ten thousand seat multipurpose arena used for a variety of events.

The sheer size and cavernous character of the Armory presented its own challenges in terms of staging the gala. But Sinatra, who had drafted in Peter Lawford to help him, couldn't help wallowing in the responsibility he had been handed by Kennedy. If the show proved a success it would achieve a number of major objectives for the organizer-in-chief. The first would demonstrate how powerful an ally the entertainment business could be to a presidential campaign and, as a consequence, cement Frank's relationship with the Kennedy people. The second would help to defray the debt the Democratic Party had run up during the campaign, estimated to be $1.7 million. Friendship was one thing but Frank had, by now, been around long enough to learn that in politics it was money that counted, and he was instrumental in the decision to set the ticket prices in a range from $100 for an individual to $10,000 for a group with favored seating and a presidential "meet and greet."

The responsibility for overseeing the most glamorous and spectacular show ever staged in the capital would, if he could pull it off, represent a personal triumph for Sinatra, who genuinely felt he had pioneered celebrity support of politicians as far back as his meeting with Roosevelt and most recently with his tireless campaigning for Jack. There's no doubt that Frank clearly felt that this endorsement would raise him to a level of social achievement and acceptance, which the heights of his musical career had never matched. It would certainly help, he felt, his rehabilitation in the eyes of the press and those who continued to question his involvement with the more dubious elements of his social circle.

All he had to do now was prove that he was worthy of the honor.

Sinatra moved quickly. With the help of Lawford he astutely began to assemble a star-studded troupe of powerful names, even persuading a couple of Broadway producers to commit to closing their shows for the night to release performers to appear in the show. He chose Roger Edens, the veteran MGM producer and the man credited with creating Judy Garland's success, to help stage the show, and the highly regarded Kay Thompson as his assistant. While not a formal creative double act, Edens and Thompson made a formidable team and had a famous, if somewhat corny, association. They shared the same birthday, November 9, and from 1942 through to 1957 had given a joint birthday party during which each presented a surprise production number using special material which featured their friends—Judy Garland, Lena Horne, Gene Kelly, Maureen O'Hara, Danny Kaye, Cole Porter, and many others—each never telling the one while rehearsing what the other was planning to present.

This duo was supplemented by Nelson Riddle, who had been central to Frank's comeback of 1953, in particular with his arrangement of "I've Got the World on a String," as well as longtime collaborators and friends Jimmy Van Heusen and Sammy Cahn, who had remained loyal to Sinatra through the trials and tribulations of the years when he was out of favor with just about everyone.

If the group behind the scenes was production royalty, the performing cast represented some of the most famous and recognizable entertainment names in the world. The first draft of Frank's running order included, among others, Ethel Merman—at the time the undisputed first lady of musical comedy—Frederic March, Bette Davis, Laurence Olivier, Sidney Poitier, Nat King Cole, Ella Fitzgerald, Bill Dana, Gene Kelly, Milton Berle, and Jimmy Durante. Sinatra reserved the role of master of ceremonies and central performer for himself.

A sour note was struck with the forced exclusion of Sammy Davis Jr. Despite his willingness to be involved in the 1960 campaign, Sammy had been largely frozen out on the instructions of Kennedy senior when Joe adjudged that Davis's engagement to white Swedish actress May Britt was too politically risky to his son in an America where interracial marriage was banned in thirty-one states. Despite Joe's vehement and continuing objections, Sinatra made a number of attempts to put Davis back on the bill, at one stage appealing directly to Jack Kennedy, but gave up when it became clear that Joe's word on the matter was final. JFK wasn't going to rock the boat over a minor sideshow to what was now promising to be a very special event. Davis was understandably devastated to be pushed out of the historic lineup, particularly given the fact that, at Joe's behest, he had delayed his marriage to May until after the election.

In Palm Beach, Jack Kennedy was putting the final touches to the Cabinet, which he intended would guide the United States for at least four years of the 1960s. The president-elect had decamped with Powers and O'Donnell for some sunshine and relaxation in the Florida sun. But as Frank agonized over his final inauguration night lineup and the exclusion of Sammy there were already some serious rumblings about Jack's choice of impresario. Bobby, for one, was already uncomfortable with the idea of Sinatra playing such a pivotal role in the inaugural celebrations. He'd already decided that continuing his crusade against organized crime would feature at the top of his agenda in the Justice Department and was acutely aware of Sinatra's less than savory connections. After all, it was he who, with Larry O'Brien, had masterminded the main strategies that had propelled his brother to the White House. For the director of elections to turn a blind eye to his father's direct line to Sam Giancana and Johnny Roselli when they were needed to turn out the vote was one thing; for the attorney general of the United States to ignore the existence of the Cosa Nostra and, by doing so, effectively endorse the continuance of their wide ranging illegal operations, was quite another. From the moment of his appointment Bobby was effectively at war with the Mob. This would put him not just at odds with his brother and father but would lead to a long-festering resentment of Bobby by Frank, which would ultimately grow to a virulent mutual hatred.

For Kenny O'Donnell, who always backed Bobby to the hilt, Sinatra represented a problem. He saw the obvious attractions of retaining the Hollywood glitz and glamour, which Sinatra had delivered, as an obvious foil to the controversies and negativities that the administration was bound to encounter. On the flip side he had been around the Sinatra-Kennedy axis for long enough to understand the potential political disasters that lay beneath the fun loving exterior of the relationship.

Along with Dave Powers, O'Donnell had become JFK's closest confidante and one of the people Kennedy relied on most for support and practical advice. Now as de facto chief of staff, his challenge would be to loyally serve the interests of his boss, the president, while maintaining his lifelong friendship with the attorney general. And on the subject of Sinatra it was clear the opinions of the two brothers differed dramatically. The list of the number of ways in which the president-elect had used Sinatra was growing; he'd availed of Frank's hospitality in Las Vegas and Palm Springs and keenly encouraged him to introduce him to as many women as he could. He and his father had covertly used the Mob, through Sinatra, during the West Virginia primary and the election, to get the vote out and to, in some cases, fix entire electoral areas. He had used Frank to encourage his Hollywood and entertainment industry friends to support the Kennedy presidential election campaign with endorsements, contributions, and personal appearances. He now intended to use him again to sprinkle some Sinatra magic on his crowning as the new, immensely attractive, and magnetic leader of the free world.

In exchange Sinatra had basked, and was about to bask even more, in the warm glow of Kennedy's celebrity. Jack's patronage was not only reaffirming Frank's boasts that he had a direct line to the president, it was, in his view, rehabilitating him in the eyes of the American people who had adored him until things had begun to unravel in the 1940s. The *From Here to Eternity* Oscar had offered personal and professional satisfaction and a way back to commercial success, but he knew many in America still regarded him as a womanizing, draft-dodging immigrant with a chip on his shoulder. Most of all he'd been unable to shake off the belief held by many, particularly in the media, that he habitually consorted with underworld figures.

In this sense, Sinatra was his own worst enemy. If you don't want to be accused of hanging around with mobsters, then don't hang around with them. Frank knew this, but his inherent loyalty to his roots, and the sense of respect he derived from his fellow Italian Americans who still idolized him, made him blind to this obvious mistake, and left him exposed to accusations of consorting with the worst of the organized crime bosses long after he should have had the sense to leave them behind.

The ten-week period between the election of Jack Kennedy in November 1960 and his inauguration in January 1961 was probably make-your-mind-up time for Sinatra. Would he choose the Kennedys and some sort of respectability and rehabilitation in the eyes of American public or the familiar faces of the Cosa Nostra? Instead of making the right decision, in fact, any decision, he continued to ride both horses; fidelity had never been Frank's strong suit—now it would be a costly mistake for all concerned.

As Kennedy returned to Washington in the early days of 1961, he embarked on a hugely expanded work schedule as the demands on the aspirant commander-in-chief began to kick in. Clark Clifford, a lawyer and former counsel to President Truman, had been liaising with the Eisenhower people on the transition. He was also responsible for filtering the hundreds of external representations and recommendations for the promotion of party members or friends into a credible panel from which the president could choose his team. Clifford, who would later serve as secretary of defense under Lyndon Johnson, understood the complex Washington political dynamic, and in particular the need for a relatively untested leader like Kennedy to balance the publics expectation for youth, freshness, and change at cabinet level with the need for experience and capability. His ultimate short list included seasoned political professionals like Minnesota Governor Orville Freeman as secretary of agriculture and Governor Abraham Ribicoff of Connecticut as secretary of health, education, and welfare. To maintain some continuity with the outgoing cabinet and to assuage the financial markets, Kennedy asked Douglas Dillon to remain as treasury secretary. But in a move that signaled his independent thinking and his desire to bring a fresh approach to US foreign policy, he appointed Robert McNamara, the president of the Ford Motor Company, as his secretary of defense. Over a thousand other government appointments were left to O'Donnell and Powers to distribute and supervise.

Meanwhile, apart from the usual round of social commitments, Kennedy's main preoccupation as the inauguration approached was the address, which he and his speechwriter and newly appointed special counsel, Ted Sorensen, were determined would leave an indelible footprint on the history of presidential inauguration speeches. Sorensen, a law school graduate from Nebraska, had been with Jack since his early Senate days of 1953 and while closer and more influential than most, still remained outside the inner-inner circle, not least because he was of Danish rather than Irish extraction. Sorensen remained somewhat detached from the Irish Mafia, O'Donnell and Powers in particular. His access to the president-elect was by virtue of his keen intellect and sharp strategic thinking, rather than the rough-and-tumble ward politics that the Irish guys thrived on. The Irish regarded Sorensen and Arthur Schlesinger, the Harvard historian who joined as special adviser shortly after the inauguration, as "egg heads," strong on intellect but weak on political reality. The Sorensen wing, which also included national security adviser, McGeorge Bundy, saw Powers and O'Donnell as somewhat uncouth, unnecessarily ruthless, and lacking in the niceties of diplomacy, a description with which the Irish were secretly delighted. Both sides had an enduring respect for each other, however, and understood that for Kennedy's administration to live up to public and media expectations, a mixture of both cultures would be essential.

In discussions about the inaugural address in late December, both speaker and writer agreed that they wanted it to be short and clearly focused, mainly on foreign policy. From the beginning it had been designed as a collaborative composition orchestrated by Kennedy but crafted by Sorensen. On December 23, Sorensen set the ball rolling in a Western Union telegram to a number of potential speech contributors including Allan Nevins, former presidential candidate Adlai Stevenson, Dean Rusk, whom Kennedy would appoint as secretary of state a few weeks later, and Harvard economics professor John Kenneth Galbraith. The communiqué said the president-elect was asking for suggestions each might have for the inaugural address. "In view of the short period of time available before inauguration day it would be appreciated if we could have your recommendations before December 31st. We are particularly interested in specific themes and in language to articulate these themes, whether it takes one page or ten pages," he wrote.

Kennedy also asked Sorensen to study other inaugural speeches and, in particular, President Lincoln's Gettysburg Address. He was determined that the content should be short, as he wanted to avoid coming across as a windbag or in any way arrogant. Lincoln's famous 1863 speech had been structured using small passages of short phrases and words and Sorensen took this as his template. The other main inspirations were the speeches of Winston Churchill. In terms of tone Kennedy wanted the speech to give him gravitas while being completely accessible to all who heard it. Fresh faced and tanned after his post-election rest, he was also somewhat concerned that he might look too young and hoped that the formal dress of the occasion (the traditional top hat and tails had been agreed, despite Kennedy's initial reservations that it might seem too pompous and old fashioned) and an effective address would portray a maturity beyond his years. Despite his adherence to the staid, almost Victorian conformities of his predecessors, Jack was making at least one concession to modern personal grooming—he had taken the opportunity to have his teeth polished.

On the evening of the of January 18, with just two days to go to the inauguration, Sorensen came to Georgetown and he and Kennedy worked once again on the content of the address. Later that evening he attended a dinner party at the home of Florence Mahoney, a major financial supporter of the Democratic Party, where he seated himself between former President Truman and the celebrated poet Robert Frost, who had become an unlikely friend of the president-elect. Frost had given the very early part of the presidential campaign an impetus when, in March 1959 at a press conference before a gala celebration of his eighty-fifth birthday party at the Waldorf Astoria Hotel in New York, in response to a question about the decline of New England he had responded, "The next president of the United States will be from Boston. Does that sound as if New England is decaying?" Despite the fact that at that stage Kennedy had not formally declared his candidacy, the national media picked up Frost's prediction immediately. This sparked off a correspondence between the poet and the young senator, which culminated—on the advice of Stewart Udall, who would become secretary of state for the interior—in Frost being invited to recite a poem at the inaugural ceremony, a historical first. Accepting, he noted, "Poetry, now for the first time taken into the affairs of statesmen."

On the morning of the nineteenth, on President Eisenhower's last day in office, Kennedy went for a meeting with him at the White House. They spent the first forty-five minutes alone as Ike explained the drill regarding to the protocol to be followed in an exercise to activate large-scale military response, including the nuclear option. The machinery available to the commander-in-chief fascinated Jack. Within minutes Ike demonstrated how communication could be established to the chain of military systems, nuclear warhead sites, bombers already in the skies, and submarines in the Atlantic and Pacific. The relationship between Eisenhower, at that time the oldest ever president of the United States, and his successor, the youngest, was cordial but lacked warmth. The formal and somewhat standoffish war general had steadfastly refused to comment publicly on the senator during the campaign, not least because Kennedy's opponent had been Eisenhower's own vice-president and son-in-law. This was despite the fact that he regarded Kennedy as "a whippersnapper" and "not up to the job" and had been less than discreet in his private descriptions of Kennedy, particularly over the previous year.

The two then moved on to a larger meeting with the old and new secretaries of state, defense, and treasury, the new incumbents being Dean Rusk and McNamara, as well as Douglas Dillon, the continuing Eisenhower man. The hot spots of the Cold War were top of the agenda, as well as China, Laos, and Cambodia. Though not described as such during the meeting, the "domino theory" of the potential fall of Southeast Asia to Communism was presented, and the means to prevent it discussed. Eisenhower expressed such action and the possibility of military intervention in the region as a high-risk poker game with no easy solution, a reality that would quickly face the new president. As far as Cuba was concerned, Eisenhower maintained that under no circumstance should the Castro-led regime be allowed to continue unchallenged, and that any guerilla operations outside and inside the country should be supported.

As the meeting broke up, Eisenhower took the opportunity to have a quiet word with Jack about a campaign ploy Kennedy had utilized—the so-called "missile gap" between the United States and the Soviet Union, something that JFK had continuously referred to and that had apparently infuriated Ike privately. The missile gap was a tactical exaggeration as opposed to an untruth, because depending on the viewpoint, the matter was certainly debatable. As far as Eisenhower was concerned the Polaris submarines and missiles gave American forces the upper hand against Russia, and he assured Kennedy of this (not surprisingly since the systems had been installed at his insistence). Eisenhower's discussions and advice to Kennedy were more than prescient that day. In time Cuba and missiles, along with the emerging storm clouds in Southeast Asia, would dominate JFK's foreign policy during his time in office.

While the White House meeting had been in session, storm clouds of a different and far more immediate kind had been gathering and sweeping from the south toward Virginia, Maryland, and the District of Columbia and with rapidly dropping temperatures the rain transformed into snow. Kennedy attended a governor's reception in the Park Sheraton Hotel, where he bumped into

President Truman for the second time in twenty-four hours and invited him back to the Georgetown house for a chat. Through the front window they could see the snow begin to fall thick and fast. The Weather Bureau had forecast a mixture of rain and snow but what was emerging was a continual downpour of iced snow and as the temperature dropped below zero the wind increased to 25 mph. By early evening, chaos ensued as all forms of transport in Washington, DC, and the wider metropolitan area, both private and public, ground to a halt. There were crippling traffic jams, vehicles locked bumper to bumper, and by evening nothing was moving and hundreds of cars were marooned and abandoned by their frustrated drivers. By now the inaugural parade route was not only heavily snowbound, but littered with abandoned vehicles. The Army Corps of Engineers teamed up with more than one thousand District of Columbia employees to try to tackle the enormous task of clearing the route in an effort to get the city moving in time for the next day's ceremonies. The iced urban landscape of Washington became a surreal vision as hundreds of dump trucks, front-end loaders, sanders, ploughs, and rotators took to the paths and streets against the backdrop of lines of flame throwers moving in formation to melt as much of the icing snow as possible before the subzero temperatures took hold.

Meanwhile, rehearsals for the Sinatra-produced gala had been going on all morning and early afternoon at the Armory. Some of the performers had returned to the Statler Hilton Hotel, where nearly all were based for a rest before the show but were now stranded. The White House fleet, along with the Washington police car pool, mounted an emergency transport operation, but progress was naturally slow with many vehicles having to use the footpaths. The cast, in dribs and drabs, finally managed to assemble at the Armory. The show, much delayed, went on.

And in spite of the very short time there had been to rehearse under the batons of Edens and Thompson, and the chaos caused by the weather, it proved to be all Sinatra had promised.

Although the appalling weather meant there were some gaps in the auditorium, the atmosphere was electric. Bette Davis began the event, summing up the spirit of the evening: "The world of enter-tainment, showbiz, if you please, has become the sixth estate just as Hawaii became the fiftieth state." She could easily have added that Frank Sinatra was now the president of the sixth, running his own inauguration ceremony.

One after another each of the twenty-four performers hit the highest note in their individual and collective acts, to rapturous and sustained applause. Ethel Merman, who had slipped away from her record breaking run of *Gypsy* on Broadway, lit up the stage like a neon light and transfixed the audience as she addressed her song directly to Kennedy in the president-elect's box:

"You'll be swell, you'll be great, gonna have the whole world on a plate."

Comedian Jimmy Durante, at sixty-seven the elder statesmen of the troupe, who had just the previous month caused his own national sensation by marrying Margaret "Margie" Little, twenty-six years his junior, delivered a heartfelt version of "September Song":

Oh, it's a long, long while from May to December
But the days grow short when you reach September
When the autumn weather turns the leaves to flame.

The Kennedy clan doubly appreciated the old trouper's choice, as it was a big family favorite. Harry Belafonte, who days before had been very vocal about the exclusion of Sammy Davis Jr. from the lineup, tugged the heartstrings of the audience with a passionate rendering of the classic folk song "John Henry," and Sinatra himself provided the icing on the cake with "You Make Me Feel So Young," followed by a reworking of his hit "That Old Black Magic" as "That Old *Jack* Magic," and finally Sammy Cahn's take on the campaign song "High Hopes" lifted the roof of the vast auditorium with:

Let's hear it now for Kennedy
Jack and Lyndon B
And let's follow their lead
They're the men that our America
They're the men that our America
They're the men that our AMERICA needs.

Finally the entire Armory erupted as Jack Kennedy, introduced by Sinatra, walked on stage. The president-elect, with just fourteen hours remaining to the moment he would fulfill his ultimate destiny, focused on the man who, more than anybody, had worked unstintingly to make the ambitious event a reality. "To a great friend, Frank Sinatra. Long before he could sing he used to poll a Democratic precinct back in New Jersey. That precinct has grown to cover the country, but long after he has ceased to sing, he's going to be standing up and speaking for the Democratic Party and I thank him on behalf of you all tonight," said Kennedy warmly.

It was an incredible tribute to the singer who had, in the first instance, been dragged by his mother, Dolly, from the humble streets of Hoboken and then, by his own talent and a little help from friends, to national and international prominence. The enormous assistance Frank had given to Jack during his election campaign had helped bring both singer and politician to this juncture. But as Kennedy stated, Sinatra wasn't just a campaign helper, he was also a "great friend."

The party was far from over, and the main contingent moved on to Paul Young's restaurant just across from the Mayflower Hotel, a favorite Kennedy haunt, for another lavish bash, this time hosted by Joe Kennedy. Jackie, exhausted and still not over the Caesarian birth of John Junior just two months previously, had gone home. At the restaurant Jack Kennedy met "Red" Fay, who was escorting the beautiful young actress Angie Dickinson. The escort part was a euphemism—Fay was acting as a cover; Angie was one of one of Jack's many current extramarital interests. Dickinson, who would go on to marry the composer Burt Bacharach, was more special than many of the soon-to-be president's dalliances, so much so that she was due to attend the inauguration ceremony the next day, again with Fay in tow as her official escort.

Kennedy got back home sometime after 3:30 a.m. He was out of bed four hours later in the heavily secured Georgetown house, immediately reaching for the now final copy of the inaugural speech, which had been closely guarded by Evelyn Lincoln. Sorensen had dropped the tweaked and approved draft over to the house the previous evening and he and JFK had spent an hour going over it line by line. At 1,364 words it was five times longer than the Gettysburg address, but in time its content would have similar impact and longevity across the United States.

Friday, January 20, 1961 dawned a crisp, steel-blue morning. The snow had stopped falling but it was incredibly cold, with the temperature ten degrees below zero. It was, however, a welcome contrast to the previous day's storm, and a huge relief to the inauguration organizers. Kennedy might, had it crossed his mind, justifiably have considered the glorious conditions a sign that the Gods were with him on the most momentous day of his life. The first president born in the twentieth century was about to take the mantle from the Supreme Commander of the Allied Forces in the Second World War. As Ike had helped redraw a continent after the Nazi destruction of Western Europe, his future successor had been a mere lieutenant in the navy. But that was of no consequence now—the winds of change were blowing and the old guard was being replaced by the new.

After a light breakfast, the Kennedy entourage, led by Jack and Jackie, walked to Mass at Holy Trinity Catholic Church, a few streets away, their eyes squinting from the intense reflective glare of the sun on the surface of the snow. The Kennedys were then driven to the White House for coffee with President and Mrs. Eisenhower. As they walked up the steps of the north portico, a crowd of twenty thousand was already gathering on the East Plaza of the Capitol. Coffee was a cordial if unexciting affair. Mamie Eisenhower lacked the glamour and appeal that the American people saw in Jackie, and, as a dutiful army and then political wife, had always maintained a discreet distance from publicity. If both women knew about their respective husbands' infidelities they were saying nothing, certainly not to each other. (It would later be revealed that Eisenhower had conducted a relationship with his wartime driver, the Irish-born Kay Summersby.)

As was the tradition, the president and first lady accompanied the Kennedys to the Capitol for the inauguration ceremony. The route through Washington was lined with thousands of people, none of whom could have had an easy journey to get there but all of whom were driven by the prospect of witnessing a slice of history. They would not be disappointed with the outcome, and few, if any, could have regretted the effort, even in the freezing conditions.

As the Kennedys arrived at the east portico, no less than sixteen members of the Kennedy family and a number of Jackie's Bouvier and Auchincloss relations were on the main platform, which seated 105 people. Right to the front were former President Truman, Vice-President Nixon, Vice-President-elect Lyndon Johnson, and Chief Justice of the Supreme Court Earl Warren, who was to conduct the swearing-in ceremony. Under the podium, there was a reserved section housing 635 people with friends, election helpers, and those who were considered vital to the election effort and victory, among them nervous speechwriter Ted Sorensen, Mayor Richard Daley of Chicago, and, fresh from the previous night's soiree, Red Fay and his "girlfriend," Angie Dickinson.

After an invocation by Boston's Cardinal Cushing and other prayers, the African American contralto Marian Anderson sang *The Star Spangled Banner* as she had at Eisenhower's inauguration four years previously. Then Robert Frost stood to recite *Dedication*, a poem he had specially composed for the occasion. However, blinded by the rays of the sun and the snow, Frost was unable to read the lines. As the ceremony began to unravel with Frost's confusion evident, Lyndon Johnson tried to shade the podium for the eighty-six-year-old poet with his top hat. Gently brushing aside the offer,

Frost then recited from memory *The Gift Outright,* which had been Kennedy's original choice for the ceremony. The last lines ran:

> Such as we were, we gave ourselves outright
> (The deeds of gift was many deeds of war)
> To the land vaguely realizing westwards,
> But still unstoried, artless, unenhanced,
> Such as she was, such as she will become.

Frost's dramatic recovery, *The Washington Post* reported the following day, resulted in the poet stealing the hearts of the crowd. However, that crowd did not include many of the artistic entourage who had been involved in the previous night's gala and post-event celebrations. Reportedly exhausted by the performances, but more likely by excessive partying, they had opted to watch the ceremony on television. Needless to say the absentees included Sinatra and Lawford.

The 59.5 percent of American households that watched the event on television now saw Kennedy divesting himself of his overcoat and top hat as he placed himself before the chief justice to take the oath of office. At 12:51 p.m., with his hand on a family bible, John Fitzgerald Kennedy uttered the thirty-five words of the oath of allegiance and became his country's president. For the Kennedy family, and for his father in particular, it was the culmination of an extraordinary personal and political journey. So many people were now basking in the power and glamour radiating from this young, tanned, handsome Bostonian, not least Frank Sinatra.

Kennedy, conscious of the cold and the discomfort of the crowds, immediately took his place at the podium to make one of the most talked about, remembered, and quoted presidential inauguration speeches of all time. From the opening lines of one of the shortest such addresses ever delivered, it became as obvious as the blinding glare from the surface of the snow that quality is always preferable to quantity. If Robert Frost had stolen the hearts of the crowd, President John F. Kennedy was about to steal both their hearts and minds. Despite the length and intensity of the previous day's activities and celebrations, and with only four hours sleep, Kennedy was remarkably self-composed and unflustered as he stepped up to begin the address. He laid the script down and would only sporadically glance at it in the thirteen or so minutes he was on his feet. His Boston drawl fitted the content perfectly and he employed his right hand as an emphatic metronome. His voice rang out as clear as the sky above:

"We observe today," he began, "not as a victory of party, but a celebration of freedom, symbolizing an end as well as a beginning—signifying renewal as well as change. . . . Let the word go forth from this time to friend and foe alike that the torch has been passed to a new generation of Americans. Born in this century, tempered by war, disciplined by a hard and bitter peace, proud of our ancient heritage."

Everything about the address was irresistible—the epic imagery, the clear but wonderfully crafted language, the searing message of change, and the calculated but perfect delivery. It came across not just easy to the voice but also to the ear of the vast audience, not only those present but also to those watching on television. It was the modern political equivalent of a Shakespearean soliloquy—the art was in the writing but hugely enhanced in the delivery, all along the way before that famous statement: "Ask not what your country can do for you, ask what you can do for your country."

Sorensen, who knew every syllable of the script, drew an almost audible sigh of relief as Kennedy concluded at just after one o'clock. In every sense here was an inaugural address that would withstand the exacting scrutiny of history. And, in time, for most who witnessed the speech in person or on the small screen, it was delivered by a man with exceptional oratorical skills, a giant political figure with extraordinary, almost magical, powers. Sorensen, curiously, however, would later remark about his boss, "He sometimes obscured his motives and almost always shielded his emotions. Jack was a natural leader—the secret of his magical appeal was that he had no magic at all." The rest of the day and evening would demonstrate another, more predictable, side of Kennedy's character summed up by Sorensen: "Not all his hours were spent at work, he liked parties and lively companions. He sought fun and laughter." There was that aplenty awaiting the new president.

After much handshaking and backslapping, a motorcade brought Jack and Jackie and the invited guests to the official lunch in the old Supreme Court chamber of the Capitol hosted by the joint congressional inaugural committee. At the same time in the Mayflower Hotel the president's father put on a magnificent banquet for the Kennedy and Bouvier relatives. Among the fabulous culinary fare was hot soups, Lobster Newburg, Alaskan king crab, shrimp cocktail, and roast turkey.

A bracing interval in the freezing afternoon followed for the inaugural parade on Pennsylvania Avenue, which took over three hours to pass, while another reception for the families of the president and first lady was held in the State Dining Room, where again there was a feast fit for royalty. As well as the inaugural balls, there were a large number of parties planned for that evening and Jack Kennedy made it his business to attend as many as possible. He made a brief show at a dinner party before attending the first of the balls given by campaign workers Jane and George Wheeler. The ever-loyal Red Fay was there, accompanied as usual by Angie Dickinson waiting patiently in the wings. (In later life Dickinson would never confirm or deny the affair with Kennedy and would many years later return a publisher's advance rather than deal with the matter publicly.)

Despite receiving invitations to all of the inaugural events, Judith Campbell did not attend, in deference, she would later explain, to Jackie Kennedy. According to Judy, who had seen Jack on at least a dozen occasions during the campaign, she did not want to flaunt herself in front of her lover's wife on the most important day of her life. Jackie did make an appearance at the second ball at the Statler-Hilton. At some stage her husband slipped away with his secret service detail and took the lift to the South American suite, where his "secretary of entertainment" was giving a party for the cast of the gala. Having thanked Frank and cast once again he rejoined Jackie.

Next stop was the biggest ball of all, in the Armory, the venue for the previous evening's gala, now squeezing in an event attended by over a thousand people. There was an enormous wave of excitement as the presidential couple arrived with a huge searchlight constantly focused on them and again much greeting, kissing, and hugging. About an hour into the visit it all became too much for Jackie, who, as she later described, "just crumpled." She returned to the White House to spend the rest of the night alone in the Queen's Room.

Jack continued his almost endless round of handshaking into the early hours. Considering the commitments, the historic inauguration speech, and the nonstop partying, people continuously remarked just how fresh and well he looked that night. Perhaps it was the easy comparison with the aging, pasty Eisenhower and his defeated son-in-law sidekick; perhaps it was adrenaline or maybe an amphetamine tablet or an injection or two. Whatever it was, Kennedy exuded energy, sex appeal, glamour, and excitement. He managed two more balls and then dropped unannounced into the Georgetown home of friend and columnist Joe Alsop where the startled journalist sat up with him for a nightcap.

At 3:20 a.m. he returned to the White House where, because there was some refurbishment work going on in the presidential suite, he slept in the Lincoln Room, soundly—not interrupted by dreams, he would later relate—"I just jumped in and hung on." Some few hours later, the golden dawn of Camelot would break. One basking in that glorious beginning was Frank Sinatra.

Chapter 13: Hoover Turns the Screw

———————◆———————

WHEN ONE GOVERNMENT administration succeeds another, the predecessor inevitably leaves political and economic legacies, which, for good or ill, impact the successor. In general there are no major surprises except, perhaps, in the deepest vaults of intelligence and security. It was in that very area that one resided when, just a week into his presidency, on the morning of January 28, 1961 Jack Kennedy was handed a thick file by Walt Rostow at the intelligence briefing.

The president scanned the heading of a twenty-five-page report, which read, "Lansdale's Trip, January 1961." The file, which had been forwarded by the CIA, first to Defense Secretary Robert McNamara, contained the stark message that there was a very serious problem developing in South Vietnam with increasing incursions from guerrilla groups from the North Vietnamese Communist regime under Ho Chi Minh.

It was a surprise and a bit of a shock as Kennedy, who, casting his mind back to the meeting with Eisenhower on the former president's last day in office, remarked that there had been no huge mention of Vietnam in the discussion about the Communist threat in Southeast Asia. The author of the report was Brigadier General Edward Gerry Lansdale of the US Air Force. It was a fancy title that belied the fact that Lansdale actually worked for the CIA and was considered a master spy with a legendary reputation, a larger-than-life character, a sort of former-day James Bond (a comparison that Kennedy himself would later make) with the looks to match, whose real life exploits were the very stuff of fiction.

Lansdale had helped build the army's intelligence division and was involved in the discovery of a huge hoard of gold amassed by the Japanese when they occupied the Philippines and then its disbursement to banks to help fund CIA covert operations. The dashing spook certainly caught the interest and imagination of the president, even if the bureaucrats in Washington considered him a maverick and, as one report on him stated, "not a team player."

In his report Lansdale urged that South Vietnam and its leader, Ngo Dinh Diem, be given more support as a bulwark against the increasingly encroaching Communist regime of the north, reputedly backed by Russia and China. Diem, according to Lansdale, was feeling increasingly isolated and somewhat unwanted by the US representatives in Saigon, which, given the fact that they were there at his behest, was something that needed a diplomatic solution, which in essence meant treat him with some respect and all would benefit. When the president finished reading he wanted to talk directly to the author. While events in that small corner of Southeast Asia would traumatize the United States later in the decade and Kennedy would ultimately be blamed for playing a part in their escalation, it was another small bastion of Communism closer to home that was about to create some serious headaches for the fledgling administration. But in one case, at least, it was the people within a government agency that had the potential to make more trouble for Kennedy than the activities of the organization itself, much as it had for Frank Sinatra a decade earlier. That agency was the FBI and its chief protagonist was, of course, the perennial J. Edgar Hoover.

If Hoover disliked Sinatra and his Mob associates, he actively despised the Kennedys, and his direct superior, Robert Kennedy, the new attorney general, in particular. Now with Frank perceived as being firmly in the president's camp, his attentions turned to how he could deal with all of them at one time. For Hoover, his continuance at the head of an organization he had had autocratic control of for almost three decades was of paramount importance. The secret of his tenure at the top bore no relation to his organizational skills, his crime fighting abilities, or even his political networking. In fact, there was nothing to suggest he was of above average capability in any of these areas. Rather, he had held his vice-like grip on power because of a series of secret files on public figures, which he'd amassed using the vast intelligence-gathering network of the bureau. He'd had politicians, movie stars, entertainers, and thousands of ordinary Americans, followed, secretly taped, photographed, and spied upon. He knew the personal, financial, and sexual secrets of his employers and his underlings. In short, he had made himself the most powerful man in the United States and, as far as he was concerned, a couple of Ivy League brat politicians weren't going to change that, not to mention a bum, Communist-leaning, draft-dodging lounge lizard like Frank Sinatra.

Hoover was sixty-six years of age, a rather toadlike figure with somewhat bulging eyes. His new boss was a tousle-headed, handsome, tanned man three decades younger than himself. The ascension of the young Kennedys to the peak of the greatest power in the western world recalled W. B. Yeats's fabled phrase "no country for old men," but J. Edgar would disagree. He had long employed his well-tried methods to stem the passage of time and change, which he intended to apply as he had always done when he felt threatened, and he did feel threatened.

With previous presidents, Hoover had set the agenda fairly smartly upon their arrival at the White House, usually by producing a file not directly connected with any wrongdoing of the incumbent, but by furnishing some data on a matter connected in some way with the new president's rise to power. The mere suggestion that the matter might "get out of hand" if Hoover was not there to control or deal with it had been enough to leave the director in situ for over a quarter of a century. Presidents Roosevelt, Truman, and Eisenhower, each of whom had been president at least twice, had tolerated his dictatorial style and his proprietorial attitude to the bureau. But the Kennedys were different. While Hoover had experienced some difficulty with the three men who preceded Jack Kennedy, and in the case of Harry Truman, some significant clashes during which the president came close to firing him, he still regarded them as men of honor, who had made something of themselves and served their country with distinction.

Kennedy, on the other hand, was seen by Hoover as the product of a privileged upbringing: a womanizer, and a keeper of bad company. And he reserved particular odium for Bobby, holding what he considered as his sense of entitlement, and that of his family, in complete contempt—that "arrogant whippersnapper," as he described him.

Within a very short time Hoover began to actively despise his boss, not just because of his interference but also because of the fact that he was so much younger. He had been used to dealing directly with the president, and now he was cut off from that privilege and had to put up with a man he frequently described as that "sneaky little son of a bitch." His resentment was amplified by the fact that the incumbent was the president's brother and therefore an even bigger threat to the hegemony of the FBI director. Bobby had made it clear from the start that while he was in charge all would change and everything under the control of the Justice Department would answer directly to him, including the FBI. Kenny O'Donnell copper-fastened this edict when he gave instructions that any attempt by Hoover to get through to the president would be blocked by Evelyn Lincoln or himself. Bobby was the boss, he said, and nobody, including Hoover, was going to go over the boss's head.

Hoover also hated the casual attire Bobby wore to work, believing it was inappropriate for a man of such high office. Hoover was the ultimate conformist who had a strict dress code among his men. Bobby often showed up at the Justice Department wearing casual trousers and an open-neck shirt. He was further discomfited when the attorney general had a direct line to his office installed so he could get to the director without going through his secretary. Hoover, in his continual and unabated state of paranoia, viewed such efficiency as the start of the erosion of his power. During one early meeting Bobby conducted the conversation with the director while throwing darts at a board on the wall of his conference room. The odd shot went astray into the oak paneling, which drove Hoover mad. He soon began to sharpen his sword.

The feeling of hatred was entirely mutual, however, and Bobby had subjected Hoover to a series of little humiliations, including the buzzer on the direct line, which he used to summon the director, knowing it irritated him to distraction. Hoover was known to have a lunch of chicken soup and cottage cheese every day at the Mayflower Hotel with his deputy director Clyde Tolson, a close confidante, rumored to be his lover. Kennedy would insist on meeting Hoover for lunch in a drugstore, knowing it would offend his effete sense of place. But he also set him to work, ordering him to clamp down on organized crime on a monumental scale, something that was a shock to Hoover's system as he had never tried to curb the activities of the Cosa Nostra in any meaningful way before. Hoover's interaction with the Mob had been limited. Yes, he had put a few mobsters in jail in his early years of the bureau and had, essentially, lived off that reputation. In recent years, however, his interest had been confined to extensive and illegal wiretapping, which could never have been produced as evidence in any court of law, and most of which was to expand his own database of information about his other enemies.

On February 10, 1961, in response to Kennedy's pressure and less than a month into Bobby's tenure at Justice, Hoover responded to the attorney general's demands for action on the Mob by sending him a memo detailing Frank Sinatra's longtime and extensive connections with organized crime figures. Hoover's file dated back to 1944 and would, in time, number over two thousand pages. But while primarily directed at discrediting Sinatra, there was another agenda. For Bobby the missive must have struck a chord of both anger and familiarity. Part of the art of politics is the bestowing of favor, and the Kennedy history had included both giving and asking favors from people of questionable character, to put it mildly. It was an effective policy used by Joe Kennedy over the years, but full of the potential for future adverse consequences.

There was one classic example of this that could not have escaped the attorney general's mind. After acting as his brother's campaign manager in the successful 1952 senatorial election, the young lawyer got a job through the intercession of his father with the country's most notorious anticommunist witch-hunter, Joseph McCarthy, the republican senator from Wisconsin, who had just won his second term.

Two years earlier McCarthy had grabbed national headlines when on February 9, 1950 he gave a Lincoln Day speech to the Republican women's club of Wheeling, West Virginia during which he produced a piece of paper that he claimed contained a list of over two hundred Communists working for the State Department. These people, he claimed, were central to "shaping national policy." The fact that there was no truth in the statement, or not one whit of evidence to back it up, did not stop people from believing it. The outbreak of the Korean War the same year and the hardening of Communist control in the European Eastern bloc made it a perfect time and opportunity for the senator to mount an obsessive and dangerous crusade.

This questionable character had an appeal to Jack and Bobby's father for two reasons. Joe Kennedy shared his anticommunist stance, and in McCarthy's popularity among Catholic communities, the vast majority of whom voted Democrat, Joe saw an opportunity that could help further Jack's political aspirations. He not only backed the red baiter with hard cash but also had him at Hyannis Port as a frequent visitor, and McCarthy even dated two of the Kennedy girls, Patricia and Eunice.

McCarthy relied in his campaigns against the alleged Communist infiltration of government on a mixture of blatant falsity and innuendo, and his modus operandi was to create a climate of fear in order to justify his tactics of threats and intimidation. His dangerous but, for a while, popular crusade was also characterized by reckless, unsubstantiated, and underhand attacks on the character and motives of his opponents.

The committee set up under Senator Millard Tydings to investigate his assertions in relation to the State Department found nothing to back them up. His charges were described as "a fraud and a hoax," the purpose of which was to divide and confuse the American people to "a degree beyond the hopes of the Communists themselves." The findings completely undermined McCarthy, but not before he had caused false alarm and spread malicious falsehoods across many sectors of American society.

None of this dissuaded Joe Kennedy from standing by the senator, and he shared the general antipathy of the liberal Democrats to this creator of smoke with no fire. Joe had continuously proved himself as totally single-minded when he smelled an opportunity and, just as in his business dealings, he was not in the least fazed by the potential downside. There was a further knot tied with the family when McCarthy was invited to be godfather to Bobby and Ethel's firstborn, Kathleen. Joe's financial and personal support of McCarthy meant his political invoice was in the hands of the senator; it was only a matter of when he would want it to be paid.

Joe called in the favor when Jack first ran for the Senate in 1952. Jack was running against Henry Cabot Lodge. McCarthy, also a Republican, refused to campaign with Lodge and was instrumental in swaying republican Catholics to back Kennedy.

Just a few months later Joe called in another favor and in January 1953 Bobby joined the staff of the Permanent Subcommittee on investigations under the chairmanship of McCarthy. Very quickly he had misgivings about the job, confirmed when Larry O'Brien called to give his opinion that McCarthy was a tyrant and was bad news. Five months after he took up the job Bobby resigned. Despite this, in an argument with Kenny O'Donnell, Bobby not only refused to recognize the shame of the Wisconsin senator's witch-hunting but defended him, prompting O'Donnell to yell at him, "What the hell is wrong with you?" Such an association with an ultimately undesirable person, however much his use in a political sense, clearly didn't provide the lesson to the Kennedys that it should have. The result was even more dangerously evident in the comprehensive memo on Sinatra that the attorney general was now perusing.

This was not the first time the shadow of Hoover had darkened Bobby's desk since his brother had taken over as president. At the outset the brothers had spoken about getting rid of the director but their father had urged caution and advised against it. Joe had cultivated a friendship with Hoover over the years and considered that he knew him as well as anyone who knew his way around Washington did. While his justification to his sons was in tandem with that old adage about keeping your friends close and your enemies closer, it's more likely he feared that, despite any friendship they might have, Hoover's dossier on him, reputedly garnered over a quarter of a century, would be equally, if not more, salacious than anything he could produce on his two sons. The general wisdom was that, with his mountain full of secrets, Hoover was potentially more dangerous outside the administration than within it, as long as he could be kept under control, and the Kennedys felt they could do that. There were a lot of things they could do but, as it turned out, this was not one of them. Hoover's main preoccupation had always been to consolidate his own power base. Fighting Communism and organized crime was a secondary consideration to his innate and all-consuming sense of survival.

From the outset he had left the attorney general with no doubt of where he stood. The sub-text could be seen as little more than blackmail. In numerous memos he recounted what he knew, and had heard, from informants about the connections of organized crime to the CIA, the president, and to Joe Kennedy. It was a demonstration of exactly how far the Joe's cultivation of the FBI director had gotten him, basically nowhere, an echo of McCarthy in another time, but in Hoover any enemy faced a monster of a different and far more dangerous hue. Hoover had also shared the rabble-rouser's hatred of Communism and had secretly provided him with information. At the height of McCarthy's popularity, the FBI director had also gone on holiday with him in California. But when the going got rough for McCarthy, Hoover faded away.

When he received Hoover's umpteenth Communist threat warning, Bobby turned to Kenny O' Donnell and thumped the desk. Calling the director a "cocksucker," Kennedy continued, "One day that fucking fruit will show up in one of Jackie's Dior creations." He then crumpled the memo and threw it in the basket calling the whole line of correspondence "a total fucking waste of time." His tirade referred to the rumors that the FBI director was a cross-dressing homosexual, a charge never satisfactorily proved but generally accepted. Admittedly, if the Kennedys and their associates, or indeed Sinatra and his Cosa Nostra pals, had been able to get their hands on any substantive proof of the widely believed gossip about Hoover, that definitely would have been the end of him. In the absence of this tantalizing evidence, the attorney general and O'Donnell began to concoct a number of other measures to put Hoover in his place.

Hoover's response was to issue a tide of memos over the next five months relating to the sexual indiscretions of people in power, including the president's weakness for casual sexual encounters. The move was entirely typical of a man who had been a scourge to every administration that he had worked under. It would be later remarked that he would have fit nicely into the Nazi regime, or indeed a Communist administration in Russia, which he so roundly detested. The reality of course would be that if he had kept files on either Hitler or Stalin he would have been consigned to a fate far worse than mere transfer to the quiet pasture of retirement. His modus operandi might well have suited the demands of a totalitarian state but the consequences of his actions were and would be far more comfortable under democracy, a state for which he showed no respect if judged by his passion for dictatorship on his own powerful patch, and his penchant to chronicle in the most underhanded fashion in an attempt to destroy the lives of others to secure his position.

Bobby fumed at the audacity of the man who he now knew had kept a file on his brother since the war, openly telling colleagues that

Hoover was a psycho. Indeed, some of his staff who had dealings with him were convinced that the FBI director was mentally unhinged, something that was probably not far from the truth. For the moment, however, he had to tolerate him, if only for the principal purpose of keeping Hoover quiet about what he knew about the Kennedy sexual indiscretions and the family's dubious connections to the Mob.

The February 10 memo was clearly directed against Frank Sinatra, who, Hoover, having had access to his agents' reports for years, had now positioned close to the top of his hate list. Sinatra had been around nearly as long as Hoover had been in the top job at the bureau, so he'd managed by now to have ticked all of the boxes. Hoover disliked him with the intensity he reserved for his serious enemies—suspicion of being a Communist, a bagman for the Chicago Mob, a sexual philanderer, and now, a friend of the Kennedys. The substance of the memo contained an unstated sub-text that Bobby was not slow to pick up on: the attorney general is conducting a huge crackdown on the Mafia and this document is all about one of its associates, namely a man the president is hanging around with.

There was fanciful and purely speculative information at the beginning of the memo. According to an anonymous complainant in 1944 Sinatra had paid $40,000 to avoid the draft. He had been connected to sixteen organizations that had been cited as Communist fronts. There was, of course, no hard evidence to back the allegations up and, most tellingly, nothing to prove that Sinatra had ever held membership of the Communist Party.

The FBI director then chronicled the connection between Frank and a host of top Mafia figures. The names rolled damningly from the pages: Joseph and Rocco Fischetti, cousins of Al Capone; New Jersey crime boss Willie Morretti; Mickey Cohen of Los Angeles; and, of course, Sam Giancana. The document went on to report that Frank and Dean Martin had also attended a soiree at the home of "notorious hoodlum" Anthony Accardo and recounted the story about Sinatra's private number being among the items in Giancana's wallet when he was arrested in 1958.

The more the attorney general read, the worse it got. The text then detailed how, in the summer of 1959, Frank had hosted a nine-day party in Atlantic City's Claridge Hotel, which had been attended by Chicago Mob members and East Coast cohorts, including Vito Genovese and Tommy Luchese. Hoover's thesis was that even if Sinatra had not been found guilty of any criminal activity, his extensive association with Mafia figures was more than sufficient proof that the Kennedy administration should have nothing to do with him.

In spite of Bobby Kennedy's hatred of Hoover, it was an argument that, at the very least, made him pause for thought. Sinatra and his brother had been very friendly but Frank had, perhaps unwittingly, brought a lot of trouble the way of the Kennedys. Hoover, of course, took pleasure in using the hated Sinatra as a stick to beat the administration's cupboard and rattle the legion of skeletons therein.

The FBI director was like a large bloated spider spinning a web so tangled that it would stretch the most active imagination. The genesis of the web, however, went back only a few months.

On October 31, 1960, just three months before Kennedy's inauguration, the FBI had discovered an illegal wiretap in the Las Vegas hotel room of comedian Dan Rowan, later to become a huge national television star as one half of the comedic duo *Rowan & Martin*. The bureau investigators established that the CIA had placed it at the behest of Sam Giancana. But why would a secretive government agency perform such an action for a notorious mobster who himself was a target of the FBI? It was part of one of the most bizarre chapters in the history of US intelligence and one of almost unbelievable narrative. Three months earlier at the beginning of September, Robert Maheu, a former FBI agent who now operated as a private security consultant, had been contacted by the CIA, who had him on a monthly retainer to do work of a minor nature from time to time. He knew from the tenor of the phone call and the identity and rank of the two men who had arranged to meet him at his house in Virginia, that this was something special.

His visitors, Sheffield Edwards, head of the agency's office of security, and another top operative called James O'Connell, told him that the assignment was top secret and would be carried out without the knowledge of Eisenhower, now in the last months of his term as president. The mission was one of assassination, the target was newly installed Cuban President Fidel Castro, and it would be Maheu's role to hire the assassin. While the international community had welcomed the overthrow of the corrupt regime of Fulgencia Batista a year and half before, it was not a view shared by the US administration who saw the new socialist government, then in the early stages of developing an alliance with Russia, as a huge potential danger to national security. Maheu could take on the political angle but assassination had not been part of his résumé. He balked inwardly, not least because he was a Catholic. But there was another twist that he could never have anticipated.

Another newly avowed enemy of Cuba was the Mafia. Castro had shut down their operations, and the huge fortunes made from casino gambling and prostitution on the island were now a thing of the past. Instead, the Mob now had to concentrate their gambling efforts in Las Vegas. The gangsters, like the legitimate American investors who also found themselves squeezed out of Cuba, just had to swallow the Cuban pill and move on. But Maheu still nearly fell out of his chair when Edwards said that the ideal assassin would be a Mob killer because the Mafia had more contacts in Cuba than the CIA. He questioned the propriety of a government security agency collaborating with a criminal organization. The agents understood his position but insisted that the whole matter was in the interest of "national security." The two men made it very clear that they were well aware that he had contacts at the highest level within the Mafia.

Maheu said he would consider the matter and get back to them the next day. When the agents left he spent the rest of the evening pondering over the implications and the possible consequences for himself. There would be a lot more risk for him as the middleman, but he would be the main man in reality, as the CIA would not want to be seen to be involved in any way. Even in his crazy world he had never come across anything like it. Maheu did indeed have a Mafia contact, a connection that had arisen in a roundabout manner. He had been asked by a client to subpoena an owner of a Las Vegas hotel who had made himself very scarce so that the order could not be served. He had turned to a friend, Edward Bennett Williams, a lawyer who regularly represented mobsters.

The man sent to him was "Handsome" John Roselli, the Western representative of the Chicago Mob, based in Los Angeles. Charming, but very dangerous, Roselli had sorted things out for Maheu, and they had become friendly and Roselli had even been invited to the Maheu home for Thanksgiving dinner. In late August they met in the Brown Derby in Beverly Hills. Roselli reacted with disbelief when told of the plot in general terms and the role he was being asked to play in recruiting the assassin. How, he asked, could he possibly get involved with such a plot when the FBI was monitoring his every move?

Perhaps the mobster protested too much, because the flip side, which could not have escaped him, was that there could be some advantage for him to cooperate with the FBI. Maheu offered $150,000 on condition that he could never be connected with the plot. Roselli agreed to collaborate but refused to take any money, considering it his "patriotic duty" to become involved. There were two further meetings in September 1960, the first at the Plaza Hotel in New York where Maheu introduced Roselli to O'Connell, who was posing as the representative of a group of wealthy industrialists who wanted to get back into business in Cuba. The Mafioso was not just a pretty face and had quickly worked that he was dealing directly with a CIA man, but he let the two men know subtly without laboring the point.

The second meeting took place at the Fontainebleau Hotel in Miami, where it was Roselli's turn to introduce two of his associates, Sam Gold and a man Johnny introduced only as "Joe," the latter of whom he said would act as a courier to Cuba. Roselli had correctly sniffed out a security operative at the Plaza, but neither Maheu nor O'Connell had any idea of the seniority of the mobsters they had just met at the Florida encounter. A short time later it became clear when Maheu picked up a copy of a newspaper supplement that featured an article on the FBI's most wanted criminals. Top of the list was Sam Gold, in reality, of course, Sam Giancana. "Joe" also made the list under his real name of Santo Trafficante, the Mob's Florida boss and former Cuban chief.

Meanwhile, Eisenhower had gone and the Kennedy administration was now in full swing but the Castro assassination plan continued unabated. Further communications between Maheu, O'Connell, Giancana, and Roselli were focused on how to kill the Cuban president. They decided on poison, the preferred method of dispatching enemies in the times of the Borgias and a favorite method of murder in Victorian times, but a very strange choice in the middle of the twentieth century. Pills containing a number of lethal concoctions were tested in the CIA's Office of Medical Services and one containing botulinum, a powerful nerve toxin, was ultimately chosen.

The pills were delivered to Giancana and Trafficante at a meeting in a suite in the Hotel Fontainebleau in March 1961. Roselli also attended, as did a disaffected Cuban by the name of Juan Orta. Many years later Roselli would testify what happened next, saying that Maheu opened a briefcase and dumped a considerable sum of money on Orta's lap along with the poison capsules. Faced with the reality of the undertaking, Orta got cold feet, and it became apparent that another assassin would have to be found, but it never happened. This is somewhat surprising given that the overthrow of Castro was such a priority for the Kennedy administration at that time, and given the lengths that they had gone to and the associated risks. If association with figures like Sam Giancana was part of the day-to-day operations of the Kennedy administration, then the Cuban threat was clearly outweighing any ethical dilemmas.

The wire in the hotel room of Dan Rowan, it transpired, had been organized by Maheu at Giancana's request because he suspected one of his girlfriends, the singer Phyllis McGuire, was having an affair with the comedian, regarded as a handsome specimen of manhood, unlike the ferret-like mobster. It beggared belief that the CIA would lay an illegal wiretap at the behest of a notorious mobster for the purpose of checking up on his mistress, but these were unusual times, as the author Phillip Roth observed: "The actuality is continually outdoing our talents and the culture tosses up figures daily that are the envy of any novelist." Nothing could be truer in this instance.

For Hoover, who had been kept informed of developments since the Rowan wiretap had been uncovered by his agents, the events were his latest insurance against any thoughts of a forced "retirement" by his superiors. He now knew that Mafia elements were involved in a Kennedy administration-sanctioned plot to kill the president of Cuba. To anyone other than Hoover this would represent the sort of revelation that would offer the opportunity to, at a minimum, seriously compromise the government. But the bureau director hated Communists more than anything else, and Castro represented the ultimate threat, so Hoover viewed his prospective liquidation with relish, no matter who was to be responsible for killing him. But Hoover had discovered something else, which was real live political dynamite, something he knew could, if it reached the ears of the American public, have the potential to destroy the Kennedys. He now knew the president had been sleeping with Judith Campbell. He knew the president was still seeing the twenty-seven-year-old and that she had been a regular visitor to the White House in the previous twelve months. Crucially, he now knew that Judy was also sleeping with Sam Giancana and that Sinatra had been the instigator of the entire ménage. Hoover knew he now had the Kennedys where he wanted them, and he was about to turn the screw.

Chapter 14: The Trip

———————————◆———————————

KENNY O'DONNELL SAT at his desk, staring into the distance, exhausted by the events of the previous week. It was evening on Thursday March 22, 1962, and his exhaustion was compounded by the fact that the next morning he, and the entire entourage of the president of the United States, were due to travel to California. The chopper to Andrews Air Force Base was due to leave the White House at 8:30 a.m. so, for Kenny that meant a five thirty start.

The California visit had been on the cards for over a year, and there were a lot of moving parts, which O'Donnell had painstakingly tried to coordinate. His carefully orchestrated arrangements had been put in place to cover not just the political bases, but also the repayment of favors to Democratic Party and social friends, as well as events that would show the president in a positive light in this most important of states. Despite the fact that California was Richard Nixon's home state, the former vice-president had won there by less than thirty-six thousand votes, the narrowest margin of any of the states he carried in November 1960. With a margin that tight, Larry O'Brien believed that only a presidential challenger from California would have the potential to secure the vital 32 electoral college votes ahead of Jack in the next election. The three-day trip was all about making sure those votes were kept warm enough for Kennedy to take them in 1964.

As well as making sure the local party faithful were kept happy, Kenny had reached out across party lines and had included a visit with former President Eisenhower in the itinerary. Eisenhower, who was spending time at the El Dorado country club in Palm Springs, probably had more to gain from the visit than Jack, whom he had continuously privately derided during his last months in office. The war general's reputation had suffered in recent months and he was now seen, by many, as relatively inactive and uninspiring in comparison to the dynamic and stylish, new, young president. Kennedy wasn't letting bygones be bygones, though; he felt the meeting would look good, particularly in the eyes of California Republicans and sentimental older voters, who still held the older man in great regard.

Kennedy was also due to visit Vandenberg Air Force base to view a "minuteman" missile in its silo. The Titan testing program was based at Vandenberg and the president was due to observe the nation's primary Intercontinental Ballistic Missile installation and tour the launch center. Add to this an honorary degree at a conferring ceremony at the University of California at Berkeley, followed by a visit to a cutting edge radiation treatment development center, and the few days had the makings of a very solid political tour.

For Kennedy, though, the centerpiece of the trip was the visit to Sinatra's place in Palm Springs. Selected members of the presidential entourage were due to stay for two nights at the newly refurbished residence, and Frank had declared himself honored and excited about the arrival of his special guest. The president knew Frank's place well, of course, and was looking forward to a little R&R in the California sunshine and, perhaps, an opportunity to reacquaint himself with some old friends.

Frank had known about the proposed presidential visit for some time. Despite the fact that the secret service had refused to confirm it, Jack had intimated that when he got around to visiting California, as he inevitably would, he would stay with Sinatra. Peter Lawford had been instrumental in ensuring that the president was as good as his intimation. Pierre Salinger had as much as confirmed things in late '62 as the schedule for the spring of the following year began to firm up, and O'Donnell had been in contact fairly regularly as the date got closer. Frank was anything but discreet about the information entrusted to him about the potential movements of the commander-in-chief.

He was, however, more than enthusiastic about the arrangements he decided to make to ensure that every comfort of his guests would be catered to.

But now the Sinatra stopover was off. What was to have been a pleasurable, undoubtedly relaxing interlude, in the heat of the California sun, away from the cold of Washington, had turned into what Bobby was now describing as "a complete and utter fucking nightmare."

The previous week had been somewhat of an administrative headache. Because the trip was to begin on Friday the twenty-third, the resulting four day week meant a busier than normal schedule, compounded even further by a busy schedule the previous weekend, which revolved around St. Patrick's Day and the Gridiron Dinner. The Irish Ambassador, Thomas McKiernan, along with two Irish American congressmen, John E. Fogarty and Michael Kirwan, had paid their respects at around ten o'clock on Saturday, and the president had kept up a round of meetings and social chats right across the morning. His engagements that day had ranged from a discussion on the Cuban situation with General Maxwell Taylor and McGeorge Bundy, to a meeting with Florence Mahoney and Lady Barbara Jackson, ten minutes with Charlie Bartlett, his journalist friend, who had first introduced him to Jackie, and lunch with Richard Rovere, another journalist. Despite his hectic schedule, Kennedy still liked to spend time with press friends like Ben Bradlee of *The Washington Post*, Joe Alsop, and Hugh Sidey of *Time* magazine. All three had been to visit or to dinner in the previous two weeks, and Jack considered their opinions and feedback a vital barometer of the public's opinion of the administration.

The members of the press were also his hosts that evening at the Capital Hilton. The Gridiron Club, Washington's oldest journalistic society, an "invitation-only" group of sixty-five of the most influential people in the media, held an annual dinner event at which the president was traditionally the guest of honor. It had been a lively, jovial affair with members engaging in satirical and musical skits about each other and political figures. Kennedy, introduced by Julius Frandsen, the UPI bureau chief and president of the club, had spoken, somewhat informally, and had spent the evening working the roomful of people whose views, he knew, had such a huge influence on America. It was a long evening, with the president spending four-and-a-half hours at the dinner before arriving back the White House after eleven thirty.

O'Donnell had been waiting at the door of the office when the president walked in at 9:35 a.m. on Monday morning. Kenny briefed him on the week's events and appointments, among them a breakfast with the legislative leaders, including the speaker of the house, John McCormack, a visit by the president of the African Republic of Togo, and the signing of the recently passed Welfare and Pension Plans Disclosure Act Amendments. The two then went over the schedule for the California trip Friday, and the Sinatra "situation," which O'Donnell had been trying to contain for the last few days. In reality it was a difficulty that he had found himself caught up in for some time and had accentuated the personal conflict that he had long feared, having to choose between his loyalty to his boss and his friend, his boss's brother. Thankfully, it now looked as if it would not come to a head but, at times, over the past couple of weeks, there had been some very tense moments between the Kennedy brothers, and Kenny had found himself in the middle.

O'Donnell had been well aware of Frank Sinatra's efforts to ingratiate himself with the president and had himself, like Jack, been somewhat blinded by Sinatra's stardom as far back as the mid-1950s. He had accompanied the senator, as candidate, on some of the visits to meet with Sinatra and had witnessed firsthand the attraction Frank had for JFK, particularly where women were concerned. But since the election Sinatra had sought access to, and approval from, the president with a new intensity. Beginning in the late spring of 1961, Sinatra had bombarded Kennedy and, to a lesser extent, Pierre Salinger, with letters, messages, gifts, and suggestions. Since Kenny saw pretty much everything his boss saw, he was aware of just how keen Sinatra was to keep close.

A pile of Sinatra material arrived in the White House while Kennedy was on a tour of South America in September 1961, prompting him to write on October 3,

"Dear Frank, a wonderful assortment of albums and three of your tape recordings awaited my return to the White House this week. I am delighted with these gifts and wanted you to know how very much I appreciate your thoughtfulness."

Two weeks later Kennedy acknowledged a "generous assortment of matches that you recently sent to me. I am delighted by your very thoughtful gesture."

In a follow up to the inauguration gala, Frank had suggested the production of a souvenir two-disc highlight record to both commemorate the event and to raise some funds to defray the expenses incurred in staging it. He had, he claimed, mentioned the idea to the president earlier in the year, and on March 30 had written to Salinger, "I think my people did a damn good job compiling it. I hope you and, of course, the president agree. Any changes you or the president think of, we can discuss by telephone." Frank was obviously taking a hands-on approach to the project, going on to write, "We are thinking of a price of fifteen dollars a copy which I think is quite fair to the buyer. We have a few ideas on how to distribute and sell them which should bring us some good loot." The note finished, "Please ask your secretary to forward the album to the president after you have seen it in Washington." Perhaps in an effort to ensure that JFK would hear the record the letter was copied to Joe Kennedy, whom Sinatra correctly assumed would raise the matter with his son, as note of June 8 from O'Donnell to Salinger confirmed, "Re: Sinatra Album. Mr. Kennedy senior has the album in hand and has discussed the matter with the president."

In the meantime, Salinger had obviously, unintentionally or on purpose, managed to mislay the discs as Kenny finished by writing, "Despite your efforts to lose the album it was found by Tish" (Letitia Baldrige, Jackie's social secretary).

As O'Donnell's relationship with Frank had moved to a more formal basis as his position within the administration became more pivotal, Pierre Salinger's dealings with him had become more frequent and warmer: "Dear Frank," he wrote upon learning of Sinatra's short-lived engagement to the actress Juliet Prowse, "Heartiest congratulations on your engagement. Everyone back here is most pleased with the news." Frank also sought to flatter the president and his administration with regular telegrams, usually through Salinger: "Dear Pierre, Please convey to the president the following message—We are in complete accord with your belief and attitudes and we applaud you." This particular telegram from July 1961 ended with the sort of teasing message that generally excited JFK with the potential for female liaisons: "Peter (Lawford) and I hope to see you in a few weeks. Frank." On this occasion, however, the meeting referred to would take place in Hyannis Port, where Kennedy's opportunities for extramarital fun were very limited and on this occasion the press had been informed that Sinatra was a guest of Lawford and Ted Kennedy, and not of the president. Following that visit, a Mr. Charles N. Stah of Hollywood, one of many correspondents to the White House on the subject of Frank, which Salinger had to field on the president's behalf, wrote in a telegram, "Recent United Press report insinuating Yves Montand and Sinone (sic) Singoret plus left wing sympathizer Frank Sinatra allegedly were your guests at Hyannis Port this weekend surely most Americans as I feel in these critical times if the story was true the company was very ill chosen."

Jack Rosenstein, the editor of the entertainment trade magazine *Hollywood Close-Up*, was more specific about Frank's behavior in his letter to Salinger of February 3, 1962: "Aside from his own small clique there is a virulent odium attached to Sinatra in the motion picture industry generally, particularly in the self-aggrandizement of the identification of himself with the President."

The note also said: "It may be of interest to you that there is a persistent rumor that Frank Sinatra is having a house constructed adjoining his residence in Palm Springs specifically as a vacation home for President Kennedy."

It was no rumor. In anticipation of the visit, work on the Sinatra property had been ongoing for some time. In addition to a remodeling of the main house, Sinatra had, among other things, commissioned the construction of additional buildings, which he intended for the accommodation of the president's secret service detail and other members of the Kennedy entourage. He'd also had a bank of twenty-five telephone lines and a switchboard wired in so the leader of the free world could remain in contact with his office, his cabinet, and the presidents and prime ministers of other countries if necessary. Add to this the installation of a concrete helipad and a presidential flagpole, like the one he'd seen in Hyannis Port the previous September, and the place had the capability to function like a sort of western White House.

Salinger, and others like O'Donnell and Bobby, didn't need the disaffected Mr. Rosenstein to tell them of Frank's insinuation or "self-aggrandizement." The man they considered the most dangerous threat to the success or otherwise of the administration already knew how badly Sinatra felt the need to tell anyone who would listen about his relationship with the president and the upcoming visit. J. Edgar Hoover's file on Frank and his activities continued to expand, and word had already reached him about the construction that was taking place on the Palm Spring property. Of most interest to Hoover, however, was the continuing relationship between the president and Judy Campbell.

Jack Kennedy's dalliance had become a serious affair over the two years since Sinatra had introduced them, and she had seen Jack on at least ten occasions between their first meeting and the inauguration, and had continued to see him in Washington throughout 1961.

By early 1962, Hoover, through his now routine surveillance of
Sinatra and Johnny Roselli, and the Dan Rowan hotel wiretap among
other sources, knew definitively about "Mr. Flood," and that she had
been carrying on a relationship with him as well as with the president. Hoover had made it abundantly clear to Bobby Kennedy that
he was in possession of this information and that he knew Sam Flood
was Giancana. He had continued to warn the attorney general about
the dangers of the president's relationship with Sinatra right across
1961, and Frank had become the become the subject of much inten-
sified FBI surveillance in this period.

Frank was also receiving attention from another unwelcome
direction. Bobby Kennedy's campaign against organized crime,
which he had begun within days of taking up office, was intensifying.
As the key adviser to his brother, Bobby was enjoying the luxury of
being able to do what he wanted at the Justice Department with the
minimum of interference. In fact, the president, compromised by his,
and his father's, ties to a number of dubious underworld personali-
ties, may even have wished to turn a blind eye to the ferocity of the
war that his brother had embarked upon. Jack would say, "If I want
something done and done immediately I rely on the attorney general.
He is very much the doer in this administration, and has an organizational gift I have rarely if ever seen surpassed." To support his crusade the attorney general had assembled what Arthur Schlesinger
described as an "outstanding" group of deputy and assistant attorneys
general, including Byron White and Nicholas Katzenbach, and this
tightly knit team had embarked on their task like zealots.

While there could never have been a formal agreement between
the Kennedys and the Mob, there was certainly an implication that
those who had helped Jack get elected in 1960 would benefit to
some degree from the largesse of the administration. Powers and
O'Donnell had supervised the distribution of thousands of jobs and
favors to campaign and long-standing loyalists. Political figures like
Mayor Richard Daley in Chicago and Senator George Smathers from
Florida (arguably JFK's best friend in the Senate) could always rely

on the support of the president if they had to call upon it. Having orchestrated so many dirty tricks on Jack's behalf during the election campaign, the Mob now expected that the status quo, which had existed up to November 1960, would, at the very least, be maintained. What they actually experienced shook the commission to the core.

By 1962 racketeering prosecutions involving the Organized Crime Section of the Criminal Division of the Department had increased approximately 300 percent over 1961 and 700 percent over 1960. Convictions had increased more than 350 percent over 1961 and almost 400 percent over 1960. By 1962 the number of individuals indicted for offences connected with organized crime had risen from 49 in 1960 to 350. Across the United States well-known mobster figures were being put away, and the central information pool that the department coordinated now had comprehensive files on the background and activities of more than 1,100 major racketeering figures. The Organized Crime and Racketeering section of the Criminal Division had been greatly expanded. Since January 1961, the personnel strength of the section had been more than tripled from seventeen attorneys to more than sixty. Permanent field units had also been set up in Chicago, New York, Los Angeles, and Miami. All of this spelled bad news for characters like Mayer Lansky, Anthony Accardo, Santa Trafficante, and, of course, Roselli and Giancana. For Sinatra it was a disaster. Not only was he the subject of intensive surveillance by the most senior and dangerous law enforcement officer in the land, he was now being regarded with increasing suspicion by the powerful Italian American gang bosses he had effectively represented as a go-between with the Kennedys, the same people who were now trying to crush the Cosa Nostra's interests. And to make matters worse, the brothers were now about to throw him overboard.

The news about the cancellation of the trip hadn't been handled very sensitively. At the removal of half a century and with all of the major participants deceased, it is difficult to piece together the sequence of events accurately, but what appears to have happened is the following:

At the end of February, Hoover dropped his bombshell. In identical memos to Bobby and Kenny O'Donnell he informed both that the president had been having a relationship with Judy Campbell and she, in turn, had been involved with Mob boss and criminal suspect, Sam Giancana. The person responsible for making the various introductions was Frank Sinatra, another subject of FBI surveillance, and as far as the director was concerned, it would be wholly inappropriate for the president to stay in Sinatra's house on his forthcoming trip to California. If the attorney general did not feel he could advise the president to adopt this course of action, then Hoover would do so himself.

Bobby may not have known about the proposed stay at Sinatra's, although this seems unlikely given his closeness to O'Donnell. He was fully aware, however, of the relationship between his brother and Frank, and was obviously more than aware of Frank's more dubious connections. Given that he was now effectively "at war" with the Mob, why he had not moved earlier to distance the administration from Sinatra is hard to fathom. The answer may lie in the fact that Jack, deep down, valued the friendship and all Sinatra had done for him, and was unwilling to cut him loose. There is also a distinct possibility that Bobby may have been agitating for this for some time without success. Hoover's ultimatum changed all that.

At what exact point the president finally acquiesced to his brother's remonstrations is also unclear. There is only one record of Bobby visiting the White House in March 1962 prior to the California trip, on Tuesday the 20, and that is in the company of Clark Clifford and also after Sinatra had been ditched. While the two spoke frequently on the telephone, the brothers were definitely in each other's company when they traveled home together from Palm Beach, after visiting their father, at his home there, on the weekend of March 10–11. They spent two hours en route from Miami together and Jack's first appointment at 9:35 a.m. the next morning, was with O'Donnell and Salinger.

The decision made, it was really only a matter of who would pull the trigger.

Kenny O'Donnell's orders were straightforward. The president would not be staying with Frank Sinatra, an alternative would have to be found, and Peter Lawford, as the man deemed closest to Frank, would be the one to break the bad news. O'Donnell was also instructed to find a plausible excuse for the cancellation.

Lawford, as the instigator of the visit, and the man now charged with the dirty work, was the last to know. He and Pat had been to the White House for a private dinner with the first couple on February 8. If Peter had known there was a confrontation with Frank on the horizon he would have steered a million miles clear of it, or at a minimum tried to keep the visit on the tracks. Peter and Pat Lawford were still very close to Frank, but they were both more than aware of his volcanic temper, and the clothes-ripping incident of 1958 must have crossed Peter's mind.

Now Lawford's loyalty was being tested, and he was in a no-win situation. "It fell to me to break the news to Frank, and I was scared," Lawford told Sinatra biographer Kitty Kelley. He went on to say, "When Jack called me, he said that as president he just couldn't stay at Frank's and sleep in the same bed that Giancana or any other hood had slept in." "You can handle it, Petah," Jack had said in his Massachusetts drawl. Jack had called only after Kenny let the president know that encouraging "Petah" to do the deed might need the weight of the commander-in-chief behind it.

O'Donnell was now faced with the task of finding suitable alternative accommodation for the presidential entourage. While providing bed and board for the president of the United States, his key staff, and secret service detail would inevitably be challenging at such short notice, the clumsiness of what happened next is the most unbelievable and insensitive part of the whole sorry chapter. Chris Dunphy, a prominent Republican supporter from Florida, was contacted, and he, in turn, made arrangements for most of the presidential party to be put up at Bing Crosby's house, just down the road at Rancho Mirage. The agents were accommodated next door at Jimmy Van Heusen's place. The reason for the change of venue was put down to security, the Secret Service deeming that they would be unable to effectively protect the president at Sinatra's the official line. Had the entire group checked into the local Holiday Inn, Frank might have bought the excuse, or at least have been able to put it about, to the numerous people to whom he had announced the visit, as a reason for the cancellation. As it was, the Kennedys had left him in a most humiliating position, salt rubbed into the wound by switching the trip to Crosby's.

When Lawford made the call, his official line quickly crumbled, and he confessed that it was Bobby who had really decided that the president could not stay with Frank. Sinatra was having none of it, accusing Lawford of setting the whole thing up at Crosby's, before slamming the phone down. Frank then called Bobby in Washington to be told that the reason for the cancellation was the disreputable company he was keeping and the need for the administration to distance itself from people such as himself. Sinatra called the attorney general every name in the book before slamming the phone down. Frank is then alleged to have gone around the house, smashing up everything in his way before taking a sledgehammer to the concrete helipad outside. Despite his temper, whether he did anything quite so dramatic is debatable. What is certain, however, is that he was deeply wounded by what he regarded as a huge personal insult to him. Unaware of the machinations behind the scenes and the urgent, if somewhat tardy, political necessity of the cancellation, Sinatra took out his rage on Bobby. He cut him off, knowing the relationship was now all but at an end.

Chapter 15: Assassination

———————◆———————

IN RETROSPECT, A trip to Texas, to the heartland of anti-Kennedy sentiment, seems like a crazy idea. But in mid-1963 the lone star state was causing all sorts of headaches for the Kennedy administration. For one, its main power broker, the vice-president, was feeling uneasy, and his supporters were also concerned. Lyndon Johnson, whether through the disregard of his boss and his brother, or his own indifference, had played a very limited role in the governing of the Unites States since the inauguration in January 1961. Having tried to carve out a more significant role, he found himself frustrated at every attempt by the Kennedy brothers, especially Bobby, who regarded him as an old-fashioned political dinosaur and a liability to the administration. Johnson was rarely consulted on matters of importance, and, as Kenny O'Donnell was to tell White House correspondent Sander Vanocur in an interview in the late 1960s, "The only time we ever heard from Lyndon was on the issue of patronage."

For Johnson, patronage, and in particular the ability to bestow favors on fellow Texans, was a key perk of the vice-presidential job and a method of political payment, which was the very cornerstone of his career. A central part of the agreement between JFK and his running mate when LBJ had agreed to accept the nomination was that, if elected, the new vice-president would be consulted on all matters pertaining to patronage where Texas was concerned. This hadn't always been the case, and Johnson had worn a well-trodden path to the oval office to complain to Jack about this supporter's son or that contributor's daughter who had failed to receive a job, appointment or contract promised by the vice-president. One appointment of significance, however, had made Johnson apoplectic with rage and driven a serious wedge between LBJ and Bobby.

Just days into office, Johnson had tried to have his long time friend and supporter, Judge Sarah T. Hughes, a judge of the fourteenth district in Texas, appointed to the United States District Court for the Northern District of Texas. The position was a federal appointment in the gift of the president and lifetime tenure, unlike her then current position, which required periodic reelection. Bobby, who, as attorney general, had sight and effective veto over all such appointments, disagreed with the elevation on the grounds of age (Hughes would have been sixty-five at the time, and the Kennedys were anxious to appoint younger judges). Johnson, who prided himself on being a man of his word had to break the news to Hughes that the favor he had promised would not be forthcoming, something he regarded as a humiliating climb-down. But it was nothing to the humiliation he would experience weeks later when Bobby then appointed Hughes to the position at the insistence of the House Majority Leader, another Texan, Sam Rayburn, who threatened to hold up legislation until he secured her nomination. Rayburn, who would die just a few months later, understandably took full credit for the appointment. The news of how Hughes secured the appointment soon did the rounds of Washington and Lyndon's embarrassment was further exacerbated.

O'Donnell, describing the debacle as a "terrible mistake," had resolved to build bridges with Johnson in an effort to bring him back onside. Key to that was to ensure that Johnson's access to the president became less complicated and that he be regarded as pre-eminent among Texan politicians. This was an aspect of the matter that needed to be handled sensitively, given the importance of the state to the forthcoming 1964 campaign. In 1960 Kennedy had secured the 24 available electoral college votes with 50.52 percent of the vote to Nixon's 48.52 percent. Johnson's prolific vote getting talent had been essential to securing the largest number of votes available in the country, excepting California. Now O'Donnell and strategist Larry O'Brien were keen to ensure that Texas delivered again and a happy Johnson was part of the key to achieving that objective. Local supporters were also dismayed by rumors in the national media that Kennedy might drop Lyndon from the 1964 ticket in favor of Senator George Smathers or North Carolina Governor Terry Sanford, rumors the Kennedys were doing little to dispel.

Furthermore, a rift had opened between two other Texan democrats, the newly elected conservative governor of the state, John Connally, and the liberal senator Ralph Yarborough. A disenchanted vice president and more widespread disenchantment among Democrats would only work to the advantage of the Republicans, and Connally, Kennedy, and O'Donnell had discussed a presidential visit as a way of mending fences. Johnson was agreeable as long as he could be seen to play a central role in the visit and an overnight stay at his ranch at Stonewall, about fifty miles west of Austin, had been built into the trip. With the exception of a brief private visit to Sam Rayburn in hospital in October 1961, Kennedy had not visited Dallas since his election, and for good reason.

The city was a hotbed of extremism and harbored many extreme anti-Communist groups. On a visit just before the election, Johnson and his wife, Lady Bird, had been attacked by a group of Kennedy detractors, mostly well-dressed women, upon their arrival at the Adolphus Hotel. They set upon the startled couple on the street, screaming and spitting at them. Close to the group a man stood holding a sign that read, "LBJ Sold Out to Yankee Socialists." On the October 25 just past, following a speech in Dallas, Kennedy's envoy to the United Nations, Adlai Stevenson, had been spat at by a young man and hit by a woman holding a placard, as a hundred or so people milled around the frightened ambassador. Segments of Dallas were clearly not enamored of Jack Kennedy and he had demonstrated his acknowledgement of this by simply staying away.

Apart from all these considerations, by mid 1963 it was simply not politically practical to put off a trip to the state any longer. The decision to make a trip was made at a meeting between Kennedy, Johnson, and Connally on June 5 at the Cortez Hotel in El Paso, Texas. The president had spoken earlier that day in Colorado Springs and had stopped in El Paso to discuss the proposed visit and the other local party issues with the vice president and the governor. The original plan was that Kennedy would spend only one day in the state, making whirlwind visits to Dallas, Fort Worth, San Antonio, and Houston. By September, the schedule had been extended over two days and included more expanded activities in the four cities and the addition of a stop-off in Austin. When Connally called at the White House just before lunchtime on October 4 to discuss the details of the visit, the two days were confirmed, and it was agreed that the local planning of events in Texas would be left largely to him, while O'Donnell would, as normal, act as overall coordinator. Johnson met with Kennedy later in the day, and the two of them signed off on what had been discussed with Connally earlier.

One point at issue, however, even at the early stages, was the Dallas motorcade. Everyone agreed that, if there were sufficient time, a motorcade through downtown Dallas would be the best way for the people to see the president. When the trip was planned for only one day, Connally had opposed the motorcade because there was not enough time. He later said, however, that "once we got San Antonio moved from Friday to Thursday afternoon, where that was his initial stop in Texas, then we had the time, and I withdrew my objections to a motorcade." For Kenny O'Donnell, a motorcade was never in doubt. "We had a motorcade wherever we went," he later said, "particularly in large cities where the purpose was to let the president be seen by as many people as possible, it would be automatic for the Secret Service to arrange a route which would, within the time allotted, bring the president through an area which exposes him to the greatest number of people."

The main obstacle to setting a definitive date for the visit was Thanksgiving, which fell on the twenty-eighth, pretty much eliminating the week beginning November 25, and the week after. The president had received an invitation to speak at a dinner in honor of congressman Albert Thomas, which was being held in Houston on Thursday the twenty-first, so it seemed logical to O'Donnell to build the trip around that event. After some to and fro and discussions with Connally and other local representatives, the main elements of the trip were finally agreed. The presidential party would first travel to the southernmost location of San Antonio to view the Aerospace Medical Center, followed by the Albert Thomas dinner, and then an overnight stay in Fort Worth followed by a breakfast event on the morning of the twenty-second. The twenty-second would also include the motorcade through downtown Dallas, followed by a speech at the city's Trade Mart, an afternoon trip to Austin for a party fundraising dinner that night and an overnight at the LBJ ranch, before jetting back to Washington on the Saturday. As with the California visit of March 1962, when the Frank Sinatra element of the trip had been aborted, O'Donnell felt this tour had the right mix of public profile, political practicality, and geographical spread to make the most of the two-day marathon. The decision to finally agree to the visit was made at the October 4 meeting and O'Donnell set about making the arrangements.

With the main elements agreed, Kenny telephoned Gerry Behn, the special agent in charge of the Kennedy secret service detail, to advise him of the itinerary. He also contacted Gerry Bruno, the White House staffer responsible for advance work on many of the presidential trips, and assigned him the task of working with Behn on behalf of the White House. On November 4 Behn appointed Winston "Win" Lawson, a member of the White House detail, as advance agent for Dallas, and Forrest V. Sorrels, special agent in charge of the Dallas office, was given the task of coordinating locally. Lawson then received an outline schedule of the Texas trip on November 8 from Roy Kellerman, assistant special agent in charge of the White House detail, who was the Secret Service official responsible for the entire Texas journey. As advance agent working closely with Sorrels,

Lawson had responsibility for arranging the timetable for the president's visit to Dallas and coordinating local activities with the White House staff, the organizations directly concerned with the visit, and local law enforcement officials. Lawson's most important responsibility was to take preventive action against anyone in Dallas considered to be a threat to the president.

Frank Sinatra, meanwhile, had begun work on his latest film project, *Robin and the Seven Hoods*. The film, produced by Sinatra and directed by Gordon Douglas, who had worked with Frank on *Young at Heart* in 1954 and would subsequently do so with *Tony Rome* (1967) and *Lady in Cement* (1968), portrayed the Robin Hood legend in a 1930s Chicago gangster setting. The movie revolves around Robbo, a gangster played by Frank, who donates money to a local orphanage and, when the papers get to hear of it, becomes a local celebrity. The film was something of a "Rat Pack" movie with Dean Martin and Sammy Davis Jr. playing co-starring roles. *Robin and the Seven Hoods* had been in the works for a while and one of the other main roles, that of the orphanage director, Allen A. Dale, had originally been earmarked for Peter Lawford, but Sinatra had dumped him from the proposed cast after the events of March 1962. Ironically Bing Crosby was now playing the part, his first movie role with Frank since *High Society* in 1956.

The week of November 18 was a varied one in terms of John Kennedy's schedule. The president had returned from various commitments late the previous week and over the weekend in Delaware, New York City, and Florida, arriving back to the White House late on Monday evening. There was a lot to cram into the two days before the Texas trip, due to begin in the early afternoon of Thursday. Apart from publicity events like the presentation of the national Thanksgiving turkey by the Poultry and Egg national board, the schedule included a legislative leaders breakfast and meetings with the ambassadors to Finland, Indonesia, Ghana, and Bolivia, as well as political discussions with Larry O'Brien (with Senator George Smathers on Wednesday morning), Dean Rusk and, of course, O'Donnell. For Kenny it was continuous pressure. The incessant demands by Johnson to ensure he received top billing along with the president on all stops was causing problems with Connally and also with Ralph Yarborough, who felt that he was being consistently slighted. The issue, somewhat childishly, came down to who would ride with whom and in what cars in the various motorcades. At one point Yarborough refused to travel with Johnson at all and it took a lot of persuasion and the promise of more prominent positioning of the senator at the Friday event in Austin to sway him. In some sense all of this was irrelevant given that the majority of people anticipated to turn out in Texas over the coming days were expected to do so to see the president, and just as importantly, Jackie, who had agreed to campaign with her husband on the trip. Jackie had lost a son, baby Patrick, after he was born five and a half weeks premature on August 7, and this was the first time since that the first lady had toured with her husband. As with every trip she had taken since the election, huge crowds were expected to follow her.

On the morning of Thursday, November 21, with things more or less in line, Kennedy had two more ambassadorial meetings, with his envoys to Gabon and Upper Volta, before departing with his entourage by helicopter for Andrews Air Force base at 10:50 a.m. At San Antonio, the first stop, Johnson, Connally, and Yarborough led the welcoming party. They accompanied the president to Brooks Air Force Base for the dedication of the Aerospace Medical Health Center. Continuing on to Houston, he addressed a Latin American citizens' organization and spoke at the Albert Thomas testimonial before flying the 250 miles to end the day with an overnight stay in Fort Worth.

It was a wet morning in Fort Worth as Jack emerged from room 850 of the Hotel Texas to give what would be his second-to-last speech, to a crowd gathered outside. He then went into the Crystal Ballroom at 9 a.m. for the Fort Worth Chamber of Commerce breakfast. Kennedy explained Jackie's absence away at the first speech: "Mrs. Kennedy is organizing herself. It takes longer but, of course, she looks better than we do when she does it." Arriving late into the ballroom, Jackie was greeted with thunderous adulation from two thousand attendees and made her way to the head table in a striking pink wool suit with matching pillbox hat. Kennedy could not refuse the opportunity: "Two years ago I introduced myself in Paris by saying I was the man who had accompanied Mrs. Kennedy to Paris. I am getting somewhat that same sensation as I travel around Texas. Nobody wonders what Lyndon and I wear," he commented to widespread laughter and applause.

After the speech and numerous handshakes, the presidential party left the hotel, traveling by motorcade to Carswell Air Force Base for the thirteen-minute flight to Dallas. Arriving at Love Field at 11:39 a.m., Jack and Jackie disembarked and walked toward where a group of well-wishers had gathered. A bouquet of red roses was presented, which Jackie brought with her to the waiting limousine. Connally and his wife, Nellie, were already seated in the open convertible as the Kennedys got in and sat behind them. The motorcade lined up with an unmarked police car at the head, containing Win Lawton and Forest Sorrels, accompanied by the Dallas Police Chief, Jesse Curry. The presidential limousine followed, driven by Agent Will Greer, with agent-in-charge, Roy Kellerman, in the other front seat. The secret service car followed closely behind, with eight agents on board (four of them on the external running boards), as well as Kenny O'Donnell and Dave Powers. Johnson, his wife, Lady Bird, and Ralph Yarborough, along with assistant special agent in charge, Rufus Youngblood, and a Dallas police driver, occupied the last of the main cars, followed by a line of other vehicles filled with press, police, and politicians.

The procession left the airport at approximately 11:55 a.m., and traveled along a ten-mile route that wound through downtown Dallas on the way to the Trade Mart, where Kennedy was scheduled to speak at a luncheon with the city's government, business, religious, and civic leaders and their spouses. The closer the motorcade progressed downtown the more enclosed the cars became, winding its way left on North Harwood Street, right onto Main Street, and then right onto Houston Street, and then left turn onto Elm Street, which would take it directly onto the Stemmons Freeway and the Trade Mart. At 12:30 p.m., the motorcade turned onto Elm Street, passing the Texas book depository building on the right. As it did so, the secret service agents on the running board in the follow-on car were able to see a curious white pergola-like structure on raised ground to the right, and the park-like expanse of Dealey Plaza to the left. Within seconds shots rang out, clearly audible to bystanders and those in the cars. Kennedy and Connally were both hit by the snipers bullets and within seconds the president's car began speeding up. Jackie was heard to scream and she climbed out of the back seat onto the rear of the limousine. At the same time, jumping from the driver's side running board of the follow-on car, agent Clint Hill managed to climb aboard and hang on, pushing Jackie back into the car. As the panic ensued the main cars raced under the triple underpass leading to the freeway. Will Greer, shouted "hospital" to the outriders and, with police motorbikes leading the way with their sirens blaring, the limousine raced to Parkland Hospital, passing the original destination of the Trade Mart on the way.

The convoy arrived at 12:38 p.m., and within moments the president was transferred to Trauma Room #1, where emergency staff, led by vascular surgeon Dr. Malcolm Perry, worked to try to resuscitate him, to no avail. Kennedy's severe head wounds meant he was most likely killed in Dealey Plaza at the moment of impact of a bullet to the right side of his head. Dr. Perry later said, "We never had any hope of saving his life,"—he was pronounced dead at 1:00 p.m.

News of the president's death moved fast. Despite the fact that the official announcement wasn't to come until half an hour later at 1:30 p.m., most television and radio networks across the United States had already broken into their schedules to inform their audiences of the shooting. The ABC radio network reported on events in Dallas as early as 12:36 p.m., while CBS was the first to break the news on television when, at 12:40 p.m., the network interrupted its live broadcast of *As the World Turns* with a "CBS News Bulletin" slide and Walter Cronkite filed an audio-only report over it: "Here is a bulletin from CBS News. In Dallas, Texas, three shots were fired at President Kennedy's motorcade in downtown Dallas. The first reports say that President Kennedy has been seriously wounded by this shooting."

On the streets of Manhattan, incredulous office workers peered into television rental stores to try to get the latest on the shooting. In towns and cities across the United States, workers huddled around radios in offices and factories. Members of the press awaited news in a nurse's classroom in the hospital. Their worst fears were confirmed at 1:30 p.m., Central Standard Time, when White House Deputy Press Secretary Malcolm Kilduff addressed the waiting press: "President John F. Kennedy died at approximately 1:00 CST today, here in Dallas. He died of a gunshot wound to the brain. I have no other details regarding the assassination of the president," he said, the emotion on his face close to breaking point.

In truth, most of the press had already had confirmation of John Kennedy's demise, although not from the official source from which they were now hearing it.

Father Oscar L. Huber of the Holy Trinity Church, who had been disturbed while eating lunch and had rushed to Parkland after a call from the hospital, had as much as confirmed the death as he emerged from giving the president the last rites. As the priest was being led away by a secret service agent, he responded to the questions of the press with, "He's dead, all right." Agents also maintained an open line to the White House from where Gerry Behn was relaying information to other key figures in Washington. It is impossible to believe that by the time Father Huber made his unwitting pronouncement, the president's fatal condition had not been conveyed to the majority of the press present.

A few minutes after 2:00 p.m., following an extraordinary confrontation between Kenny O'Donnell, supported by Secret Service agents with their weapons-drawn, and Earl Rose, the Dallas County medical examiner, who insisted the body could not leave the state without an autopsy, President Kennedy's body was removed and driven straight to Air Force One. It was another in a chain of events surrounding the entire tragic episode that have remained the subject of intense scrutiny and controversy to this day.

Frank Sinatra was filming a scene for *Robin and the Seven Hoods* in a Burbank, California cemetery when news reached the set that Jack had been assassinated. Stunned by the news, Sinatra reportedly became very withdrawn and took a series of long walks away from the set, thinking about the tragedy as production executives tried to decide what to do (right across the United States businesses were grinding to a halt as the news spread—Hollywood was no different). He also called the White House from the set and spoke briefly to someone there. There was utter confusion on the White House switchboard with thousands trying to get through, and Sinatra, despite his celebrity, was just another caller that afternoon. He then returned to the waiting film crew and said, "Let's shoot this thing, 'cause I don't want to come back here anymore." After the scene was finished Sinatra immediately went to Palm Springs. According to later reports, he "virtually disappeared" for three days, speaking to no one. He would later say of Kennedy, "For a brief moment, he was the brightest star in our lives. I loved him."

Peter Lawford was appearing in Lake Tahoe with Jimmy Durante when he heard the news. He quickly made arrangements to be released from the shows planned for the weekend and hurried back to be with Pat. By the weekend they were in Washington, DC, Lawford standing in solemn support of his wife and family alongside the other Kennedy brothers-in-law, Steve Smith and Sargent Shriver.

Representatives from over ninety countries attended the state funeral on Monday, November 25. The late president was buried at Arlington National Cemetery in Virginia. Approximately twelve hundred invited guests had attended the Requiem funeral Mass in St. Matthew's cathedral. The mass was celebrated by the Archbishop of Boston, Cardinal Cushing, who had witnessed and blessed the marriage of Jack and Jackie in 1953. The casket was borne by caisson on the final leg to Arlington National Cemetery for burial. Earlier that morning the State Department also issued the following directive:

> Upon the conclusion of the ceremonies at the Cathedral, those attending the Mass enter their cars and join the procession from the Cathedral to Arlington National Cemetery in the following order of precedence: Mrs. Kennedy and members of the immediate family, The President and his Party, Chiefs of State, Heads of Government and Chiefs of Special Delegations, The Chief Justice and the Supreme Court, Members of the Cabinet, Leadership of the Senate, Governors of the States and Territories, Leadership of the House of Representatives, Joints Chiefs of Staff, Personal Staff of President Kennedy, Close Friends of the Family.

Despite all of the nights they had spent together, the shared secrets and girlfriends, the dirty election tricks, and the enormous personal sacrifices, Frank Sinatra was not, despite Kenny O'Donnell's best efforts, invited to take his place as a "close friend" of John Kennedy.

Moments after the casket was carried down the front steps of the cathedral, Jacqueline Kennedy whispered to three-year-old John Junior, after which he saluted his father's coffin. Ever the showman, Peter Lawford managed to position himself in the second row of the mourners, standing behind and between Jackie and Teddy, as the most iconic moment of the funeral was recorded for the world to see.

In a strange postscript to the tragic events of the previous seven days it later emerged that Richard Nixon had been in Dallas the night before the assassination and had attended a party held at the home of Clint Murchison, the owner of the Dallas Cowboys football team. The gathering had also included many influential and super-rich local businessmen, including the oil magnate HL Hunt. According to Madeleine Brown, LBJ's mistress since 1948 (who had allegedly borne him an illegitimate son in 1950), the vice president had also attended. Even more curiously, J. Edgar Hoover and his companion and assistant director, Clyde Tolson, had been there, and the entire event had apparently been held in Hoover's honor. What three of the most powerful men in the United States were doing in the same room on the night before the still-unexplained assassination of their president is anyone's guess.

Chapter 16: The Wilderness Years

———————◆———————

A DARK CLOUD HUNG over the United States in the days and months following the events in Dallas. Few families had the stomach to fully celebrate Thanksgiving, which fell six days after the president's assassination, and in the run up to Christmas 1963, a palpable sense of grief and loss remained across America. Nowhere was this felt more acutely than in the White House and in the homes of those who had accompanied Jack from his early days in Congress right up to his finest hours during the thousand days of his presidency.

Kenny O'Donnell and Dave Powers, in particular, grieved deeply. Both had invested the best part of their adult lives in their boss's career and had been just yards from him when the bullets cut him down in Dealey Plaza. Watching his immediate and brutal elimination, they also believed they were witnessing the end of their own associations with national politics. Larry O'Brien, who had joined the team later than the others, but had become just as indispensible, found it extremely difficult to pick up the pieces. But for all three there was to be some element of continuity with the Kennedy White House.

Johnson, anxious not just to maintain a strong connection between his administration and Jack's, but also to ensure that what was now being widely perceived as the martyrdom of Kennedy remained uncontaminated by him, was keen to retain as many of the senior staffers as possible. Powers, O'Brien, and O'Donnell in particular were prevailed upon by the new president to stay in the jobs they had previously held, despite their reticence to serve a man whom they had little respect for over the previous three years. O'Donnell had found the whole episode so traumatizing that he was unable to visit his office for the remainder of 1963. He recalled the period in an interview given to Paige E. Mulhollan in 1969: "I didn't go to the White House for another two or three weeks. He (Johnson) used to call me every day. I just didn't have the stomach for it. I came back some time in January, and he wouldn't let me out of his sight. Lyndon is a rather demanding fellow. He was frightened I was going to leave. I was pretty invaluable at that moment, and I didn't mind trying to help him."

As far as O'Donnell was concerned, his arrangements with Johnson were temporary in nature, a stopgap until he could find someone else to do the job:

> I considered myself a loyalist, yes, but I was not going to stay in the White House with Lyndon Johnson. Firstly, because I knew I couldn't get along with him, which is not any more his fault than my fault, and, secondly, I don't see where there's a job for me. When you work for President Kennedy, and when you work for the President as his appointments secretary you live with him.

But Johnson appeared to have other ideas about his adoption of the members of the Irish Mafia. In retrospect it appears that Johnson's thinking was that he could thrive as president, evoking the memory of John Kennedy, until the election of 1964. After that he would have to sink or swim on his own reputation if elected. To get there, though, required all of the elements, which had made Jack such a success in his short tenure. Keeping Kenny and the other Irish loyalists on side was a key element of this strategy:

> I think President Johnson trusted me. He didn't think I was a liar; he may not have liked my attitude upon some occasions.

But I think without any question that if I had been willing that I would have been appointments secretary. He came out one day and said, "I don't want anybody [else] ever to sit at this desk as long as I'm president of the United States." And he meant it. He had great confidence in my judgment politically, and we talked every single day. He chased me all over the place.

LBJ also love-bombed Jackie Kennedy, although his conversations with her reflect a genuine affection. She might have been the nation's heroine, but his calls, particularly in the period between the funeral and the New Year, show real sympathy for a young woman widowed with two children at the age of thirty-four, as this call, placed two days before Christmas, demonstrates:

JBK: Mr. President?
LBJ: I hope that you're doing all right.
JBK: Oh, I'm doing fine, thank you.
LBJ: Well, this Congress is getting pretty rough up here and I may have to send for you before it gets through.
JBK: I hope you get home for Christmas. Will you?
LBJ: I don't know.
JBK: You're so nice to call me, Mr. President. You must be out of your mind with work piled up.
LBJ: I have a few things to do, but not anything that I enjoy more than what I'm doing now.
JBK: You're nice.

Johnson was on the phone again to Jackie on New Year's Day, and a week later on the ninth of January. Her calls with him were very personal and it appears that he had developed a far closer relationship with Jackie than he had enjoyed with her late husband:

JBK: Will you please start to take a nap after lunch?
LBJ: I'm going to.

JBK: It changed Jack's whole life.

LBJ: I'm going to.

JBK: He was always sick. And when we got to the White House, he did it every day, even if you can't sleep. And you know, Churchill did that. And you just, now that you've got your State of the Union over, you just can't tear around.

LBJ: I'll start it the day you come down here to see me, and if you don't, I'm going to come out there to see you.

JBK: Oh, Mr. President—

LBJ: And I will just have all those motor-sickle cops around your house, and it will cause you all kinds of trouble, and—

JBK: I can't come down there. I wanted to tell you. I've really gotten ahold of myself. You know, I would do anything for you. I'll talk to you on the phone. I'm so scared I'll start to cry again.

LBJ: Oh, you never cried—honey, I never saw anyone as brave as you.

If the president's relationship with his predecessor's wife had become warmer, the diametric opposite could be said of Johnson's dealings with his brother. Bobby Kennedy described his new boss as "mean, bitter, vicious . . . an animal in many ways." Johnson felt Kennedy was a "grandstanding little runt." The animosity between the two had not been tempered in the slightest by Jack's death. If anything, Bobby's resentment that Johnson, of all people, had succeeded to the highest office in the land and was now sitting in the chair where, just weeks before, his beloved brother had sat, had driven his hatred to new levels. He grudgingly acquiesced to Johnson's pleadings with him to remain as attorney general, mainly because he didn't really know what else to do in the short term, and because the president convinced him that any public disagreements between them would serve only to cast an unnecessary shadow on his brother's memory, something the American public would not thank either of them for.

In *Robert Kennedy: Brother Protector*, author James Hilty writes of Bobby's disposition in the aftermath of November 22:

> For weeks (he) seemed barely able to function. He failed to attend meetings, walking into Lyndon Johnson's first cabinet meeting only by chance; he left mail unanswered and never, in fact, responded to letters regarding the details of the assassination. (He) displayed many of the symptoms of clinical depression, including sleeplessness, lack of concentration, preoccupation with death, brooding, feelings of sadness, despair, and melancholy—except he also felt anger.

And that was the anger he took out on anyone who would listen to his feelings about Johnson. Having handed over most of the day-to-day running of the Justice Department to his deputy, Nicholas Katzenbach, Bobby tried to get himself back on his feet and to plan his next move, as far away from Lyndon Johnson as possible. Bit by bit he began to integrate himself back into a normal routine and to make contact with friends he had shut himself away from in the first six months after Jack's death. Frank Sinatra was not one of those friends.

Two weeks after the assassination, nineteen-year-old Frank Sinatra Junior was kidnapped. On December 8, 1963, Joe Amsler, a twenty-three-year-old former high school classmate and friend of Frank's daughter Nancy, along with two accomplices, abducted Frank Jr. from his hotel room in Lake Tahoe. A distraught Sinatra called Peter Lawford and, without any niceties, asked him to ring Bobby and get him to get the FBI on the case. Bobby told Lawford they were pulling out all the stops, with agents and other law enforcement officials sweeping through Nevada and California, and road blocks at all major traffic points on the state borders.

The next night, a visibly distraught Sinatra and his attorney, Mickey Rudin, met with four FBI agents, including Dean Elson, the FBI's special agent in charge of Nevada. Bobby called, promising more help. Sam Giancana also called. Two days later, Sinatra and an FBI agent delivered $239,985 to the kidnappers in Los Angeles. Frank Jr. was returned unharmed, and the kidnappers were picked up within three days.

As far as special agent Elson was concerned, the whole event marked a fundamental change in the relationship between the FBI and Frank. The FBI agents he worked closely with over the intense days of the kidnapping felt they had gotten to know him. An FBI memo of April 17, 1964, stated that Elson now had a "close personal relationship" with Sinatra. "Elson believes his relationship with Sinatra is so close that he might be able to induce Sinatra to cooperate with us." The idea made its way up to Hoover's inner circle. "I don't think the leopard will change his spots, but I recommend SAC Elson try his hand at this," commented Alan Belmont, the Hoover assistant who looked after the Sinatra file. "I do not agree," wrote Tolson. "I share Tolson's views," replied Hoover, and that was the end of the matter.

In the aftermath of the kidnapping one would have thought there might have been some thaw in Sinatra's attitude toward Bobby Kennedy, but time would show that the grudge against the attorney general was too embedded in Frank's dysfunctional psyche. But while Sinatra had a remarkable ability to bear grudges he also had extraordinary blind spots, which made him unable to grasp the simple implications of an event and act accordingly. This was evident in his attitude toward the Mob and his inability to shake off the temptation to mix with such dubious and dangerous company.

His association with Sam Giancana, in particular, had contributed hugely to his rift with the Kennedys and, yet again he found himself in trouble because of the same notorious hoodlum and Bobby Kennedy's relentless pursuit of the his Cosa Nostra associates. Giancana, under constant surveillance by the FBI, had been seen in July of that year in Sinatra's Cal Neva Hotel and gaming joint, which, like all of those establishments, was strictly off limits for the mobster.

He had stayed there with his mistress, Phyllis McGuire, who was performing there, and had been involved in a physical alteration in the bar late one night. Sinatra had been spending a lot of his time with Sam in Palm Springs, Hawaii, New York, and now at Lake Tahoe, and the association provided the FBI with an opportunity they were not going to miss. The irony is that FBI wiretaps showed that by this stage Giancana was completely disillusioned with Sinatra for failing to deliver the promised détente between himself and the Justice Department. Giancana was heard bitterly remarking that Frank "wasn't worth a quarter."

The FBI tipped off the Nevada Gaming Control Board about Giancana's stay at Cal Neva, and the fact that there had been an incident involving a fight in the bar. This prompted an investigation headed up by Ed Olsen of the Nevada Gaming Commission, who arranged an interview with Sinatra. Frank admitted that he had seen Giancana coming out of Phyllis McGuire's room, but that, he said, was all he knew. All Sinatra had to do was to play it cool, accept and apologize for the oversight, and make a firm pledge that Giancana and his like would not visit again and he would probably have walked away with a caution.

Instead he impeded agents involved in the investigation that came to the premises and, at first, refused to cooperate. During the conversation with Olsen he was aggressive, in his usual crazed and foul-mouthed manner. The upshot, no surprise, was that the Board of Control issued charges and sought to revoke his gaming license in both the Cal Neva and the Sands Hotel. He had managed, through his own stupidity, to incur the wrath of the most powerful of authorities, who could, and would, inflict severe financial damage on the shareholders of both establishments.

Jack Kennedy had shown some residual loyalty toward Sinatra, when he had visited Nevada in 1963. While in Las Vegas, Kennedy remarked to Governor Grant Sawyer that, in his view, they were going a bit hard on Frank. He received a polite, curt reply from Sawyer that the matter was out of his hands. There had been considerable media coverage of the matter at this stage so the president did not seek to exert any further influence. The licenses were revoked and Sinatra was now faced with disposing of his interest. Giancana

was furious, estimating his losses at just short of half a million, vow-
ing to never darken Sinatra's door again. Frank was now completely
out of favor with the man responsible for him falling out of favor
with the president of the United States.

When Bobby announced his candidacy for the 1968 Democratic
Presidential nomination campaign, Sinatra announced that he would
support Bobby's main rival, vice president Hubert Humphrey, with
the same intensity and commitment that he had on Jack's campaign,
letting people know that, in his view, Bobby was not qualified to do
the job. Bobby had taken a long time to commit to a run for president. Johnson, elected with a landslide in 1964, was a strong incumbent, despite the difficulties that the civil rights movement and the
Vietnam War had created for him. There was also the dark shadow
of Hoover lurking in the background with dirt on Bobby, which he
could choose to leak at any time. Then there was the matter of the
public exposure, which could leave him vulnerable to enemies, not
least of which were the hugely disgruntled members of the Mafia.
Despite his transformation into a less abrasive, more caring individual, with a real interest in social justice, Bobby had a lot more enemies
in 1968 than Jack had had five years before. After the announcement that he would seek the nomination, Jackie confided to Arthur
Schlesinger, "Do you know what I think will happen to Bobby, the
same thing that happened to Jack. There is so much hatred in this
country and more people hate Bobby than hated Jack."

Frank Sinatra was among that army of haters but he was translating his odium into political action against Bobby. The campaign
was conducted against a backdrop of political turbulence and civil
unrest. In one week, two major events shook the United States.
Johnson landed a bombshell on the nation on March 31 when he
announced: "I shall not seek, and I will not accept, the nomination
of my party for another term as your president." Then widespread
riots followed the assassination of Martin Luther King Jr. on April 4.

Sinatra announced that he would travel to ten cities to support Humphrey but he could not get any of his troupe from the

Jack Kennedy days to join him. As it became obvious to many that Frank's support of Humphrey was primarily motivated by his enmity toward Bobby, old Jack Kennedy supporters, like Shirley McLaine and Sammy Davis Jr., melted away. Hollywood was not keen on Humphrey, the old Kennedy magic still attracted the stars, and Sinatra would be alone in backing the older man with a losing track record.

All was to change on the evening of June 5 when the Kennedy team arrived into the Ambassador Hotel in Los Angeles after over a week of punishing hours on the campaign trail. It was an occasion for celebration, as the campaign team had just learned that Kennedy had won the South Dakota primary with 50 percent of the vote. The Royal Suite was bustling with a mixture of celebrities, supporters, and Kennedy insiders with the sound of victory ringing in their ears, and the promise of more to come.

Just after midnight, and within moments of leaving the stage, Bobby was shot as he walked through the kitchens of the hotel, gunned down mercilessly by a disaffected Arab Palestinian, Sirhan Sirhan. Bobby's body reposed for two days in St. Patrick's Cathedral while thousands filed by, before funeral Mass was celebrated on June 8. Delivering the eulogy, Teddy Kennedy, now the last of the four brothers in whom Joe Senior had invested so much, spoke to a congregation numbed with shock.

> My brother need not be idealized, or enlarged in death beyond what he was in life; to be remembered simply as a good and decent man, who saw wrong and tried to right it, saw suffering and tried to heal it, saw war and tried to stop it.
>
> Those of us who loved him and who take him to his rest today, pray that what he was to us and what he wished for others will someday come to pass for all the world. As he said many times, in many parts of this nation, to those he touched and who sought to touch him: "Some men see

things as they are and say why. I dream things that never were and say why not."

The Kennedy nightmare had returned with a vengeance and Jackie's premonition had been tragically realized.

Perhaps Frank Sinatra shed a few crocodile tears, who knows? But while the object of his hatred no longer existed, he continued his obsession with walking the corridors of power, even if it meant dumping a lifetime commitment to the Democratic cause. He had absolutely no grasp of either loyalty or morality in life, so why should this be different in the heady arena of political action? Sinatra would hang on to the coattail of the Devil himself if he saw an advantage to it.

The ever-present ghost of his Mob loyalty was once again at his shoulder and he could not, and would not, be able to banish its corrupting presence. A week before the Democratic Convention in August, the Wall Street Journal ran a front-page story profiling the usual Mafia suspects that graced his company, including Giancana, Moretti, Fischetti, and Luciano. In the wake of Jack's assassination, President Johnson had concurred with Bobby's view that Sinatra was tainted by the Mafia connection and should always be considered an electoral liability. Humphrey was asked by his advisers to distance himself from Sinatra, and Frank had to maintain a far lower profile than he would have wished as the convention approached, all the more so because it was being held in Chicago, the principal fiefdom of Sam Giancana.

Humphrey won the nomination and stepped up from second in command to run for the presidency. Sinatra remarked that he would continue to campaign for the Democratic candidate, "anything to defeat that bum Nixon," words he might have choked on later when he began to flirt with the very object of his disdain. In time he would behave the same way with Ronald Reagan, someone he called "a bore" who "couldn't get into the pictures." Frank proved that he would never be a leopard when he dramatically changed his political spots two years later by backing Reagan in the race for the governor-ship of California against Jesse Unruh, the former Speaker of the California Assembly, and a former supporter of Bobby Kennedy. He didn't only signal his betrayal of the Democratic Party, his roots in which went all the way back to Hoboken and the very beginnings of his career, but also demonstrated that death had not quelled his hatred of Bobby.

He slipped even lower down the greasy political pole when he espoused and championed Spiro Agnew, Nixon's vice president. Agnew was totally in tune with Sinatra's loathing of liberal views, his detestation of intellectuals, and, in particular, newspapers such as *The New York Times* and *The Washington Post*. They became great pals, and Agnew stayed regularly in Palm Springs where he occupied the suite of rooms built by Sinatra for Kennedy.

Although he was more than comfortably off, Sinatra was in an entertainment wilderness. His record sales had bottomed out and his movie roles became infrequent. In 1971, at age fifty-five, he announced his retirement with a farewell concert in Los Angeles, with his new Republican friends, Agnew, Reagan, and Henry Kissinger in the audi-ence. A year later he became the object of much derision, even with his own family, when he supported Richard Nixon's reelection campaign.

He was in Washington on election night in early November 1972 to celebrate Nixon's landslide victory, and in January was back to host a series of parties in advance of the inauguration. On that trip he disgraced himself by attacking Maxine Cheshire of the *Washington Post*. When she dared ask him a question he thought impertinent, he turned on her, showering her with foul-mouth invective, which included calling her a "two dollar prostitute" who was "laying down for two dollars all her life." It was a disgusting attack for which he got the usual treatment in the media, once again proving an embar-rassment to his political master. But when the dust settled he was forgiven by Nixon, who invited him to the White House to perform for the Italian prime minister as part of his official visit.

In 1973 Agnew was investigated on suspicion of taking bribes, extortion, and conspiracy, and was forced to resign from the doomed Nixon administration, and was replaced by Gerald Ford. In October of that year he became only the second vice president to resign office after he pleaded no contest to the criminal charges of tax evasion. Had he managed to remain, he would have become president a year later after Nixon was forced to resign in the wake of the Watergate scandal. Agnew had been an embarrassment to everyone around him, with the exception of Sinatra. When Nixon's special assistant, John Ehrlichman, asked the president why he'd kept him on the 1972 ticket, Nixon replied, "No assassin in his right mind would kill me because they would get Agnew (as President)."

Sinatra had not only swapped political allegiance, but had backed the most corrupt administration ever to occupy the White House. His reward for his betrayal of the Democrats was that he would now always be associated with the disgraced Nixon, and with the crooked Agnew, who had been a visitor at Palm Springs no less than eighteen times.

Sinatra would go on to back Ronald Reagan, the man he considered a bore, in the presidential campaign of 1980, and to organize the inaugural ball in January of the following year, as he had two decades earlier for Jack Kennedy. The same year he launched a legal challenge against the decision of the Nevada Gaming Control Board to revoke his license. Affidavits to his generosity came from numerous Hollywood stars including Bob Hope, Kirk Douglas, and Gregory Peck. President Reagan also recommended that the Board return the license and the board concurred.

Frank Sinatra was now an old man of pensionable age and, at sixty-six years of age, he was in the autumn of his career and his voice was not what it used to be. It was a fact that his vanity would not allow him to admit. The Kennedy brothers had been long, and honorably, interred but Frank Sinatra would never be allowed to forget them because the legend of Camelot had grown, not faded, in the interim. He would remain a pale shadow in the wake of their greatness and

Jack Kennedy's in particular. He might have occupied a larger space but his weakness for the masters of the dark arts prevented that from ever happening. Instead of preserving his mother's political legacy, he betrayed it, and became part of a gallery of shame along with Agnew and Nixon and the dubious accomplishments of other politicians he supported, whose reputations would diminish with the passage of time. The Kennedys, for all their human frailties, would occupy the land of legend.

Chapter 17: The Final Curtain

———————◆———————

NOSTALGIA, A SENSE of loss of time and love, had always been at the center of Frank Sinatra's art. Memory and desire had provided a focus for him long after his capabilities as a performer had waned and, in recent years it had become clear that his time to abandon the stage was long overdue. He had, to a large degree, escaped the effects of hard living and the punishing schedules of an international star for decades, as well as the storms of a turbulent emotional life. It appeared to many that Sinatra was indestructible. But by the early 1980s it was clear to most who witnessed him in concert that the crown of the greatest singer of the modern age was beginning to slip.

While Frank was still trying to defy the years, the Grim Reaper was picking off the major figures from his life with increasing tempo from the mid-eighties to the mid-nineties. The first to go, and the first of the Rat Pack to die, was Peter Lawford. Although he and Sinatra had not spoken since the aborted visit of March 1962, except for briefly during the days of the kidnap of Frank Junior, his death must, for Frank, have been an intimation of mortality, not to mention some sense of regret about the social disaster that journalist Gay Talese, writing in *Esquire* magazine in 1966, had pointed out that Sinatra was never likely to forget.

In keeping with the pattern of his turbulent existence, Lawford had married his fourth wife, seventeen-year-old Patricia Seaton, in

July 1964 before his drink and drug habits finally brought his life to a close just six months later. He suffered a heart attack after kidney and liver failure and died at the Cedars-Sinai Medical Center in Los Angeles on Christmas Eve 1984. He was just sixty-one.

Two years later in 1986, Ava Gardner, who was by now living in London, suffered two strokes and was left partially paralyzed and bedridden. Sinatra paid for an air ambulance and medical expenses to have her treated back in the United States. After decades of cigarette smoking she had also developed emphysema. A fall at her London home brought on pneumonia and she died from the effects on January 25, 1990. Her posthumous memoir, *My Story*, stated that Sinatra was the love of her life but also chronicled in detail the many shameful episodes in their turbulent two-year marriage including numerous beatings by Frank. To be reminded at this stage of his life of such unsavory behavior must have made Sinatra uncomfortable at the very least. In May of the same year, Sammy Davis Jr. became the second member of the Rat Pack to pass. Davis, whom had remained loyal to Sinatra, although not close as a friend in latter years, died of throat cancer after decades of smoking, alcohol, and cocaine abuse.

There was worse to come. In 1992 Jilly Rizzo, who Sinatra had first met in the Copacabana in 1956, and who had maintained a friendship that had endured many of Frank's difficulties, was killed tragically. Rizzo was the owner of the bar and restaurant Jilly's Saloon in Manhattan, which had become one of the most popular hang outs for celebrities in the 1960s, largely through Sinatra's patronage and association. Rizzo had graduated to become what Nancy Sinatra described in her memoir as "Dad's right hand man," providing professional and personal comfort on the singer's tours and recording sessions over three decades.

In May of 1992 Rizzo had been making preparations for his seventy-fifth birthday that he was hosting the following day at his Rancho Mirage home with eighty guests including Sinatra due to attend. Just past midnight he got into his white Jaguar to drive to his girlfriend's home. As he drove carefully across Gerald Ford

Drive, a Mercedes driven at 80 mph by twenty-eight-year-old alcoholic Jeffrey Perrotte plowed into the right side of the Jaguar, which exploded into flames. Perrotte, saved by the airbags in his car, abandoned the vehicle and fled the scene while Rizzo, whose cries for help were heard by witnesses, was burnt to death beyond recognition. Just one year before Sinatra had included the deceased in his will to the tune of $100,000. "If Jilly Rizzo does not survive me," it read, "this gift shall lapse and be considered as part of the residue of my estate." It would, but Sinatra was utterly devastated by this loss. It was said that he would break down in tears at the very mention of his old and best friend's name. He buried Jilly in the family plot next to Dolly and Marty.

Barbara Sinatra, in her memoir of her life with Frank, described the impact on him of the death of close friends: he would shut himself in his den, which he had built for the planned JFK visit, and sink into deep periods of solitary mourning. It was significant that he chose this room—evidence, were it needed, that he continued to remember that terrible humiliation. The bell of mortality tolled again in September of 1993 when a third member of the Rat Pack, Dean Martin, was diagnosed with lung cancer. He died on Christmas Day 1995 and Sinatra did not attend the funeral. Publically he put out the excuse that he had had enough of such unrelenting loss, but in reality his body was finally beginning to break down and his memory was starting to fade.

There had been other losses that had affected him greatly too. On January 6, 1977, his mother, Dolly, opted to travel with her friend Ann Carbone to the opening of Frank's show in Las Vegas, rather than travel with her son and Barbara. Dolly chartered a Lear jet so she could travel in comfort from Palm Springs. Just four minutes after take off, the jet crashed into the San Gorgonio Mountains at 375 mph, causing the plane to disintegrate, scattering wreckage over half a mile and killing the two crew and their passengers instantly. The loss of such a formidable influence and constant confidante devastated Sinatra and the nature of the tragedy weighed heavily on him for the rest of his life.

Some others with whom he had been closely associated, less important personally, but just as significant in his life story, also met violent endings. On the night of June 19, 1975, Sam Giancana was cooking a dish of sausage and peppers at home for someone he knew (police have always assumed it was a friend because Giancana could not eat spicy foods owing to his heart problems). As he was at the cooker, the still-unknown visitor shot him in the back of the head and then six more times in the head and neck. He was sixty-seven. Handsome Johnny Roselli had been hauled twice before the Church Committee investigating the plot to kill Castro in June and September of the same year. On April 23, 1976 he had appeared before the committee now investigating the assassination of JFK. He was recalled a couple of months later but had been missing since July 28. On August 9, Roselli's decomposing body was found in a fifty-five-gallon drum floating in a bay near Miami. He was seventy-one.

Few humans accept the iniquities of age with equanimity. The loss of power and faculty is difficult enough in private, but Frank Sinatra would not surrender either in private or public and it was entirely characteristic of him to rail against his failing faculties. Frank was still going in his late seventies but displaying memory loss and distortion, mixing up the past with the present, generally regarded as the first signs of dementia. In truth the weakening of his voice and the appearance of physical frailty had been obvious by his late-sixties not just as a result of the natural aging process but by the effects of hard living. In 1986, aged seventy-one, he collapsed onstage at Atlantic City. He was diagnosed with diverticulitis and surgeons removed twelve inches of intestine and put in a temporary colostomy bag. His response when he recovered was, characteristically, to up his annual concert output.

To celebrate his seventy-fifth birthday he launched a seventy-five-city world tour and in 1992 he managed to complete a schedule of eighty-four concerts. The previous year he had been fitted with a hearing aid and the following year he had two operations to remove cataracts. He had spent all his life in the spotlight both on and off stage and he was determined to prove his enduring longevity even when the majority of his performances were but pale fire when compared to his best years.

Speaking to one of his few media pets, Larry King, on his show, he displayed that he had a poor grasp of the meaning of a legend: "I don't know what a legend means. I'm not a stupid man, but the definition of a legend is so broad, I don't know what it means. . . . It's longevity. I think if you are around long enough, people become aware, your name comes up in conversation. People write about you."

Sinatra had been a legend for a long time, and at this stage of his life he had nothing else to prove. Jimmy Dean was a legend but had only three films behind him when he died in his mid-twenties. Frank's former lover Marilyn Monroe had provided another example of the fact that longevity is not a prerequisite to legendary status. The importance of longevity is to be found in the art and not the artist, and on that score Frank had already qualified.

By 1994 Sinatra was seventy-eight years of age and no longer wearing it well. Physically diminished, the once tolerable stage toupee now looked more than faintly ridiculous, a silver ill-fitting crown, sitting precariously over the wrinkled folds of the face in which those famous blue eyes had sunk into hooded obscurity. Incredibly, though, his career was undergoing a revival.

Two years previously he had been approached with the idea of recording an album of duets. Legendary engineer and music producer Phil Ramone, Sinatra's manager Eliot Wiseman, and the producer Don Rubin discussed the details at Sinatra's Palm Springs home and he agreed to participate provided that the duet partners would not be in the studio while he was singing his part. While from a technological point of view that was not a problem, the trio espoused the view that it certainly would take away from the spontaneity and chemistry of the project.

Ramone, who was to produce the album, was all too aware of this drawback, but got on with the job of enlisting the duet partners. Sinatra, he surmised, was an old man, his voice not as in his prime, and he might be somewhat intimidated or nervous of the younger stars' immediate presence. In truth, Sinatra had seen it all and was intimidated by no one. A couple of days in studio with a bunch of reverential, even obsequious, performers could be an irritating experience. It would be better to do his own thing with no distractions.

The final lineup included luminaries such as Tony Bennett, Barbra Streisand, Aretha Franklin, and Luther Vandross, as well as relative newcomers Bono, Gloria Estefan, and Anita Baker. Their contributions would be recorded and transmitted to the Capitol Studio in Los Angeles by ISDN telephone lines. Meanwhile, Ramone rehearsed the orchestra at the studio with traditional Nelson Riddle arrangements and when he completed this, Sinatra came into record the songs toward the end of June 1993.

His first day was not good; he complained that his voice was not what it should be and he went home, leaving a nervous Ramone wondering if the album would happen after what was an already-considerable financial outlay. Frank turned up again on June 30 and, full of confidence, recorded nine songs in the five-hour session. Duets 1 was on its way, hitting the Billboard top ten at number two in the run up to Christmas, with preorders totaling over one million units. It would go on to sell three million albums in the United States and a half million overseas. Sinatra may have looked down but he was far from out. Duets 2, the fifty-ninth and last studio album Sinatra ever recorded, would be made the following year, selling over a million copies in the American market.

A newly reinvigorated Frank agreed to a series of concerts planned for 1994 with Don Rickles as the warm-up act and a fifty-piece orchestra under the baton of Frank Jr. The itinerary included Atlanta, Georgia and Richmond, Virginia in January and February; Wilmington, five nights at the Foxwoods Casino in Connecticut in March and April; three nights at the Sands Hotel in Atlantic City, New Jersey, in May; and two more at the same venue in early August.

The opening concert in the Omni Center in Atlanta was half-full. After Don Rickles had completed his routine the lights dimmed and the spotlight came on Frank as he launched into "I've Got the World on a String." There was no sign of faltering but in truth devoted fans would have paid to see him in a wheelchair singing children's nursery rhymes. The presence of the legend was more than sufficient. They may have noticed but paid little attention to four large teleprompter screens placed on either side of the stage.

These provided the running order and lyrics of the Sinatra set. His normally upbeat introductions were flat and repetitive. He fumbled some lyrics and repeated others. The fans could not have cared less. One of them, Aubrey Hammack, writing in the *Upson Home Journal*, saw nothing amiss and proclaimed a fantastic evening with Sinatra looking and sounding great. Richard Williams of the *English Independent* disagreed, however. He commented on the memory lapses and repetition but also described the singer as disturbingly quiet, "a cruel caricature of his former self."

The *Independent* correspondent had something to compare. He'd seen Sinatra in concert in London four years previously, where he'd noted a slightly shaky voice but a far more solid physical presence. It was becoming clear that this solidity was a thing of the past.

At the beginning of March, while onstage in Radio City to accept a lifetime achievement award, Frank began to ramble and the director of the live CBS telecast cut to an ad-break. This was perceived by Sinatra's management as a grave insult and the network was forced to apologize. Just four days later, on March 6, 1994, after complaining to the audience about the heat of the auditorium during a concert at Richmond, Virginia, Sinatra collapsed while singing "My Way." He fell off the stool, hit his head on the speaker, and landed on the floor. He was brought to hospital for tests but after a few hours he discharged himself and flew back to Palm Springs.

The Richmond incident should have given Sinatra pause for thought but he had lived his life, all his life, in sprint mode, and even at this late stage would not be content to slow to a jog. Thirty years previously, actor Brad Dexter, who had starred with Frank in *Von Ryan's Express*, had summed it this way: "He has an insatiable desire to live every moment to its fullest, because I guess he feels that right around the corner is extinction." In the interim that corner had considerably narrowed and the possibility of extinction was looming larger.

There was the other matter of his greatest asset and raison d'être, his voice. The aforementioned Gay Talese had been promised an interview with Sinatra three decades previously but, suffering from a cold, Frank had declined, instead allowing the writer to hang out with him and observe. Talese became the eyewitness as opposed to the interrogator and the result, published in *Esquire*, provided a searing insight into Sinatra's character when at the height of his powers.

Today those observations provide a clue to why Francis Albert did not want to let go of the power, however much the march of time made him physically diminished. Then, it was November 1965, the month before his fiftieth birthday, and the press was hounding him over his dating of the twenty-year-old Mia Farrow. A CBS documentary was about to air on his life and he was due to star in an hour-long NBC entertainment show, *Frank Sinatra: A Man and His Music*. He had his own film company and record company, a private jet, and all the trappings of wealth and success. He was on top of the world but had a cold, which for most mortals would be considered trivial. Not for Sinatra, as Talese wrote,

> Sinatra with a cold is Picasso without paint, Ferrari without fuel—only worse. For the common cold robs Sinatra of that uninsurable jewel, his voice, cutting into the core of his confidence, and it affects not only his psyche but also seems to cause a kind of psychosomatic nasal drip within dozens of people who work for him, depend on him for welfare and stability. A Sinatra with a cold, can in a small way, send vibrations through the entertainment industry and beyond as surely as the President of the U.S. suddenly sick can shake the national economy.

Three decades on, substitute old for cold. If Sinatra was depressed and discommoded by a condition that would pass, he must have been ten times more depressed by the prospect of a condition for which there was no cure. Except, perhaps, even temporarily, in the warm glow of the stage spotlight and the adoration of the non-discriminating fans. All of that considered, he was simply not up to the mark when it came to performing. Even the travel, once fun-filled and exciting, had become extraordinarily difficult. He played his final public concert at the Marriott Desert Springs Resort, for convenience just down the road from his house, in February 1995.

His family situation was also deteriorating. When he and Barbara celebrated the twentieth anniversary of their marriage in 1996, an occasion on which they renewed their marital vows, none of Sinatra's children or grandchildren were present. The long standing enmity between Barbara and the children would later spill into a major feud over the ownership of licensing rights while Frank was still alive, and would become extremely upsetting for him. Whatever effect that may have had on him, his health continued to go downhill and in November that year he was admitted to the VIP wing of the Cedars Sinai Medical Center with an apparent pinched nerve. He was placed on a heart monitor and was treated for a minor case of pneumonia and was released after eight days. In January 1997 he was hospitalized again with a suspected heart attack having just been released after another shorter stay.

In that year the *Wall Street Journal* published details of the fight centered on aspects of his $200 million fortune, reflecting very badly on Nancy, Tina, and Frank Jr., portraying them as more concerned about money and self-casting than about the welfare of the man who had made it all possible. In all reports Tina was described as having adopted the role of keeper of the flame, which translated, in most readers' minds, as the desire to make as much money as possible from the licensing of merchandising using her father's name, image, and, even, his voice.

She had taken over as CEO of Sheffield Enterprises Inc., the company that ran Sinatra's commercial affairs, when her father had begun to fail physically and mentally. She proceeded to ruthlessly exploit his name on posters, pens, hats, calendars, and even pasta sauces. The company, under her direction, reissued videos and recordings with what can only be described as indecent haste. Tina and her siblings knew that the bulk of Sinatra's estate would be left to Barbara, and the possibility of Tina remaining in charge of any assets whatsoever after her father's death was unlikely.

Barbara was opposed to the cheap exploitation that Sheffield Enterprises practiced, but the rift ran even deeper when it came to managing the music legacy. Sinatra had granted his children royalty rights to all his recordings from 1960 onward, while Barbara was given the rights to all recordings before 1960, ensuring that she made a personal fortune from the contract he signed with Capitol Records, which gave her 20 percent of royalties. His wife managed reissues of Sinatra music from the 1940s but the children claimed they had a moral right and had threatened legal action. Though this was eventually not pursued, it amplified the toxic relationship between his children and the wife who had provided the most stable and enduring marriage of his life.

As Sinatra became increasingly beset by incrementally slow and cruel illnesses he had one last card to play on his disunited family. In the drafting of his will as far back as 1991 he had inserted a condition that would deal effectively with the posthumous family fallout he anticipated and which was looming larger as each year passed. A "no contest" clause stated that any of the beneficiaries who contested the will would be disinherited.

By the mid-1990s Sinatra had become increasingly reclusive, his behavior similarly erratic. He'd invite friends to visit for card games and then ignore them, opting instead to watch television in his room, constantly switching channels. He sat about for days on end in his monogrammed pajamas and had even abandoned his toupee. As well as his other infirmities he had developed cancer of the bladder and as the dementia progressed he would wander around the house, at times not knowing where and who he was. All of this provided a heartbreaking sight for his friends, who knew that all his life he had hated to be alone. Some visited frequently, among them Jack Lemmon, Jerry Vale, writer Larry Gebert, comedian Tom Dreesen, Artie Funair, and Quincy Jones.

On one occasion Frank told Funair, who had been his assistant and had become a good friend, that he wasn't a man anymore and there was no reason to live and he wanted to die. Funair left the house in tears. Tom Dreesen, who had toured with Frank as his opening act in the late 1980s, said that he had lost the will to live once his singing days were over. Frank had also made it clear to his family he did not want any heroic interventions to keep him alive. There was only temporary retreat from illness. Nancy Sinatra posted on the official family website on Thanksgiving 1997, "We realize that he has been through a lot in his eighty-one years and that God may have a schedule other than what we would like but he is tough and who is to say that he won't get back into the race? Maybe we can have a small miracle together." The sentiment was obviously rather in hope than expectation. After meeting him around this time, Bill Miller, his pianist for more than four decades, remarked, "He just kind of looked at me, like I know you from somewhere." On December 12, 1997, Frank's eighty-second birthday, there were one hundred thousand greetings on the website from all around the world. But the time for celebration was well past and the tide of illness was turning again.

On January 23, 1998, looking gaunt and exceptionally frail, Sinatra was taken to Cedars Sinai and treated for high blood pressure. He was kept overnight for observation and returned home to Palm Springs by ambulance the next day. Just over two weeks later he was back in hospital again for tests. On Sunday May 10, rather than joining his pals for the regular card game, in which he hardly participated, he sat in his room where he had a meal of barbecued spare ribs and watched television, constantly flicking the channels.

By now he had two nurses looking after him around the clock and it was clear to all who visited that Frank's time on Earth was coming to a close. On May 14 he had lunch with Barbara on the patio and was in a cranky mood, which she took as a good sign. He later urged her to go out to a previously planned dinner at Morton's with some friends and enjoy herself. At just after 9 p.m. he summoned the nurse on duty and told her that he was experiencing chest pains and dizziness. Just minutes later he suffered a heart attack and at 9:15 p.m., the nurse rang 911. The ambulance arrived within five minutes and by 9:30 p.m. he was admitted at the emergency entrance to Cedars Sinai. The speed with which the ambulance reached the hospital would later be attributed to the fact that so many Los Angeles residents were tuned to the final episode of *Seinfeld*, which was airing around the same time.

In the interim, Barbara had been contacted and one of the dinner guests took her from Morton's to home and then to the hospital, where first indications were that Frank had been stabilized. As she entered the emergency room it was clear that he was in distress. Taking him in her arms she urged him to "Fight, fight, fight." The whispered reply was "I can't." He was pronounced dead at 10:50 with the official cause of death noted as cardiorespiratory arrest.

His body, dressed in a blue suit, was moved to the mortuary in Inglewood for a five-day wake. In New York the top of the Empire State building was bathed in blue, the casino tables in Las Vegas stopped spinning for a minute, and the tower of Capitol Records in Hollywood was draped in black. There was an outpouring of tributes, salutation, and genuflection by the media, which he had never stopped hating all his life with a tiny cadre of notable exceptions including Pete Hamill, Larry King, and James Bacon. The rest he regarded, right to the end, "as pimps, whores, and bastards."

Illustrating how deeply he felt the cuts and slashes of the fourth estate and how long, if ever, the wounds would take to heal was the hate he harbored for Lee Mortimer (the writer he had punched outside El Ciro in 1947). The powerful, but spiteful, columnist had not only attacked the singer for cavorting with mobsters but said that the un-American activities committee had regarded Sinatra as "one of Hollywood's leading travelers on the road of Red Fascism." Mortimer had died of a heart attack in New York on March 1, 1963 aged fifty-nine. Shortly afterward Sinatra and a couple of associates visited his grave, which received the dubious honor of a stream of the Frank's urine and a short eulogy that went, "I'll bury the bastards. I'll bury them all."

He had indeed outlived his most prominent critics, such as Robert Ruark and the detestable Walter Winchell. But as he well knew they would simply be replaced by another generation, Dorothy Kilgallen, Barbara Walters, Liz Smith, and his unauthorized, and very brave, biographer, Kitty Kelley, who withstood the might of his legal assault and an abandoned $2 million lawsuit.

One way or another he was given a mighty send off. Mia Farrow visited and slipped a ring on his finger, which carried the word "dream." Barbara was less than pleased. Nancy added tootsie rolls, and put blackjack gum and cherry lifesavers in his pockets. The casket was brought to the Good Shepherd Roman Catholic Church in Beverly Hills covered in gardenias for a rosary service on May 19. The next day's funeral Mass was celebrated by Cardinal Roger Mahony and attended by a galaxy of Hollywood and music stars in the church filled with white roses and cherry blossoms. After tributes from the altar Frank was laid to rest in Desert Memorial Park, Palm Springs, alongside his parents and Jilly Rizzo.

The headstone read:

THE BEST IS YET TO COME
FRANCIS ALBERT SINATRA
1915–1998
BELOVED HUSBAND AND FATHER

Sinatra's own assessment of himself could have been added, "An 18 carat manic-depressive who liked a life of violent emotional contradictions with an over-acute capacity for sadness as well as happiness." While he had, as a son of Italian immigrants, provided the very definition of the American dream of moving from rags to riches, he both experienced and recognized that dreams can become nightmares and good fortune and fame can be a curse. His musical achievement was staggering in volume, quality, and popularity and delivered riches and a lifestyle way beyond what even Dolly's imagination and ambition had dreamed for him.

He looked back on his life in a morose, almost depressive manner in an effort to discover a meaning, which he failed to find: "Sometimes I think I know what it was all about, and how everything happened. But then I shake my head and wonder. Am I remembering what really happened or what other people think happened? Who the hell knows after a certain point."

He had related to Pete Hamill the impact of his origins on his fame: "Half the troubles I've had were because my name ended in a vowel. They tried to put me together with all the other stuff that happened. I wasn't the only one. But there I was up on that goddamned stage. I was pretty easy to see, a good target."

Sinatra was no fool and he knew well that was part of the deal of fame, for both the man and the artist to play out both lives in the public eye, but it was a deal that Sinatra had found virtually impossible to accept all of his life. Rejection or humiliation had an effect on him that almost belied the position of power he eventually occupied. He had become a legend in his own lifetime but toward the end, it had come to mean nothing. The glory of fame and success had been replaced by infirmity of body and mind.

The latter had never come to John Fitzgerald Kennedy, or indeed to his brother Bobby. Their sudden and tragic deaths preserved their youth and glamour. Sinatra's later flirtations with Nixon and Reagan meant nothing to him compared to the acceptance by President Kennedy of his role in his historic election victory and Kennedy's speech about him given at the magnificent triumph that was the Gala performance at the Armory. Sinatra could have looked back at that night as his greatest moment above all others, and as one where he had achieved a very public success, and a very public endorsement of his talents and connections.

But he had never allowed himself to, because of the events of March 1962. As Kennedy's iconic status in political history grew in the decades after his death, so did Frank's resentment of the way he was treated. There is little doubt that the singer felt this as a betrayal, which it certainly was. But was it justified? In the context of both Carlos Marcello and Sam Giancana's help in the presidential election campaign and their roles in the CIA plots against Castro, it probably was.

Ironically, in one of the tributes after the singer's death, a writer drew a comparison to the reaction after the president's assassination and called Kennedy the Sinatra of politics. Frank would have loved that, but it was too late.